Schoenberg's Chamber Music, Schoenberg's World

For

Nuria Schoenberg Nono,

Ronald Schoenberg,

and

Lawrence Schoenberg

Schoenberg's Chamber Music, Schoenberg's World

James K. Wright and Alan M. Gillmor, editors

PENDRAGON PRESS

HILLSDALE, NY

Library of Congress Cataloging-in-Publication Data

Schoenberg's chamber music, Schoenberg's world / James K. Wright and Alan M. Gillmor, editors.

p. cm.

Includes bibliographical references.

ISBN 978-1-57647-130-2 (alk. paper)

1. Schoenberg, Arnold, 1874-1951. Chamber music. 2. Chamber music--20th century--History and criticism. 3. Chamber music--20th century--Analysis, appreciation. I. Wright, James K. (James Kenneth), 1959- II. Gillmor, Alan M.

ML410.S283S377 2009

785.0092--dc22

2009010764

Table of Contents

OTTAWA SYMPOSIUM AND
CHAMBER MUSIC FESTIVAL

PERFORMANCE, RECEPTION, AND
INTERNATIONAL INFLUENCE

Foreword

Lawrence Schoenberg

We met in Ottawa—my brother Ronald and I from Los Angeles and my sister Nuria Nono from Venice—to inaugurate the Canadian presentation of a multi-media exhibition that we had produced about our father, in the hope that it would inspire others to learn about his life and works. Professor James Wright invited us to Ottawa to open the exhibition, which he had rescued from the east coast of the United States, and to attend a concert series and symposium devoted to our father's work, hosted by Carleton University. We were all impressed by the schedule of events and felt that through the comprehensive presentation of lectures, concerts, and the exhibition, others would have the opportunity to experience the breadth of our father's life and works. Professor Wright had not only transferred the multi-media exhibition to Canada but had organized an imposing series of events that would encourage the performance and study of Arnold Schoenberg's compositions. Canada has a history of being Schoenberg-friendly (one thinks of the film producer Larry Weinstein, and, of course, Glenn Gould, among others), and our family was delighted to accept this invitation to take part in the events, and to visit Ottawa for the first time.

The presentations by participants from Canada, the United States, Austria, and Australia were consistently engaging and excellent. As a non-musicologist, I acknowledge that I prefer listening to *music about words* rather than *words about music*. But the combination of lectures and performances resulted in an altogether satisfying and music-enhancing experience.

Our family contribution included the opportunity to add a personal touch to the proceedings by discussing our early memories of growing up in Los Angeles. Following the chamber music theme we were able to recall the many visiting performers and ensembles that had performed in our home. But we also revealed the music that we sang together—our ladies club and gentleman's anthems, of course composed by our father, and a special song that he had written for Nuria (the "Nullele-Pullele" lied). And we had the opportunity to discuss and display the many games that he made for us, the tennis scoring system which he developed for my brother in order to help them both analyze the match, and some of his "tinkering" inventions. I was especially pleased that my visit to Ottawa allowed me to discuss in detail an ambitious Coalition Chess Project with computer scientist Michel Paquette, one of the conference presenters, who is creating an internet version of the four-player game invented by my father.

We also talked about our father, a non-film composer, working in Hollywood, and about his relationship with George Gershwin. This neatly led us to a small tribute to the Canadian film composer Eldon Rathburn. I was aware of his interesting correspondence with my father, and I had listened to and played many times for my guests his ingenious composition "Schoenberg vs. Gershwin" ("How many tunes can you name?"), but I had never before had the opportunity to discuss with him his experiences with my father in Los Angeles. Nuria, Ronald, and I had first met Eldon when he visited my father in our Rockingham home in 1945. To meet him again some sixty-two years later added another memorable event to our Ottawa visit.

One of my favorite stories that we related about my father was a memory of a family automobile trip up the Pacific Coast Highway. We would often stop at a roadside stand that served freshly squeezed orange juice. During the summer of 1947, on our way to the Music Academy of the West in Santa Barbara, we made our usual detour to the "Santa Claus Lane" orange juice stand. The stand had a large Santa Claus figure displayed over the roof with an outdoor loudspeaker from which Christmas songs would blare all year long. But this time something very special happened. When we drove up, my mother and father acted strangely and were apparently alerted to something unexpected. Then we found out what was happening: instead of the usual "Jingle Bells" resounding from the loudspeaker, it was *Transfigured Night*! My father was so pleased and amused. We never had any trouble convincing him to stop there in the future.

The concerts we heard in Ottawa were superb. They included a dramatic *Ode to Napoleon* with baritone Peter McGillivray in the role of the narrator, and a sensitive performance of the *Book of the Hanging Gardens* by the young Canadian soprano Martha Guth. I enjoyed the Vienna Trio's performance of the Steuermann Trio arrangement of *Transfigured Night* (with apologies to those who expected Schubert), a spirited *Emperor Waltz*, and enthusiastic performances of the early piano duets and Cabaret Songs. In collaboration with Carleton University, the Ottawa International Chamber Music Festival treated us to a full spectrum of excellent performances, characterized by understanding and enthusiasm.

Happily, this book—in the spirit of James Wright's symposium, concerts, and exhibition—will allow a wider audience to gain knowledge regarding the works of Arnold Schoenberg. And the written words will once again lead one to the music!

Lawrence Schoenberg
Los Angeles, July 2008

Preface

Though a great deal has been written about the life and work of Arnold Schoenberg, it is an astonishing fact that no substantial English language monograph has been published exclusively on Schoenberg's chamber music. We hope that this collection of essays will begin to address that lacuna. The book issues in part from an international symposium that took place at Carleton University, Ottawa, during the summer of 2007, in conjunction with a series of concerts sponsored by the Ottawa International Chamber Music Festival (OICMF), featuring Schoenberg's chamber works. It was a particular honor to host these events in Canada. Canadian advocacy of Schoenberg's music has always been strong: one thinks of the pianists Glenn Gould, Léo-Pol Morin, and Karl Steiner, composers John Weinzweig, John Beckwith, Jean Coulthard, Otto Joachim, and Udo Kasemets, film documentarists Franz Kraemer and Larry Weinstein, and an impressive number of Canadian Schoenberg scholars, some of whose work appears in this volume. Canada is clearly Schoenberg-friendly territory. Perhaps there is a certain affinity between the Canadian identity and Schoenberg's indefatigable spirit. Like Schoenberg, Canadians often tend to see themselves as benevolent but embattled outsiders vis à vis more dominant forces of contemporary culture.

The Ottawa conference team was frequently reminded of Schoenberg's spirit as we prepared for the summer of 2007. Two anecdotes are worth recounting here. On New Year's Eve, 2006, we towed a large multi-media exhibition on Schoenberg's life and work from Boston to Ottawa in a thirty-foot truck. The exhibition had been mounted by the Schoenberg Center in Vienna, in collaboration with the Schoenberg family. It had visited thirty-five cities, but had never been viewed in Canada. When we encountered severe snow storms in the White Mountains of New Hampshire, and were nearly forced to return to Boston, we feared that the Canadian public might never view the exhibit. Our initial elation upon arrival at the Canadian border was dampened when we were detained overnight by Canada Customs for interrogation about the nature and legitimacy of our load. The stand-off ended when a new shift of Customs agents arrived, one of whom was an amateur musician who knew very well of the importance of Arnold Schoenberg. Lawrence Schoenberg later reminded us that, when asked about what contemporary music needed most, his father once quipped: "We need many good amateur musicians." Thankfully we found one at the Custom's office that early New Year's morning.

In his preface, Lawrence Schoenberg alludes to another incident that took place at one of the OICMF concerts. When they heard that the Schoenberg family would be in attendance for the second half of their July 29 concert, the Vienna Trio instantly decided to change their planned finale, dropping a Schubert trio and replacing it with Eduard Steuermann's piano trio arrangement of *Transfigured Night*. When the substitution was announced at the top of the program, the large crowd responded by stomping their feet, loudly, in protest. A short time later the same audience rose to its feet in approval after the Trio gave a shimmering performance of Schoenberg's early tone poem. The ovations were deafening. Arnold Schoenberg had had the last word. The power of his music had triumphed over the comfort of the familiar, and the concert had served an educational role.

Some of the essays in this volume address historical, analytical, and cultural issues, while others focus more on matters of performance and reception. The reader will be struck by the breadth of perspectives that our thirteen contributors have brought to bear on Schoenberg's chamber output. The following brief paragraphs summarize their contributions in order of appearance.

In 2007 the Arnold Schoenberg Center in Vienna mounted a special exhibition, "The Young Schoenberg," with the intention of exploring the composer's earliest musical impressions, influences, and models. Christian Meyer, the Center's Director, explores the earliest stages of the compositional journey of Schoenberg who, as a child of nine, began producing waltzes, polkas, and marches, as well as violin duets modeled on the style of Viotti and Pleyel, some of which have survived. As other papers in this volume will explore, Schoenberg's love affair with the popular music of his time would surface periodically throughout his creative life. As Meyer concludes, the decade of the 1890s, "when the 'nervous splendor' of fin-de-siècle Vienna was in full flower," saw the young composer work through and consolidate a number of influences—Brahms, Wagner, Richard Strauss, and his teacher Zemlinsky, in addition to a variety of popular musics—culminating, symbolically at the century's end, in the masterful *Transfigured Night*.

James Deaville explores the role of the *Allgemeine Deutsche Musikverein* in the dissemination of new music in the German-speaking world at the turn of the twentieth century. Beginning in 1901, under the presidency of Richard Strauss, the organization sponsored festivals of new German music in various locations in Austria, Germany, and Switzerland. With the strong recommendation of no less than Mahler and Strauss, who used their special status to circumvent the normal adjudication process, the 1907 festival, held in Dresden, programmed Schoenberg's Op. 7 String Quartet. It would be, of course, neither Schoenberg's first scandal nor his last. The critics, as they had in the aftermath of the Vienna premiere earlier that same year, expressed their dismay, perhaps no more vividly than the critic for the *Neue Zeitschrift für Musik* for whom the piece was "a brooded-up pile of the most intolerable discords."

Alexander Carpenter and Áine Heneghan return to the world of popular music and its symbolism for Schoenberg. As Carpenter notes, waltzes in particular, that prime musical symbol of turn-of-the-century Vienna, are "meaningful personal signifiers that are connected to intimate and intense feelings," often appearing in Schoenberg's music at moments of personal crisis. For Carpenter, the waltz was a metaphorical means of "connecting past and present." The ensuing discussion of the Op. 7 and Op. 10 String Quartets reveals the central role of the waltz in intensely private autobiographical works; in the later piece it takes the form of the celebrated Viennese folk song "Ach, du lieber Augustin," the symbolism of which is the centerpiece of Severine Neff's essay later in the volume. Similarly, Carpenter teases out autobiographical significance for the waltzes in the Op. 24 Serenade and the Op. 29 Quintet.

Áine Heneghan's essay examines what she calls the "popular effect," particularly as revealed in the Op. 24 Serenade. Heneghan argues that popular forms, "as Schoenberg understood them, played an important role in the evolution of dodecaphony." For Schoenberg, this "primitive" form of music, based as it is on stable, and non-hierarchical, motivic organization, could provide linkage techniques, transparency, and comprehensibility as a substitute for the form-building tendencies of tonality in large-scale dodecaphonic structures.

It is a particular honor to be able to include an important essay by Allen Forte in this volume. Preeminent among American music theorists of the twentieth century, Forte has devoted a large body of his analytic work to Schoenberg's chamber music, a subject to which he has repeatedly returned during his remarkable career. In the present study, Forte focuses his analytic lens on the Three Pieces for Chamber Orchestra (1910). Identifying a number of Webernesque features in Schoenberg's vocabulary and approach in this work, Forte boldly suggests that perhaps "Webern, not Schoenberg, was the innovator with respect to the non-tonal music of the Second Viennese School."

In her contribution to this volume, Severine Neff joins a long line of Schoenberg scholars who have commented on Schoenberg's quotation of the folk song "Ach, du lieber Augustin" in the Scherzo of the Second String Quartet, Op. 10 (others include Friedheim, Haimo, Brinkmann, Budde, Frisch, Graubart, Kolisch, Newlin, Simms, and Stuckenschmidt). Drawing on a range of analytical, biographical, and cultural observations, Neff offers new insights into the question of why the composer opted to integrate such a well-known popular tune into this mature and pivotal work.

Don McLean's essay deals with a question that preoccupied Schoenberg as both composer and theorist: how are form-functional gestures to be articulated in an atonal context? Alluding to opening and closing passages in selected symphonic works of Bruckner, Strauss, Mahler, Debussy, Schoenberg, and Berg, McLean contrasts beginnings that gently materialize and endings that dissipate ("whimpers"), with beginnings and endings that assert themselves more forcefully, enthrallingly, and dramatically ("bangs"). He then discusses these and other issues pertaining to formal function in Schoenberg's Chamber Symphony, Op. 9, a pivotal work in which kernels of the composer's later thinking and method begin to manifest themselves.

In the First Chamber Symphony, Op. 9, Murray Dineen deftly uncovers a form of "tonal orientation" that focuses not on a central pitch, but on intervallic relationships. He discusses how this approach can be viewed as an antecedent to Schoenberg's later atonal and serial practice. Dineen's discussion then turns to Adorno's critique of Schoenberg's twelve-tone method, according to which the shaping forces of thematic development and freely evolving tonal relationship are wholly absent. The essay provides a conceptual framework for understanding both Schoenberg's over-arching preoccupation with the control and emancipation of tonal relationships, and Adorno's nuanced appreciation of the composer's importance and contribution.

Schoenberg frequently emphasized the notion that there was an essential continuity of tradition between first and second Viennese Schools. Brian Proksch's essay examines how, both in his teaching and in his compositional practice, the composer elevates and emulates Haydn's models. Proksch shows how Schoenberg's analyses of Haydn's chamber works can be used to point to striking parallels between central aspects of Haydn's style—phrase structure, harmonic motion, and developing variation in particular—and features of Schoenberg's own works.

Chronicling the influence of *Pierrot Lunaire* on the music of several generations of American composers, Sabine Feisst argues that Schoenberg's chamber masterwork ultimately "infiltrated American consciousness" as much as its impact resonated throughout Europe. Feisst discusses American conceptions and misconceptions of *Pierrot*, examines the work's reception history in the United States, and identifies evidence of its apparent influence on a striking number of American chamber works.

Pianist Yoko Hirota provides an overview of Schoenberg's little-known seventeen piano fragments. Hirota traces Schoenberg's exploration of timbre, sonority, articulation, and expressivity in these incipient works, and shows how an examination of the fragments can inform our understanding of the evolution of Schoenberg's compositional language in Opuses 11, 19, 23, 25, 33a, and 33b, the published piano works.

Canadian music scholar Elaine Keillor traces the critical reception and performance of Schoenberg's music in Canada from the early twentieth century through to 1960. She chronicles the impact of the Canadian Broadcasting Corporation, reviews published both in newspapers and scholarly journals, and a number of prominent Canadian performers, composers, and conductors — including Alfred Laliberté, Alberto Guerrero, Léo-Pol Morin, Rodolphe Mathieu, Franz Kraemer, Gerald Strang, John Weinzweig, Jean Coulthard, Emmy Heim,

Claude Champagne, Serge Garrant, John Beckwith, Ethel Stark, Eldon Rathburn, and Glenn Gould—on the dissemination of Schoenberg's music and ideas in Canada.

Among the post-war generation of pianists, Gould was one of Schoenberg's most ardent and gifted advocates and interpreters. James Wright's essay describes how the Canadian pianist's boundless passion for Schoenberg was expressed in his writings, his many lecture-recitals on Schoenberg and the Second Vienna School, his recording of the complete chamber works involving piano, and his own compositional work. In particular, the essay focuses on the Russian reception of Schoenberg's music, and the way in which Gould courageously championed Viennese modernism in lecture-recitals given at the Moscow and Leningrad Conservatories during his 1957 tour of the Soviet Union, at a time when Soviet culture was emerging from the artistic repressions of the Stalin years.

* * * * * * *

We wish to thank the many organizations who supported the Ottawa symposium and concerts as well as preparation of this book, including Carleton University, the Ottawa International Chamber Music Festival, the Austrian Embassy in Canada, the Austrian Cultural Forum, Austrian Airlines, the Arnold Schoenberg Center, the Canadian Broadcasting Corporation, Christ Church Cathedral, Library and Archives Canada, the Ottawa Sheraton Hotel, Air Transat, the National Arts Centre, and Peller Estates Wines. Our most sincere thanks are due also to Thomas Annand, Lena Brabec, Jack Coghill, Colin Cooke, Rebecca Danard, William Danard, James Deaville, Ernst and Donna-Ellen Dunshirn, Charles Enman, Eike Fess, Madeleine Forte, John Frecker, Bryan Gillingham, Martha Guth, Otto Heberlein, Mike Heffernan, Elaine Keillor, Hartmut Krones, Jill Laforty, Tristan Lauber, Brady Leafloor, Stéphane Lemelin, Karen Lobentanz, Peter McGillivray, Anne McNamee, Justin Mariner, Kim Matheson, Nate Meneer, Christian Meyer, Elsa Miller, Kate Morrison, Therese Muxeneder, Severine Neff, Karin Nemec, John Osborne, Sigurd Pacher, Michel Paquette, Michael Parsonage, Joseph Peller, Curtis Perry, Kate Porter, Peter Revers, Karen St-Aubin, Daniel Salinas, Anne Schoenberg, Barbara Schoenberg-Zeisl, Randol Schoenberg, Dennis Spiteri, Sarah Stephens, David Thies-Thompson, Jean-Jacques Van Vlasselaer, Erica Vincent, Sarah Westbrook, Arnold Whittall, and the late Eldon Rathburn.

It is impossible to adequately express our appreciation to Dianne Parsonage, who devoted countless hours to her role as Symposium co-chair, and who has provided invaluable assistance with the preparation of this book. Chief librarian with the Immigration and Refugee Board of Canada by day, Dianne brought boundless energy, experience, and enthusiasm to the Symposium team, as well as her substantial logistical, financial, managerial, and editing expertise. Without her support, guidance, and unfailingly level-headed counsel, the Symposium would not have taken place.

Finally, we want to offer our most heartfelt thanks to Nuria Schoenberg-Nono, Ronald Schoenberg, and Lawrence Schoenberg, to whom this book is warmly and respectfully dedicated. A conversation with Lawrence in September of 2006, over schnitzel in the cellar of a Heuriger near his father's Mödling home, was the initial inspiration for the symposium and concert series. We were deeply honored that all three of Arnold and Gertrud Schoenberg's children accepted our invitation to Ottawa. During our many memorable hours together, we came to admire how each has inherited the intelligence, warmth, good humor, integrity, resolve, and commitment to music that is the Schoenberg legacy. We only hope that the words that follow will serve to further their efforts to preserve that legacy, by leading the reader to the music itself.

James Wright
Alan Gillmor
Ottawa, April 2009

5

HISTORICAL PERSPECTIVES

The Young Arnold Schoenberg

Christian Meyer

Schoenberg's early years are clearly worth exploring in order to understand the genesis of the composer's extraordinary art and thought. While ample resources and documentation are available for Schoenberg's work in the early twentieth century, little is known about the decade before 1900, the period during which he took the initial steps in his artistic development. Hoping to shed light on new evidence concerning Schoenberg's early years, our team at the Arnold Schoenberg Center mounted a special exhibition in 2007, titled "The Young Schoenberg," which compiled and displayed original documents and manuscripts, as well as biographic and artistic sources archived at the Schoenberg Center and elsewhere.[1] A scholarly symposium on the topic was also presented from 4-6 October 2007.

At the turn of the century, Vienna, the capital of the Austro-Hungarian Empire, was one of the largest metropolises in the world. As the center of the

---

[1] I wish to acknowledge the work of the Schoenberg Center's archivists Therese Muxeneder, Eike Fess, and archival apprentice Christoph Edtmayer. Published studies of Schoenberg's early period include Walter Frisch, *The Early Works of Arnold Schoenberg, 1893-1908* (Berkeley: University of California Press, 1993); Alan Lessem, "Sound and Sense: The Search for a Unified Expression in the Early Songs of Arnold Schoenberg," in *German Literature and Music: An Aesthetic Fusion, 1890-1989*, ed. Claus Reschke and Howard Pollack (Munich: Verlag Wilhelm Fink, 1992): 85-94; Ena Steiner, "Schoenberg's Quest: Newly Discovered Works from His Early Years," *Musical Quarterly* 60/3 (July 1974): 401-20; Leonard Stein, "Toward a Chronology of Schoenberg's Early Unpublished Songs," *Journal of the Arnold Schoenberg Institute* 2/1 (October 1977): 72-80; R. Wayne Shoaf, "Acquisitions of Early Manuscripts," *Journal of the Arnold Schoenberg Institute* 10/2 (November 1987), 188-209; Harald Krebs, "Schoenberg's 'Liebeslied': An Early Example of Serial Writing," *Journal of the Arnold Schoenberg Institute* 11/1 (June 1988): 23-37.

Christian Meyer is Director of the Arnold Schoenberg Center and Foundation, a center for exhibitions, concerts, and lectures, as well as a repository for the extensive Arnold Schoenberg legacy, consisting of music manuscripts, documents, Schoenberg's writings and paintings, a library, and historical photographs. Dr. Meyer has directed the Foundation since its inception, from the shipping of the Schoenberg Legacy from Los Angeles to Vienna in 1997, to the Center's opening in 1998. During the first decade of the Center's existence, he has overseen exhibitions on themes such as "Schoenberg, Kandinsky, Der Blauer Reiter and the Russian Avant-garde," "The Painter Schoenberg," "Schoenberg and his God," "Schoenberg's Dodecaphonic Inventions," as well as more than a dozen international symposia, more than five hundred concerts, and a multitude of worldwide collaborations in the name of Arnold Schoenberg. He also serves as principle editor of the *Journal of the Arnold Schoenberg Center*.

multi-ethnic state of Austria-Hungary, the city became home to a wide variety of nationalities, language groups, and religious confessions. At the same time it was home to avant-garde artists, renowned scientists, and rebellious intellectuals who comingled to give rise to a unique cultural ambiance. The work of thinkers and artists working in a wide variety of fields seemed to be interwoven in unprecedented ways.[2]

Figure 1. Vienna ca. 1874: The imperial Ringstrasse and the earliest of its representational buildings have just been erected; on the top right the second district with the Prater gardens can be seen, Schoenberg's place of birth.

Arnold Schoenberg was born on 13 September 1874, at Obere Donau-strasse 5 in Vienna's Second District, where he went to school and spent his childhood in modest circumstances. His Father, Samuel Schoenberg (1838-89) was an enthusiastic chorister and his mother, Pauline Nachod (1848-98), came from a family of cantors in Prague. Schoenberg began studying violin when he was eight, and a year later he made his first attempts at composing music: initially waltzes and pieces for violin, then polkas, marches, and his first songs.

[2]See, for example, Allan Janik and Stephen Toulmin, *Wittgenstein's Vienna* (New York: Simon & Schuster, 1973); Carl E. Schorske, *Fin-de-Siècle Vienna: Politics and Culture* (New York: Vintage Books, 1981); Thomas Harrison, *1910: The Emancipation of Dissonance* (Berkeley & Los Angeles: University of California Press, 1996); Massimo Cacciari, *Posthumous People: Vienna at the Turning Point* (Palo Alto: Stanford University Press, 1979); William M. Johnston, *The Austrian Mind: An Intellectual and Social History, 1848-1938* (Berkeley and Los Angeles: University of California Press, 1972). Steven Beller, *Vienna and the Jews, 1867-1938: A Cultural History* (Cambridge University Press, 1991).

"As a child of less than nine years," he wrote, years later, "I had started composing little, and later large pieces for two violins, in imitation of such music as I used to play with my teacher or with a cousin of mine. When I could play violin duets of Viotti, Pleyel and others, I imitated their style."[3] Thanks to his cousin, the singer Hans Nachod (1883-1966), some of these early pieces, including several violin duets, have survived.[4]

Figure 2. The house at Obere Donaustrasse 5, where
Arnold Schoenberg was born.

When his father died in 1889, Schoenberg was only fifteen years of age. In order to provide for the family's livelihood, he left his school in Vereinsgasse and accepted a job at the private Viennese bank Werner & Company in 1890, where he worked for five years. Nevertheless music was his only passion. His sister Ottilie recalls that the bank manager complained after a short time to their mother that Arnold "scribbles music all over his papers—let him become a musician, is my advice."[5]

[3]Arnold Schoenberg, "Introduction to My Four String Quartets," program notes commissioned by Dean Mark Schubart and the Julliard String Quartet in 1949, but never printed (file T70.02, Arnold Schoenberg Center, Vienna).

[4]The Hans Nachhod Collection is held in the Archives of the North Texas State University, Denton, Texas. Fine recordings of some of these early works can be heard on a recently released CD by the Rangzen Quartet (and Strings), with Christina Fong (violin), *Arnold Schoenberg: Early and Unknown String Works*, OgreOgress Productions 45400 (2006).

[5]Letter of 6 August 1951 from Ottilie Blumauer-Felix to Gertrud Schoenberg (Arnold Schoenberg Center, Vienna [Gertrud Schoenberg Collection]).

Figure 3. David Joseph Bach, chalk drawing by Oskar Kokoschka.

Music groups playing light music in the nearby Prater parks were an early opportunity for Schoenberg and his friends to enjoy music performed publicly. David Josef Bach, his closest friend at the time, later recalled:

> It was in front of the Erstes Kaffeehaus on the main avenue of Vienna's Prater park; among the other young onlookers there stood a young lad in a short, light yellow overcoat, speaking loudly about music in general and about the music resounding from the park pavilion. That is my first memory of Arnold Schoenberg, and that initial image has not been blurred over the years to this very day. There we were, all of us, seventeen and eighteen, standing there at the fence, listening to the music free of charge. A young military bandmaster . . . used to play chunks of Wagner (once he even gave something from Meistersinger), and that was in 1891 or 1892. . . . For most of us, it was the only opportunity to really hear a bit of music. . . ."[6]

[6]David Josef Bach, "Aus der Jugendzeit," in *Musikblätter des Anbruch* 7/8 (August/September 1924): 317-20. Bach founded the celebrated Workers Symphony Concerts series in 1905, and in 1919 he was appointed director of a leftist artistic movement known as the Sozialdemokratische Kunststelle. In 1924 he organized an important "Theatre and Music Festival" that aroused controversy for its leftist politics. See also David Bach, "A Note on Arnold Schoenberg," *The Musical Quarterly* 22/1 (1936): 8-13; Jared Armstrong and Edward Timms, "Souvenirs of Vienna: The Legacy of David Josef Bach," in *Austrian Studies: Culture and Politics in Red Vienna* 14 (2006): 61-98.

David Bach was a "philosopher, connoisseur of literature, mathematician and quite a fine musician, who had a strong influence on my character," Schoenberg recalled.[7] It was through Bach that Schoenberg met Josef Scheu and came into contact with working-class singers, who would provide him with a source of income after he left his job in the bank.

Figure 4. A band playing in the Prater park (ca. 1890).

Oskar Adler, another of Schoenberg's friends during the period, says that the military bandleader and composer Karl Komzak, whose powerful and energetic way of conducting delighted Viennese audiences, was one of Schoenberg's earliest models. From Adler Schoenberg received first instruction in music theory and also in the poetic arts and philosophy

Among his early friends and acquaintances, Schoenberg singled out Alexander von Zemlinsky as "the one to whom I owe most of my knowledge of the technique and the problems of composing." And he continued:

---

[7]Arnold Schoenberg, "My Evolution [1949]," in *Style and Idea: Selected Writings*, ed. Leonard Stein (London: Faber & Faber, 1975), 80.

Figure 5. Oskar Adler (left); Alexander Zemlinsky
and Arnold Schoenberg (ca. 1900).

I have always thought and still believe that he was a great composer. Maybe his time
will come earlier than we think. One thing is beyond doubt, in my opinion: I do not
know one composer after Wagner who could satisfy the demands of the theatre
with better musical substance than he. . . . I had been a "Brahmsian" when I met
Zemlinsky. His love embraced both Brahms and Wagner and soon thereafter I
became an equally confirmed addict. No wonder that the music I composed at that
time mirrored the influence of both masters, to which a flavour of Liszt, Bruckner,
and perhaps also Hugo Wolf was added. . . . But the treatment of the instruments,
the manner of composition, and much of the sonority were strictly Wagnerian.[8]

At the age of nineteen Schoenberg progressed to writing complete pieces,
among which a charming Piece for Violin and Piano (ca. 1893-94) is a fine
example. Schoenberg's first Lieder, written when he was twenty years of age,
are indications of his artistic goals at the time. Many of them are very simple, in
the style of folk song. Others are more ambitious, such as his *Schilflied*, a setting
of a poem by Nikolaus Lenau, which earned him a first prize from the amateur
orchestra Polyhymnia. Music written simply for the pleasure of playing together
with others included the Six Pieces for Piano Four Hands, dedicated to one of
his music friends, Bella Cohn, the Three Piano Pieces, as well as the *Songs Without
Words*, one scored for strings, and another for piano, which he had originally
conceived as a *Notturno* for orchestra.

[8]Ibid., 87.

Figure 6. Arnold Schoenberg: Piece for Violin and Piano (1893-94).

The most advanced piece from this period is Schoenberg's String Quartet in D major (1897). After he had composed an initial draft, Schoenberg showed the piece to Zemlinsky, who found the piece in need of serious editing and revision. Following his teacher's guidance, Schoenberg completely rewrote the first movement, and exchanged the second and third movements. With Zemlinksy's help, a small private performance was arranged, following which

Figure 7. *Schilflied* (1894) (left); Six Pieces for Piano Four Hands (cover, right).

the first public performance was given in the Vienna Bösendorfer Hall on 20 December 1898 by the Fitzner Quartet. Both audience and press received the piece well, the latter commenting that "a true talent" had been discovered.[9] While the formal design of the quartet derives from Mozart, Beethoven, and Brahms, the melodic *ductus* shows similarities to Antonín Dvořák's music, tendencies which Schoenberg soon abandoned when he turned to another idol: Richard Strauss.

The same year that the String Quartet in D major was performed for the first time, Schoenberg wrote his two Songs, Op. 1 (1898), *Dank* and *Abschied*, after poems by Karl von Levetzow. Opuses 2 and 3 (1898-99) consist of ten more songs, following which he composed the string sextet *Transfigured Night*, Op. 4, which appeared on the threshold of the twentieth century. Wagnerian influence is obvious in this musical translation of Richard Dehmel's poem from the cycle *Woman and World* (1896), employing "leitmotiv" technique and the use of sequence and motivic repetition to intensify the development of dramatic passages. The sextet's advanced harmonic language and the persistent use of vagrant harmonies prompted a member of the Vienna "Tonkünstlerverein" jury to say of the work, "it sounds as if someone had wiped off the score of 'Tristan' while the ink was still wet."[10] While the juror's sense of Wagnerian

---

[9]*Neue musikalische Presse*, 25 December 1898, No. 52.

[10]Quoted in Alexander Zemlinsky, "Jugenderinnerungen," in *Arnold Schönberg zum 60* (Wien, Universal, 1934), 33-35.

influence in the piece was not entirely wrong, Schoenberg's harmonic language had developed well beyond Wagner's in this early piece, which has since become one of the most popular pieces of chamber music from the period.

Figure 8. Arnold Schoenberg, *Transfigured Night*, manuscript (1899).

On the whole, the 1890s were a time of camaraderie and artistic awakening for the young Schoenberg, when the "nervous splendor" of fin-de-siècle Vienna was in full flower.[11] During this period Schoenberg created his first songs, solo and chamber music—works of remarkable authenticity and beauty—and established his essential confidence, competence, and artistic vision, which prepared him for the years of personal, professional, and compositional upheaval that lay ahead.

---

[11]The heady atmosphere of late nineteenth-century Vienna is well captured in Frederic Morton's popular history *A Nervous Splendor: Vienna 1888/1889* (Boston: Little Brown, 1979).

Schoenberg's String Quartet No. 1 in Dresden (1907): Programming the Unprogrammable, Performing the Unperformable

James Deaville*

The performances of Arnold Schoenberg's *Verein für musikalische Privataufführungen* (1918 to 1921) have received attention in scholarly biographies and studies devoted to Schoenberg, not least as a performance organization devoted to modern musical works under the direction of a leading modernist composer.[1] We are most likely also familiar with his participation in the Vienna-based new music societies the *Wiener Tonkünstlerverein* (1879-1912),[2] the *Ansorge-Verein* (1903-10),[3] and the *Vereinigung schaffender Tonkünstler* (1904-05),[4] the last an association that he

*This study would not have been possible without the generous support of the Social Sciences and Humanities Research Council of Canada, which funded my research into this and other Allgemeiner Deutcher Musikverein-related publications. The staff of the Goethe- und Schiller-Archiv, Klassik-Stiftung Weimar, have been quite helpful in securing access to the sources. I am grateful to my Carleton University colleague James Wright for his comments and insights, and to student assistant Sarah Stephens for her assistance with the tables. Unless indicated otherwise, translations are by the author.

[1] Individual studies of the Society are provided by Regina Busch, Thomas Schäfer, and Reinhard Kapp, "Der 'Verein für musikalische Privataufführungen',," *Journal of the Arnold Schoenberg Center* 3 (2000): 77-83; and Ivan Vojtěch, "Einige Anmerkungen zur Idee des 'Vereins für musikalische Privataufführungen' in Wien," ibid.: 107-13.

[2] Uwe Harten, "Wiener Tonkünstler-Verein," in *Oesterreichisches Musiklexikon*, ed. Rudolf Flotzinger (Vienna: Verlag der Österreichischen Akademie der Wissenschaften, 2006), V, 2668-69. The association began in 1879 as an informal circle of musicians that was incorporated in 1885 and served as an opposition to the progressive *Wiener Akademische Wagner-Verein*. I thank Peter Revers for his help in clarifying the dates and bibliography for this organization.

[3] Eike Rathgeber and Christian Heitler, "Der Wiener Ansorge-Verein 1903-1910 (Verein für Kunst und Kultur)," in *Kultur—Urbanität—Moderne: Differenzierungen der Moderne in Zentraleuropa um 1900*, ed. Heidemarie Uhl, in *Studien zur Moderne* 4 (Vienna: Passagen Verlag, 1999), 383-436.

[4] Wolfgang Behrens, "'... Dieses Jahr war nicht verloren': Die 'Vereinigung schaffender Tonkünstler in Wien' und ein nicht von Schönberg verfasstes Memorandum," in *Jahrbuch des Staatlichen Instituts für Musikforschung Preussischer Kulturbesitz 2003* (Stuttgart: J.B. Metzler, 2003), 249–64.

James Deaville is an Associate Professor in the School for Studies in Art & Culture, Carleton University. He has published in *Journal of the American Musicological Society*, *Journal of the Society for American Music*, *Nineteenth-Century Music Review*, *Journal of Musicological Research*, *Canadian University Music Review*, *Liszt and His World*, *Cambridge Companion to Liszt*, *Cambridge Companion to the Lied*, and *Music in the Post-9/11 World*, among others. Regarding the *Allgemeine Deutsche Musikverein*, he has authored contributions about the relations of Reger and Delius with the society, as well as the *New Grove* entry for it.

founded with Alexander Zemlinsky. However, during the first decade of the century, Schoenberg also associated himself with a broadly based, well known, and long-standing performance society for new music, the *Allgemeine Deutsche Musikverein*.

Founded in 1861 by Franz Liszt and his New-German colleagues, the ADMV took as its mandate the cultivation of music by living "greater German" composers, staging the premieres of such important works as the oratorio *Die Legende von der heiligen Elisabeth* by Liszt and the Sixth Symphony of Mahler.[5] Its annual festivals occasionally featured larger "consecrated" works by German composers of the past, especially Bach, to serve as validation for its activities on behalf of the younger generation.[6] Unlike Schoenberg's various Musikvereine in Vienna, the ADMV had no one city as its locus, but rather met each year in a different German city, including locations in Austria, Switzerland, and East Prussia.

1901	Heidelberg	F. Steinbach, F. Draeseke, J.L. Nicodé, S. Ochs, E. Humperdinck
1902	Krefeld	M. Schillings, F.S., J.L.N., S.O., E.H.
1903	Basel	M.S., E.H., J.L.N., A. Obrist, P. Wolfrum
1904	Frankfurt a/M	M.S., E.H., A.O., P.W., S.v. Hausegger
1905	Graz	M.S., E.H., A.O., P.W., S.v.H.
1906	Essen	M.S., E.H., A.O., P.W., H. Pfitzner
1907	Dresden	M.S., E.H., A.O., P.W., H.P.
1908	München	A.O., E.H., J.L.N., M. Fiedler, F. Hegar
1909	Stuttgart	A.O., E.H., J.L.N., M.F., F.H.
1910	Zürich	A.O., J.L.N., H. Abendroth, V. Andreae, A. Zemlinsky
1911	Heidelberg	S.v.H., J.L.N., H.A., V.A., A.Z.
1912	Danzig	S.v.H., J.L.N., H.A., V.A., H. Bischoff
1913	Jena	S.v.H., J.L.N., H.A., V.A., H.B.
1914	Essen	S.v.H., J.L.N., H.A., V.A., H.B.

Table 1. Festival Locations and Program Committees, ADMV, 1901-1914.

Since 1901, the Society had experienced an upswing through the presidency of Richard Strauss, who through the ADMV promoted the cause of such "new" German composers as Richard Strauss, Max Reger, and Arnold Schoenberg. As is well known, Strauss assisted Schoenberg in receiving a teaching

---

[5]James Deaville, "Allgemeiner Deutscher Musikverein," in *The New Grove Dictionary of Music and Musicians*, rev. ed., ed. Stanley Sadie (New York: Macmillan, 2001), I, 303-04.

[6]This process of "consecration" of the avant-garde is described by Pierre Bourdieu in "The Production of Belief: Contribution to an Economy of Symbolic Goods," in *The Field of Cultural Production*, ed. Randal Johnson (New York: Columbia University Press, 1993), 76-78.

appointment in Berlin in 1902.[7] A decade later, they were to trade barbs, with Strauss famously and injudiciously writing to Alma Mahler in 1913 that "the only person who can help poor Schoenberg now is a psychiatrist," to which Schoenberg responded in 1914, "he is no longer of the slightest artistic interest to me, and whatever I may once have learnt from him, I am thankful to say I misunderstood."[8] However, in the intervening years, Strauss personally interceded on behalf of Schoenberg with the ADMV's relatively conservative Board of Directors (under Max Schillings's vice-presidency), so that the younger composer received not insignificant financial support and a performance outside of Vienna at a crucial time in his career.[9]

Why Schoenberg became a member of the ADMV is not clear from the documentary record. Under the influence of Strauss in Berlin, Schoenberg may have recognized the value of belonging to this supra-regional performance organization. Or it could have been the matter that, in order to receive financial assistance from the organization, he had to become a member. As is apparent from the cases of Mahler and Reger and the ADMV, composers tended to avoid joining organizations unless they were convinced of some advantage for themselves, primarily the possibility of performances.[10] Whatever the case for Schoenberg, in 1902 he became well acquainted with Strauss, who recommended him for a harmony position at the venerable Stern Conservatory. Schoenberg's first ADMV membership card dates from November, 1902—he is there called "Arnold Schöntag"[11]—and not coincidentally, one month later Strauss reported to Schillings that he has "urgently recommended the man, who is in the most severe need and is *very* talented, for a multi-year scholarship in the amount of 1000 marks."[12]

---

[7]Michael Kennedy, *Richard Strauss: Man, Musician, Enigma* (Cambridge: Cambridge University Press, 1999), 172-73.

[8]Ibid., 173

[9]Regarding Strauss's support for Schoenberg, see, for example, Roswitha Schlötterer, *Richard Strauss—Max von Schillings: Ein Briefwechsel* (Pfaffenhofen: W. Ludwig, 1987), 10-11, and Matthew Boyden, *Richard Strauss* (Boston: Northeastern University Press, 1999), 156-57. Even though they detail Strauss's financial interventions on behalf of the younger composer, the authors do not mention his support as provided through the Dresden performance of Schoenberg's Quartet.

[10]Deaville, "'... Nicht im Sinne von Franz Liszt ...': Reger and the Allgemeine Deutsche Musikverein," in *Reger Studien 6: Musikalische Moderne und Tradition: Internationaler Reger-Kongress Karlsruhe 1998*, ed. Alexander Becker, Gabriele Gefäller, and Susanne Popp, in *Schriftenreihe des Max-Reger-Instituts Karlsruhe*, Vol. 13 (Wiesbaden: Breitkopf & Härtel, 2000), 121-43.

[11]Postcard from Gustav Rassow to Arnold Schoenberg (Bremen, November 1902); reproduction, ID 22665, Arnold Schoenberg Center, Vienna, from Arnold Schoenberg Collection, Library of Congress, Washington, D.C.

[12]Letter from Richard Strauss to Max von Schillings (Charlottenburg, 18 December 1902); in Schlötterer, *Richard Strauss—Max von Schillings*, 78. "Ich habe den Mann [Schoenberg], der in bitterster Not und *sehr* talentvoll ist, dringend zu mehrjährigem Stipendium von je 1000 M. empfohlen. Bitte unterstütze mich und schreibe ihm auch Du ein glänzendes Zeugniss. Du wirst ebenfalls finden, dass die Sachen, wenn auch noch überladen, doch von grossem Können und Begabung zeugen."

At the same time, Strauss had the *Gurrelieder* score sent to Schillings, about which the former wrote in his letter, "if also overladen, it demonstrates great ability and talent." He expected nothing less than a splendid letter of recommendation from Schillings, which Strauss called a matter of supporting himself. This was a period of the strongest rapport between Strauss and Schoenberg, though apparently also a time when Strauss did not know where Schoenberg was headed compositionally. From the literature, we are well aware of Strauss's financial support of Schoenberg, but the personal risk Strauss took only becomes apparent when we look at how Schillings responded.

The letter from 27 December 1902 was not what Strauss would have liked to read: "My first impression was a true shock. . . . Where are the misunderstood scores of R. Strauss leading these super-disciples! Everywhere colors, splashes of colors, confusion of colors, and almost no drawing, no line, no nature. . . . I do not believe that I can warm myself up for this artistic expression, this acrobatics of instrumentation. . . . However, knowing life's fate and the situation of the 'accused' Schoenberg, the idealism . . . and the self-attained ability of the score has so impressed me, that I will not delay in supporting your splendid recommendation with the Liszt Foundation's Board of Trustees according to my powers. In any case, Sch. deserves every support in the spirit of Liszt!"[13] Schoenberg eventually received the letter of award for 1000 Marks in mid-March, 1903, which is the same amount he would receive for 1904.

If Schoenberg's hyper-romantic *Gurrelieder* had a disquieting effect upon the conservative Schillings, one can only speculate regarding how the Vice-President of the ADMV must have felt about the First String Quartet! Unfortunately, the name Schoenberg does not again surface in the correspondence between Strauss and Schillings, despite the 1907 performance. The scholar must look elsewhere to reconstruct this facet of the work's *Rezeptionsgeschichte*.

For the Dresden festival that was to take place between 29 June and 2 July 1907, Schoenberg submitted two scores, the String Quartet and the *Orchesterlieder*. We know this from the "Verzeichnis der eingereichten Werke" that is originally dated 1 December 1906, and lists 135 total submissions.[14] However, the two

---

[13]Max von Schillings to Richard Strauss (Munich, 27 December 1902); Schlötterer, *Richard Strauss—Max von Schillings*, 79. "Mein erster Eindruck war ein echter Schrecken. . . . Nun, wohin führen die missverstandenen Partituren von R. Strauss diese Überjünger!! Überall Farben, Farbenklexe, Farbenwirrwarr—und fast keine Zeichnung, keine Linie, keine Natur. . . . Ich glaube nicht, dass ich mich für diese Kunstäusserung, diese Instrumentations-Akrobatie erwärmen könnte. . . . Nachdem ich aber die Lebensschicksale und die Situation des 'Angeklagten' Schönberg kenne, imponiert mir der in der Partitur zu Tage tretende Idealismus und auch das selbsterrungene Können derartig, dass ich nicht zögere Deine glänzende Empfehlung beim Lisztcuratorium nach Kräften zu unterstützen. Im Sinne Liszt's verdient Sch. jedenfalls alle Förderung!"

[14]Tonkünstlerversammlung in Dresden, 1907 (Akten Musikausschuß—Aloys Obrist); Archiv des Allgemeinen Deutschen Musikvereins, Goethe- und Schiller-Archiv, Klassik Stiftung Weimar, 70/190

Schoenberg entries, No. 44½ for the quartet and No. 98½ for the songs, are both later additions. Program committee chair Alois Obrist wrote a short, undecipherable comment about the songs, which Dreililien-Verlag sent in on 8 January 1907.[15] However, Max Marschalk notes the following about Schoenberg's submission in his accompanying letter:

> Herr Arnold Schönberg (Vienna) requests that we send you the enclosed 6 orchestral songs (Op. 7 [sic], No. 1 through 6) for the Allgemeine Deutsche Musikverein. Herr Schönberg submits these works, as far as we know, under special agreement with Herrn Dr. Richard Strauss.[16]

There exist none of the obligatory assessments for the Quartet, which did not receive definitive approval until May—it may not have been submitted for Dresden until early February. On 6 February 1907, Mahler wrote the following to Strauss:

> Dear Friend:
> I heard the new Schoenberg Quartet yesterday and found it so profound and impressive that I cannot but most emphatically recommend it for the Dresden Festival. I enclose the score and hope you will have time to look at it. The Rosé Quartet offers to interpret it if their traveling expenses are paid. Forgive me for pestering you, but I think you will have much pleasure from this. . . .[17]

So, Strauss's hand was clearly at work here, enabling Schoenberg not only the late submissions, but also essentially allowing his Quartet to enjoy the status of favored work, which did not require committee approval. This latter step was important, for it explains how the work could have escaped the close scrutiny of the rather conservative program committee, which consisted of Schillings; Alois Obrist (chair), Kapellmeister in Weimar; opera composer Engelbert Humperdinck; Heidelberg composer/organist Philipp Wolfrum; and the young composer/conductor Hans Pfitzner. It also answers direct and indirect questions by the reviewers of the Schoenberg scandal in Dresden, who wondered how such music could have been selected for performance.[18] In reality, it was

[15]Dreililien-Verlag of Berlin was Schoenberg's first major publisher, responsible for Opp. 1-4 and 6-7. It was succeeded by the Viennese firm Universal as the composer's primary publisher.

[16]Unpublished letter from Max Marschalk (Dreililien Verlag) to Alois Obrist (Hallensee-Berlin, 8 January 1907); Archiv des Allgemeinen Deutschen Musikvereins, Goethe- und Schiller-Archiv, Klassik Stiftung Weimar, 70/190. "Herr Arnold Schönberg/Wien bittet uns Ihnen die beiliegenden 6 Orchesterlieder (Op. 7 [sic] Nr. 1 bis 6) für den Allgemeinen Deutschen Musikverein zu übergeben. Herr Schönberg reicht diese Arbeiten, soviel uns bekannt ist, im besonderen Einverständnis mit Herrn Dr. Richard Strauss ein."

[17]Letter from Mahler to Strauss (Vienna, 6 February 1907); *Gustav Mahler—Richard Strauss Correspondence 1888-1911*, ed. Herta Blaukopf (Chicago: University of Chicago Press, 1984), 96.

[18]See, for example, O.K. [Otto Keller?], "Eindrücke und Nachklänge vom Dresdner Tonkünstlerfest," *Neue Musik-Zeitung* 28 (1907): 429-34.

not debated by the program committee, a privilege that only a few living composers enjoyed: Strauss, Mahler, Reger, and also Schillings.[19] This is how Strauss was able to get around the issue of the Quartet's "unprogrammability," by circumventing the normal adjudication process. We thus see Strauss's support for Schoenberg extending in a concrete way beyond their mutual years in Berlin.

With regard to performability, questions about the performing ensemble did arise as the festival dates approached. The festival's resident quartet, the Petri Quartet of Dresden, collectively and individually possessed the first rights for performance of chamber music on the program. In this light it should be noted that all of the festival chamber-music offerings were new compositions, although of varied stylistic directions, difficulty, and instrumentation (see Table 2 for a listing).

June 29, 1st Chamber Concert
1) W. Middelschulte: Passacaglia, D-moll for organ
2) A. Reuss: Streichquartett, D-moll, Op. 25 (Petri Quartet)
3) B. Sekles: Serenade für 11 Soloinstrumente (fl., ob., clar., horn, bsn., 2 vln., vla., vc., cb., harp), Op. 14
4) W. Rohde: Pfte.-Trio, F-moll, Op. 21

June 30, 2nd Chamber Concert
1) Arnold Schönberg: Streichquartett (in einem Satz), Op. 7
2) W. Courvoisier: 8 Lieder
3) H. Pogge: Quartett in einem Satz f. vln., clar., vc., pf.
4) W. Kienzl: 3 Lieder

Table 2. Chamber Music Concerts at ADMV Dresden Festival, 1907.

An interesting, unpublished letter by ADMV Secretary Friedrich Rösch from 14 May makes clear the issues surrounding the Dresden performance of the Schoenberg Quartet. While the Petri ensemble knew the difficulties of the work, the quartet declared itself prepared to perform it, as a matter of honor:

> At a meeting with Music Director von Schuch, I insistently pointed to the difficulties of the work and also to the fact that the Rosé Quartet has already studied and performed the work and may be ready to play [it] also in Dresden. After Herr Petri and colleagues declared themselves prepared to take on the work, however, we will have to wait to see whether they have dedicated themselves to study the work not just with enthusiasm but also with such endurance that they are not frightened by its difficulties. Meanwhile I received the impression in Dresden that just the difficulties of the work have goaded on the ambition of the Dresden gentlemen, so

---

[19]See Deaville, "'...Nicht im Sinne von Franz Liszt...'," 134-35.

that they would not be happy to have the work played by the gentlemen from Vienna.[20]

Rösch made no promises, however, and in the final instance, the Rosé Quartet—which from the start had offered to play the Quartet itself—ended up giving the Dresden performance. From the letter we may draw the inference that the Petri Quartet ultimately found the First String Quartet "unperformable," at least on relatively short notice; however, we must keep in mind that the players had to learn four other new compositions on the program, although none of the extent and difficulty of the Schoenberg offering. Though Rösch mentions the name of festival director Ernst von Schuch, who was the principal conductor of the Dresden *Staatskapelle*, there is no reason to believe he had much more than an advisory role. Still, Schuch was a Dresden supporter of Strauss and Schoenberg, and given the difficulties with the Quartet, he may have taken an active role in ensuring that the composition stayed on the program.

All composers involved in the festival were strongly recommended to submit self-analyses of their compositions, which would be published in *Die Musik*, the *Neue Zeitschrift für Musik,* and the *Allgemeine Musik-Zeitung* in advance of the event for the benefit of concert-goers. Max Reger's self-analyses were notorious for their biting humor,[21] but Schoenberg himself provided a sober, straightforward analysis of Op. 7.[22] On the one hand, he argues for the piece's *"Einsatzigkeit,"* on the other furnishes a Roman-numeral breakdown of the Quartet into what appear to be the traditional four movements, although his closer analysis points out motivic unity within the composition as a whole. The analysis is too well known to Schoenberg specialists to necessitate further

---

[20]Unpublished letter from Friedrich Rösch to Arnold Schoenberg (Berlin, 14 May 1907); reproduction, ID 11729, Arnold Schoenberg Center, Vienna, from Arnold Schoenberg Collection, Library of Congress, Washington, D.C. "Ich habe bei einer Besprechung mit Herrn Generalmusikdirektor von Schuch auf die Schwierigkeiten des Werkes eindringlich hingewiesen und auch darauf, dass das Quartett Rosé das Werk bereits früher studiert und auch schon aufgeführt habe und event[uel]l bereit sei, das Werk auch in Dresden zu spielen. Nachdem sich nun aber die Herren Petri und Genossen zur Uebernahme des Werkes bereit erklärt haben, wird man vorläufig nur abzuwarten haben, ob sie sich dem Studium des Werkes nicht nur mit Eifer hingeben, sondern auch mit einer solchen Ausdauer, dass sie durch die Schwierigkeiten des Werkes nicht abgeschreckt werden. Ich habe indessen in Dresden den Eindruck gewonnen, dass gerade die Schwierigkeiten des Werkes den Ehrgeiz der Dresdner Herren aufgestachelt haben, sodass sie nicht gern geneigt wären, sich das Quartett von den Wiener Herren vorspielen zu lassen."

[21]"Streichquartett op. 74 in d-moll," in "Zum 40. Tonkünstler-Fest des Allgemeinen deutschen Musikvereins in Frankfurt a. M.," *Die Musik* 3/16 (1904): 244-47; "Variationen und Fuge über ein Thema von Joh. Seb. Bach für Klavier zu zwei Händen op. 81" and "Variationen und Fuge über ein Thema von Beethoven für Pianoforte zu vier Händen op. 86," in "Zum 41. Tonkünstler-Fest des Allgemeinen deutschen Musikvereins in Graz," *Die Musik* 4/16 (1905): 316-17; "Der 100. Psalm für Chor, Orchester und Orgel op. 106" and "Quartett für Violine, Bratsche, Violoncello und Pianoforte op. 113," in "Zum 46. Tonkünstler-Fest des Allgemeinen deutschen Musikvereins in Zürich," *Die Musik* 9/16 (1910): 225, 248-49.

[22]Arnold Schönberg, "Streichquartett Op. 7," in "Die 43. Tonkünstler-Versammlung des Allgemeinen Deutschen Musikvereins zu Dresden (28. Juni-2. Juli)," *Die Musik* 6/18 (1907): 332-34.

elaboration here;[23] nonetheless, it is important for us to consider this self-analysis within the broader context of its purpose. It would appear that the composer here was giving the audience—many of whom were not musicians, but members of the Dresden public-at-large—signposts that draw upon recognizable morphological homologies with the standard eighteenth- and nineteenth-century repertory. Schoenberg himself refers to these meta-musical topoi in his brief preface to the analysis: "the thematic types of the [traditional] four movements are still used. . . ."[24] The pedagogy of the self-analysis cannot be faulted, since he clearly sets out changes in character, tempo, and meter for the readers, even if they might not be conversant with the details of motivic similarity (or even musical notation). Here the problem is that none of the critics appear to have acquainted themselves with the tool that the ADMV created to facilitate understanding of the new music they were presenting.[25]

As might be expected, the result was a scandal, akin to the premiere in Vienna earlier in 1907,[26] as documented by Martin Eybl in his review collection *Die Befreiung des Augenblicks: Schönbergs Skandalkonzerte 1907 und 1908.*[27] In order to examine the much maligned Viennese critical response to the first two String Quartets and the *Kammersymphonie,* Eybl focuses almost exclusively on the Viennese premieres, so that the Dresden performance does not figure in his documentation. However, the scene was not that different: reviewers noted how the work could only be completed against a growing unrest, with a battle afterwards between numerous whistlers and a small but dedicated group of supporters (from Vienna) who stamped and vigorously clapped.[28] Members of that Viennese

[23]For example, Walter Frisch uses it (as well as Schoenberg's "Notes on the Four String Quartets" from 1949) as the basis for his own analysis in *The Early Works of Arnold Schoenberg, 1893-1908* (Berkeley: University of California Press, 1993), 181-220. Christian M. Schmidt discusses this "self-analysis" in detail in "Schönbergs analytische Bemerkungen zum Streichquartett op. 7," *Österreichische Musikzeitschrift* 39 (1984): 296-300.

[24]"Die Thementypen der vier Sätze sind zwar angewendet . . . ," Schönberg, "Streichquartett Op. 7," 332.

[25]In *Die Musik,* which was founded in 1901, the previews began with the 1902 Krefeld festival (the first under Strauss's leadership of the ADMV) and extended through the Jena festival of 1913.

[26]Thirty years later, Schoenberg still remembered the Dresden scandal: "When, for example, my First String Quartet was played at a festival of music in Dresden in 1906 [sic], the performance provoked the same tremendous scandal that it had at its first performance a few months before in Vienna." Arnold Schoenberg, "How One Becomes Lonely," in *Style and Idea: Selected Writings,* ed. Leonard Stein, trans. Leo Black, 2nd ed. (Berkeley: University of California Press, 1984), 42.

[27]Martin Eybl, *Die Befreiung des Augenblicks: Schönbergs Skandalkonzerte 1907 und 1908* (Vienna: Böhlau, 2004).

[28]The reviewer O.K. from the *Neue Musik-Zeitung* described it with the following caustic words: "The public had a right to reject the piece. After three-quarters of an hour of the most tortured listening, it was further provoked by the brash applause of several friends of the author." ("Das Publikum hatte ein gutes Recht, das Stück abzulehnen. Nach dreiviertelstündigem meist qualvollem Hören wurde es durch den aufdringlichen Beifall einiger Freunde des Autors auch noch provoziert.") O.K., "Eindrücke und Nachklänge vom Dresdner Tonkünstlerfest…," 431.

group included Alban Berg and Erwin Stein. The reviewers were by and large unfavorable, although those in *Die Musik* and *Neue Zeitschrift für Musik* both admitted that closer study might yield fruits (in other words, if they had read Schoenberg's self-analysis, they might have responded differently). There is no need to rehearse the various points of the critics, which the reader can anticipate from other reviews of the works in Vienna.[29] However, the *Neue Zeitschrift* review by Paul Pfitzner deserves mention for his comparisons and succinct vitriol:

> Strauss's *Salome* and Reger are innocent orphans in comparison with the Viennese *Himmelstürmer*. . . . It may be that my impression will improve with closer study, but it is by no means deeply felt music. Rather, at the best it is a brooded-up pile of the most intolerable discords.[30]

The negative press and even the scandalous concert-hall response in Dresden, as well as Strauss's departure from the Society's Presidency, were not enough to dissuade Schoenberg from remaining a member of the ADMV and even from contemplating participation. He considered sending in something for the 1910 festival in Zurich, which happened to include Alexander Zemlinsky on the program committee. In an unpublished letter from 15 December 1909, Schoenberg asked Obrist whether he could still make a submission, even though the deadline of 1 December—which he thought was 1 January—had passed.[31] Apparently Schoenberg made no submission, for on 31 January 1910, Zemlinsky wrote to Obrist that, in light of the poor level of compositions received so far, he "unconditionally recommends unsubmitted orchestral songs by Arnold Schoenberg [Op. 8], who by far is the most original talent of all of them."[32] Fellow program committee member Volkmar Andreae also mentioned the desirability of programming Schoenberg in a communication with the ADMV Board: "I have also looked around in Austria for young talents and would like to recommend to you most warmly: Arnold Schoenberg (Vienna), String

---

[29]For the Viennese performance on 5 February 1907, Eybl's documentation includes favorable reviews from the *Neue Wiener Journal* (Elsa Bienenfeld), *Die Zeit* (Richard Wallaschek), and *Wiener Allgemeine Zeitung* (Carl Lafite), and negative ones from *Das Vaterland* (Richard von Kralik), *Musikalisches Wochenblatt* (Theodor Helm), and *Neue musikalische Presse* ("Florestan").

[30]Paul Pfitzner, "Tagesgeschichtliches. Musikbriefe und Berichte. Deutsches Reich. Dresden, den 3. Juli. Tonkünstlerfest vom 29. Juni bis 2. Juli," *Neue Zeitschrift für Musik* 74/28 (11 July 1907): 617. "Strauss's 'Salome' und Reger sind unschuldige Waisenknaben gegen diesen Wiener Himmelstürmer. . . . Möglich, dass sich der Eindruck bei genauerem Studium bessert; empfundene Musik ist's keinesfalls, sondern höchstens eine ergrübelte Anhäufung unleidlichster Missklänge."

[31]Unpublished letter from Arnold Schoenberg to Alois Obrist (Vienna, 15 December 1909); Archiv des Allgemeinen Deutschen Musikvereins, Goethe- und Schiller-Archiv, Klassik Stiftung Weimar, 70/166.

[32]Unpublished letter from Alexander Zemlinsky to Alois Obrist (Vienna, 31 January 1910), in Archiv des Allgemeinen Deutschen Musikvereins, Goethe- und Schiller-Archiv, Klassik Stiftung Weimar, 70/234. "Dagegen möchte ich *unbedingt* vorschlagen nicht eingereichte Lieder mit Orchester v. *Arnold Schönberg*, der von all diesen das *weitaus* originellste Talent ist."

Quartet."[33] Despite all of this effort, no work of Schoenberg was heard at the festival of 1910, which may have to do with the absence of former protector Strauss from the organization.

Although Schoenberg's music appeared on three festival programs in the 1920s, none of them represented his most recent direction. The ADMV ultimately was not the place for the performance of Schoenberg, nor of his associates Berg or Webern, even though their earlier, established music did occasionally figure in programs of the 1920s.[34]

Schoenberg

1920 (Weimar), Fünf Stücke für Orchester, Op. 16 (Ernst
    Latzko, conductor)
1924 (Frankfurt a. M.), *Friede auf Erden*, Op. 13 (Hermann
    Scherchen, conductor)
1929 (Duisburg), *Die glückliche Hand* (Paul Drach, conductor)

Webern

1922 (Düsseldorf), Passacaglia, Op. 1 (Webern, conductor)
1928 (Schwerin), String Trio, Op. 20

Berg

1924 (Frankfurt a. M.), Drei Bruchstücke aus *Wozzeck*, Op. 7
    (Ludwig Rottenberg, conductor)
1930 (Königsberg), Konzertarie "Der Wein"

Table 3. ADMV Festival Performances of Schoenberg, Webern,
and Berg during the 1920s.

The Society never resolved the challenge posed by atonality, which would continue to cause difficulties for submissions by avant-garde composers of the 1920s like Hindemith and Krenek and make the Donaueschingen festival of the 1920s look like a welcome alternative.[35] However, posterity must give Richard Strauss and his organization credit for having taken a chance with the newly

[33]Unpublished letter from Volkmar Andreae to Alois Obrist (Zurich, 4 December 1909); Archiv des Allgemeinen Deutschen Musikvereins, Goethe- und Schiller-Archiv, Klassik Stiftung Weimar, 70/234; "Ich habe mich auch in Oesterreich nach jungen Talenten umgesehen und möchte Ihnen da aufs wärmste empfehlen: Schönberg (Wien) Streichquartett. . . ."

[34]To the extent that these works had entered into the "modernist canon" or, to use Bourdieu's term, the "consecrated avant-garde," the Society was taking no risk by programming them.

[35]See Josef Häusler, *Spiegel der neuen Musik: Donaueschingen. Chronik—Tendenzen—Werkbesprechungen* (Stuttgart: Metzler, 1996).

composed First String Quartet in Dresden in May of 1907, after the Viennese audience and press had rejected the same composition. One could also argue that, regardless of the negative critical reception accorded the Quartet, the Dresden festival concert brought Schoenberg's name in general and the First String Quartet in particular to a larger and more diverse audience than that of the Viennese *Skandalkonzerte* of 1907 and 1908. A host of prominent central-European composers and conductors were in attendance, including Strauss, Ernst von Schuch, Felix Mottl, Wilhelm Kienzl, Hermann Abendroth, Hans Pfitzner, Siegmund von Hausegger, Emil von Reznicek, Albert Fuchs, and Hans Sommer—they *heard* Schoenberg's music, whatever they may have thought about it. The Dresden episode should make the Schoenberg scholar aware of the value of turning our attention from Vienna to other sites of performance in the early years, in attempting to develop the broadest and most comprehensive *Rezeptionsgeschichte* for that crucial period of his emergence onto the international music scene.

A Bridge to a New Life: Waltzes in Schoenberg's Chamber Music

Alexander Carpenter*

As of 1905, Schoenberg's life, including his marriage to Mathilde Zemlinsky, was not particularly happy. The joyful early days of courtship behind him, the struggling composer was now a young husband and father, caught up in the financial worries and domestic strife that would plague his household off and on for much of the next two decades. Schoenberg documented the emotional foment of 1904-05 in the "secret program" of his String Quartet, Op. 7, which is of course now no longer a secret.[1] The program describes a series of emotional ups and downs, hinting at the on-going conflict between, presumably, Schoenberg and Mathilde ("He and She" in the program) and Schoenberg's unsettled state. Early in the Quartet, after an intense and fractious opening, a waltz appears. Relative to the program, this waltz marks what Schoenberg identifies as a "transition," a bridge passage, ultimately leading towards a temporary "struggle" and culminating in a section titled "Feeling new life."[2] For Schoenberg, waltzes are meaningful personal signifiers that are connected to intimate and intense

---

*I would first like to thank Dr. James Wright for the initial invitation to participate in the symposium *Schoenberg's Chamber Music, Schoenberg's World* in July of 2007. I also wish to acknowledge Dr. Robert Falck for obliquely providing the impetus to study Schoenberg's waltzes in the first place. Finally, I am grateful to my ever-patient wife Stacy for reading, correcting, and ultimately improving several drafts of this paper.

[1] For the text of the secret program, see Joseph Auner, ed., *A Schoenberg Reader: Documents of a Life* (New Haven: Yale University Press, 2003), 48-49.

[2] Schoenberg identifies it thus in the program (see ibid.):

> d) Transition to
>> 3. Struggle of all the motives with the determination to begin a new life.
> e) Mild disagreement
> ♭ II. 1) "Feeling New Life"

Mark Benson calls this transition the "first development section," leading into the Scherzo. See Benson, "Schoenberg's Private Program for the D minor String Quartet, Op.7," *Journal of Musicology* 11/3 (Summer 1993): 377.

Alexander Carpenter is a musicologist and music critic. He holds a Ph.D. in historical musicology from the University of Toronto, an M.A. in music criticism from McMaster University, and a Bachelor of Music from Brock University. His research interests include the music of Arnold Schoenberg, music and psychoanalysis, the history and theory of music criticism, the music and culture of Vienna, and popular music. Dr. Carpenter teaches at the University of Alberta, Augustana Campus.

feelings: they are abundant in his music, and serve a number of different functions. In the chamber music, it is especially clear that they have a particular significance, namely as gestures that mark moments of crisis and change, and that also often bridge these moments, metaphorically connecting past and present. Schoenberg once remarked to Egon Wellesz that "[m]y music is solely the representation of myself";[3] waltzes, it can be argued, are used by the composer as an important facet of this self-representation. They are used programmatically, autobiographically, and perhaps even psychologically; as commentary and reflection; and as a means to glance backwards, but also to move forward, and to forget. Closely tied to crisis and change, Schoenberg's chamber music waltzes are a key aspect of what Bryan Simms calls "the objectification of [Schoenberg's] private world."[4]

The exact nature of Schoenberg's marriage to Mathilde Zemlinsky may never be fully understood. Mathilde is mentioned only in passing in much of the secondary literature on Schoenberg. She was either marginal or marginalized, depending on the source consulted.[5] She emerges briefly as a locus of crisis in 1908, the year of her affair with the young painter Richard Gerstl, a crisis concomitant with Schoenberg's decisive move to atonality. Mathilde then gradually fades to grey in the background, lacking a profile for the next fifteen years and only reemerging briefly with her death in 1923. She was a naturally introverted

---

[3]Schoenberg's remarks to Wellesz are cited in Bryan Simms, "'My Dear Hagerl': Self-Representation in Schoenberg's String Quartet No. 2," *19th Century Music* 26/3 (Spring 2003): 258.

[4]Simms, "'My Dear Hagerl'," Ibid., 259.

[5]Malcolm MacDonald describes Mathilde as "forever overshadowed by her forceful husband . . . a dim figure to biographers." See MacDonald, *Schoenberg* (London: J. M. Dent and Sons, 1976), 7. Hans Heinz Stuckenschmidt refers to Mathilde only occasionally in his biography of Schoenberg: she does not appear in the index, and her illness and death in 1923 are summed up in several brief, dismissive sentences. See Stuckenschmidt, *Arnold Schoenberg: His Life, World and Work,* trans. Humphrey Searle (London: John Calder, 1977), 292. In Joan Allen Smith's oral history of Schoenberg and his Viennese circle, Mathilde is mentioned, again, in passing and only in relation to the Gerstl affair: she does not rate her own entry in the book's "Biographies" appendix, appearing only in Alexander Zemlinsky's entry as "Zemlinsky's sister." See Smith, *Schoenberg and his Circle: A Viennese Portrait* (New York: Schirmer Books, 1986), 288.

Mathilde was also evidently marginalized in the marriage itself, as Albrecht Dümling suggests that Schoenberg "found it difficult to integrate his wife into the circle of his friends." See Dümling, "Public Loneliness: Atonality and the Crisis of Subjectivity in Schönberg's Opus 15," in *Schönberg and Kandinsky: An Historic Encounter,* ed. Konrad Boehmer (The Hague: Harwood Academic Publishers, 1997), 111. Stuckenschmidt writes that Schoenberg kept friends and acquaintances out of his private life, with the result that Mathilde was largely isolated: "Schoenberg kept her apart from his circle of friends; she did not accept invitations to Mahler's house and her name was not mentioned in Schoenberg's exchange of letters with Strauss." Stuckenschmidt, *Arnold Schoenberg,* 88. Allen Shawn, who describes Schoenberg as "high-spirited but also splenetic," wonders "how frequently his scorn was directed against his wife," in particular during the period of 1907-10, when Schoenberg was attempting to launch a second career as a painter, a period of artistic crisis and financial stress. See Shawn, *Arnold Schoenberg's Journey* (New York: Fararr, Straus, and Giroux, 2002), 46.

person, and is remembered by Schoenberg's friends and acquaintances as a withdrawn and unobtrusive figure in the Schoenberg household after 1908: the "silent woman," in the recollection of Alexander Zemlinsky's second wife Luise.[6] Schoenberg did describe Mathilde in warmly appreciative terms to Alma Mahler, insisting that his wife was intelligent and a good conversationalist, "due to her remarkable astuteness, her rare tact and sense of comportment"[7]; however, the fact that he, and the marriage, never recovered from the Gerstl affair is evident in the ambivalent poem Schoenberg began in 1922 and completed for Mathilde following her death, entitled "Requiem." In the poem, Schoenberg equivocates about his wife, first praising her "capacity for arousing such great love" but then recalling that she was worthy of his love "rarely, and hate often."[8]

While Mathilde was apparently musical, intelligent, and a largely supportive domestic partner for Schoenberg, it is clear that she lacked many of the characteristics that Schoenberg was attracted to in his second, much younger, wife Gertrud Kolisch: the latter was sociable, lively, witty, and not afraid to criticize her husband, a trait that Schoenberg particularly admired.[9] There are several reasons for Mathilde's low profile in the musicological literature. She herself was taciturn, and because she and Schoenberg never fully reconciled after the Gerstl affair she remained partially isolated from the composer's circle. Gertrud's attitude towards Mathilde also contributed to the latter's obscurity: Mathilde's memory was largely obliterated in the Schoenberg household after 1924, with the composer going so far as to remove Mathilde's name from the score of the String Quartet, Op. 10, and to re-dedicate it to Gertrud.[10] As Anthony Beaumont notes, Schoenberg and his new wife made every effort "to suppress all memory of Mathilde," as if she had never existed: "in Gertrud's presence the name of Mathilde was anathema."[11]

---

[6]Luise Zemlinsky, quoted in Anthony Beaumont, *Zemlinsky* (Ithaca, N.Y.: Cornell University Press, 2000), 166. Raymond Coffer has recently shown that Mathilde may not have been such a "mousy, demure hausfrau," as she is so often represented; rather, he has uncovered evidence to suggest that she was quite vivacious, though clandestinely so, having apparently had at least one other affair—or, an attempted affair—through the complicity of Alma Mahler and Helene Berg. The affair, with one of Schoenberg's students (Hugo Breuer), took place in 1920. See Coffer, "Soap Opera and Genius in the Second Viennese School: The affairs of Mathilde Schönberg in Alban Berg's Chamber Concerto" (paper presented at The Peabody Conservatory, Baltimore, 26 February 2005), http://igrs.sas.ac.uk/postgraduate/students_pages/Raymond_peabodypaper.htm (accessed April 18, 2008).

[7]Letter from Schoenberg to Alma Mahler (16 November 1910). Quoted in Beaumont, *Zemlinsky*, 323.

[8]Schoenberg, "Requiem," quoted in Beaumont, *Zemlinsky*, 324.

[9]Beaumont, *Zemlinsky*, Ibid., 325.

[10]See Severine Neff, "Background and Analysis," in Arnold Schoenberg, *The Second String Quartet in F-sharp minor, Opus 10*, ed. Severine Neff (New York: W.W. Norton and Company, 2006), 113.

[11]Beaumont, *Zemlinsky*, 325.

Mathilde is invoked here because Schoenberg's early chamber waltzes were written for her. The String Quartet, Op. 7, documents a marriage and household in some difficulty; its waltz appears to play a metaphorical role in the struggle for domestic tranquility and happiness. The prominence of the waltz in the first movement is rather striking, especially when linked to the secret program: the waltz connects the tumult of the opening section—a circular journey from "Revolt, Defiance, Longing, Rapture, Dejection, Despair," to "unaccustomed feelings of love ... Comfort, Relief (She and He)" back to a "New outbreak" of "Dejection, Despair"—with a preface to the Scherzo in which there is a "struggle of all the motives with the determination to begin a new life," then leading to the beginning of the Scherzo, which is linked to the phrase "Feeling New Life" in the program. Mattias Schmidt notes that Schoenberg would later insist that the program was deeply private and belonged to the genesis of the work, not to its "aesthetic substance,"[12] and that he had modeled the Quartet on Beethoven's *Eroica* (the Quartet thus being primarily a working-through of the fundamental formal challenges of the symphony). Nevertheless, the Op. 7 Quartet's autobiographical program—important enough to Schoenberg to be a closely-guarded secret—cannot be ignored. It is clear that at least some of the musical working-through (for example, the "struggle" of the motives) is allegorical.[13] In this Quartet, then, the waltz signifies mediation and change, serving as a bridge between a despairing past and the "aggressively joyful strength" of a new life.

Schoenberg's String Quartet, Op. 10, completed in 1908, is also in large part a musical commentary on his marriage and artistic struggles. Its final, texted movements, settings of poems by Stefan George that document heartbreak ("Litanei") and a desire for transcendence ("Entrueckung"), are commonly taken as autobiographical reflections on Schoenberg's compositional crisis of that same year—leading to the advent of atonality—and his wife's infidelity. The Quartet was dedicated to Mathilde, its completion roughly concomitant with

---

[12]"Unequivocally, Schönberg made it very clear in later years, that although he had laid down such a 'program,' it was however of a completely private nature and belonged to the genesis of the work, and not to its aesthetic substance. Instead, he always pointed out, not without pride, the constructive achievement of this generously dimensioned work." Mattias Schmidt, "Arnold Schönberg: Quartett (d-Moll) für 2 Violinen, Viola und Violoncello op. 7 (1904–1905): Program notes," Arnold Schoenberg Centre, http://schoenberg.at/6_archiv/music/works/op/compositions_op7_notes_e.htm (accessed July 25, 2007).

[13]Benson cautions that "the discovery of the 'private program' does not automatically turn Schoenberg's Opus 7 into a tone poem for string quartet," and suggests that the program was a temporary solution to a technical impasse in the completion of the Quartet. Benson, "Schoenberg's Private Program for the D minor String Quartet, Op. 7": 394-95. Walter Bailey suggests that, while it is "tempting to surmise" that all of Schoenberg's music is programmatic, this aspect of Schoenberg music is "only one facet of the circumstances which spurred Schoenberg's creativity." See Bailey, *Programmatic Elements in the Works of Schoenberg* (Ann Arbor: UMI Research Press, 1984), 129.

her affair with Gerstl in the late summer of 1908. This Quartet also contains a striking waltz, albeit a very different and rather enigmatic one. Schoenberg quotes the Viennese folksong "Ach, du lieber Augustin" in the Scherzo movement. The tune dates back to the plague years of the late seventeenth century and refers to the legendary character Augustin, whose comically grotesque misfortunes begin with him stumbling drunkenly along the streets of Vienna until he passes out; he is subsequently picked up by the corpse patrol and is unceremoniously dumped into a mass grave. The text of the song recounts the down-and-out Augustin's bad luck, as he has lost everything—his girl, his money, and his coat—and fate seems to be conspiring against him:

> Ach, du lieber Augustin
> Alles is hin!
> Geld ist hin, Mädl ist hin, alles ist hin, Augustin!
> Ach, du lieber Augustin, alles ist hin!
> Rock ist weg, Stock ist weg, Augustin liegt im Dreck.

> Oh, beloved Augustin
> All is lost!
> Gold is gone, girl is gone, all is gone, Augustin!
> Oh, beloved Augustin, all is lost!
> Coat is gone, staff is gone, Augustin's on his ass.

This is all compounded by the plague, which marks the end of the good life—"Jeder Tag war ein Fest/jetzt haben wir die Pest!" (Every day was a party/ now we have the plague)—leaving Vienna a city of death, a big corpse party ("ein großes Leichenfest"). The song concludes resignedly: all is lost, and so Augustin might as well go lie down in his grave ("Augustin, leg' nur ins Grab dich hin!").

"Augustin" is an anomalous little tonal quotation in the context of the highly chromatic, occasionally atonal, Op. 10, and is clearly set as a waltz. Its appearance is shocking and brief: after a few measures, it dissolves back into the frenetic texture of the Scherzo.[14] The main interest in the passage hinges on the poignant textual reference—"All is lost"—that would have been readily recognized by contemporary audiences. While a number of scholars suggest that this quotation is a comment on both Schoenberg's artistic and personal crises—tonality is lost, love is lost—others insist that this nihilistic statement be

---

[14]Neff calls the entrance of the "Augustin" quotation a "stunning juxtaposition" and identifies it as the "compositional centerpiece" of the Scherzo. Neff, "Historical Background and Analysis," 149.

understood as an ironic gesture, or as a joke; Schoenberg, for his part, described it as a tragic-comic statement that should be taken literally.[15] The appearance of this quotation as a waltz is significant: it is another example of the waltz-as-bridge. Here, the waltz connects and signifies change. It occurs in the music as a transitional passage, linking the recapitulation of the Trio with the recapitulation of the Scherzo, and also has potent, if ambiguous, extra-musical implications. The quotation is a poignant comment on the end of one musical tradition and the dawning of the next; it also represents personal reflection on a marriage that perhaps had been slowly unraveling for years.

While there is some debate over the date of completion of the second movement, it seems that Schoenberg began working on an old fragment of the Scherzo in July of 1908, finishing it before the end of July, just a few weeks before Mathilde would run away with Gerstl; the "Alles ist hin" quotation evidently was conceived as part of the movement that same month.[16] The Scherzo, with

[15]Neff has summarized the many different interpretations of this quotation, noting that some scholars regard it as a joke, some as a self-mocking gesture, some as a serious meditation on the inevitable collapse of tonality, and some as related to Schoenberg's marriage. Neff prefers to think of the quotation as connected to Mahler: the tune had a particular psychological significance for Mahler, made manifest through treatment with Freud; its incongruous appearance in the Op. 10 Quartet also suggests Mahlerian juxtapositioning. See Neff, "Background and Analysis," 149-50.

Simms suggests that a personal interpretation is the "least credible" (see Simms, "'My Dear Hagerl'," 273-75); however, given that the Quartet was written during the summer of Schoenberg's discontent, why wouldn't this be a personal statement? It is appropriate to the situation (though Schoenberg's marriage was still intact as of July 1908, it is quite possible that a combination of anger, suspicion and distrust of Mathilde and Gerstl would have led to the resigned, presumptive conclusion "all is lost"), and is appropriate to the idea of the artistic and the personal as innately wedded. See Schoenberg's *Testaments-Entwurf* (in Auner, *A Schoenberg Reader*, 53-56) as evidence of Schoenberg intertwining personal and artistic crises in 1908.

[16]Simms suggests that the "Alles ist hin" quotation "was conceived as part of the movement only in July of 1908, based on the appearances of the tune in Schoenberg's sketchbooks. See Simms, "'My Dear Hagerl'," 272-73. Ethan Haimo insists that Schoenberg likely did not initially realize the seriousness of his marital problems and that, as of the first part of the summer, would not "have reason to believe that 'alles ist hin'." The sentiment expressed in the Augustin quotation, in Haimo's interpretation, would not have been appropriate until late August. See Haimo, *Schoenberg's Transformation of Musical Language* (Cambridge: Cambridge University Press, 2006), 270. Haimo's interpretation does not take into account the correspondence between Mathilde and Schoenberg from the early part of the summer of 1908, in which the problems in their marriage are readily apparent: she attempts to assuage Schoenberg's suspicions about Gerstl and his doubts about her love and fidelity, and defends herself against his accusations, writing, for example, on June 21, "Am I really always so disgusting to you?" See Simms, *The Atonal Music of Arnold Schoenberg*, 40, and Neff, "Background and Analysis," 108. Simms notes too that Schoenberg had already developed "an intense distrust of his wife" as of May of 1908, after learning from his daughter Gertrud that she had seen Mathilde and Gerstl kissing. See Simms, "'My Dear Hagerl'," 267. Clearly, May and June of 1908 were months of intense emotional foment; with Gerstl and Schoenberg arriving simultaneously—explosively, suggests Simms—in Gmunden at the end of June to join Mathilde and her children on holiday, it stands to reason that over the course of the following month, Schoenberg would have recognized that his marriage was in serious crisis. That summer, the Op. 10 Quartet transmogrified into a direct expression of Schoenberg's feelings towards his wife.

its nihilistic little waltz, was thus composed during what must have been an emotionally stressful and very awkward summer holiday—Gerstl was vacationing with the Schoenbergs that summer—in Gmunden on Lake Traun, the culmination of months of domestic instability, suspicion, and anger. The texts of the two final movements of the Quartet clearly express Schoenberg's loneliness as a modern artist and angst as a cuckolded husband—the final stanza of "Litanei" reads "Kill now my longing/close the wound,/Take from me love,/give me thy peace!"; "Entruekung" describes leaving behind "strife and tumult" and being "Carried aloft beyond the highest cloud/I am afloat upon a sea of crystal splendor"—but, the "tragic-comic" Scherzo, with its strange little waltz, though situated as the second of the four movements, may well have been the last composed, serving as Schoenberg's Augustinian sigh of resignation in advance of an anticipated collapse.[17] Here, at the moment of "Alles ist hin," it is as though Schoenberg himself is standing on a bridge, simultaneously looking forwards and backwards, as the Quartet makes its final tonal "retrenchments" while breaking with the past and taking steps towards free atonality[18]; it is also a moment of decisive personal rupture, an intimation of what would prove an unhappy decade to follow, as Schoenberg's troubled marriage was about to be broken beyond repair.

Neither Mathilde nor Schoenberg ever fully recovered from the marital crisis of 1908: "a cloud" hung over the house, and in a letter to Gerstl's brother Alois, Mathilde hints that she wished she could have followed Richard—who committed suicide shortly after the end of their affair—down the "easier path; to have to go on living in such a situation is terribly hard."[19] The Schoenbergs' marital difficulties would remain unresolved when Mathilde died in 1923. In the few years leading up to and following Mathilde's death, another period of personal and artistic crisis and change, there are more waltzes, and Schoenberg used them to build new bridges, as a means to leaving behind both his musical and personal pasts in search of a "new life."

The Serenade for clarinet, bass clarinet, mandolin, guitar, violin, viola, cello, and baritone voice, Op. 24, connects the early crisis years and the advent of the twelve-tone method, and does so in part with a cluster of waltzes. Schoenberg began sketches for the Serenade in 1920, completing it in April of

[17]Simms, *The Atonal Music of Arnold Schoenberg*, 41. Simms gives the date of 11 July 1908 for the completion of the third movement; the fourth movement cannot be precisely dated, but was most likely composed sometime during the summer of 1908, either in July or August; the first movement had already been completed the year before; the Scherzo movement, Simms claims, was finished by July 27th. It is thus possible that the inclusion of the "Augustin" quotation was one of Schoenberg's final compositional gestures for the Quartet.

[18]Simms, *The Atonal Music of Arnold Schoenberg*, 40.

[19]Letter from Mathilde Schoenberg to Alois Gerstl (9 November 1908). Quoted in Beaumont, *Zemlinsky*, 166. Beaumont suggests that the "cloud" over the Schoenberg household persisted for the intervening fifteen years between the Gerstl affair and Mathilde's death (323).

1923. It is comprised of seven movements: March, Minuet and Trio, Theme and Variations, Sonnet by Petrarch, Dance Scene, Song (without words), and Finale. One of the interesting things about this piece is that it is contemporaneous with what seems to be a fresh welling up of negative feelings towards Mathilde, evident in both the text of the Petrarchan Sonnet that forms the fourth movement and in the roughly contemporaneous "Requiem" poem.[20] In each text, the despairing and disparaging sentiments of 1908 seem to be reborn, as the Sonnet begins "Oh, that I might find relief from that resentment against her,/Who assails me by glance and speech alike"; the "Requiem" likewise invokes the alienation of the crisis years of the first decade of the century, directly recalling the despair and loneliness of 1908: "Hopeless: perhaps we pass each other by/perhaps forever."[21]The Serenade is a locus of these feelings, and this work and its sentiments connect directly to the past by way of the waltz. As Schoenberg marked his grief, isolation, and nihilistic feelings with waltzes in the atonal music of 1908-12, so the waltz returns with a vengeance as that period is recalled more than a decade later; at the same time, as the early crisis years portended the advent of a new technique, so the crisis years of the early 1920s, replete with waltzes, mark the birth of dodecaphony.

Depending on how they are counted, there are at least three waltzes in the Serenade: the darkly evocative Sonnet is effectively framed by them. The opening movement, March, is essentially a waltz, its duple meter frequently interrupted by a triple meter lilt. The fifth movement, Dance Scene, includes a waltz and a *Ländler* (and it is worth noting that Schoenberg, in a highly unusual gesture, repeats the full *Ländler* melody and countermelody several times, untransposed, attesting to its importance). The final movement, Finale, comprises what Schoenberg called a "potpourri" of material from the preceding movements, including the *Ländler* theme. According to the sketches of 1920, Schoenberg had been working on an additional waltz movement for the Serenade, titled

---

[20]Simms, *The Atonal Music of Arnold Schoenberg*, 215-16. It is possible that Schoenberg's renewed ill will towards Mathilde had something to do with the fact the Schoenberg family had returned, for the first time since the Gerstl affair, to Lake Traun for summer holidays in 1921, returning again in 1923. See Ena Steiner, "Schoenberg on Holiday: His Six Summers on Lake Traun," *The Musical Quarterly* 72/1 (1986): 28-50. Also, if Raymond Coffer is correct, Mathilde had gone through a rather licentious period in 1920, chasing around younger men, in particular a student of Schoenberg's. See Coffer, "Soap Opera and Genius in the Second Viennese School."

[21]Schoenberg, "Requiem," quoted in Simms, *The Atonal Music of Arnold Schoenberg*, 216. This theme of alienation and misrecognition also appears in Schoenberg's 1909 psychoanalytic monodrama *Erwartung*, in which the protagonist (the unnamed "Woman"), quoting from an earlier song by Schoenberg entitled "Am Wegrand," recounts: "Tausend Menschen ziehn vorüber … ich erkenne dich nicht" (A thousand people pass by … I do not recognize you).

In his *Testaments-Entwurf*, written in the summer of 1908, Schoenberg writes despondently, and somewhat schizophrenically, about his emotional and spiritual alienation from Mathilde: "My wife's soul was so remote from mine that I had neither a truthful nor a false relation with it. . . . We never knew each other. I don't even know what she looks like." See Auner, *A Schoenberg Reader*, 53-56.

"Tempo zwischen langsamem Walzer u. Polacca," that was never completed.[22] The Sonnet is central to the work, and is a movement in which objectivity, parody, and a classical sensibility—the main characteristics of the Serenade as a whole—are eschewed for a much more personal statement.[23] That the Sonnet is bookended by waltzes seems sensible enough: they often appear in Schoenberg's music when strong personal sentiments are expressed. Schoenberg's ostensibly Mozartean, neo-classic Serenade, then, is ironically replete with the expression of self; here, in a work perched on the brink of a new, forward-looking compositional endeavor, waltzes evoke a troubled past, framing and effectively re-contextualizing the text of the Sonnet, a text that speaks of grief and alienation.

The Quintet for flute, oboe, clarinet, bassoon, and horn, Op. 26, is another important example of a piece in which waltzes serve as a bridge to a "new life." Begun before Mathilde's death, interrupted by her illness and death, and completed during his courtship with Gertrud Kolisch, the work spans the end of one part of Schoenberg's life and the beginning of the next. As Therese Muxeneder has noted, it "was begun in one of the composer's most difficult years and completed in one of his happiest."[24] The third movement, *Etwas Langsam*, contains an unmistakable waltz passage, complete with idiomatic "oom-pah-pah" accompaniment. The entire work, composed using the twelve-tone method and structured according to the sonata principle, is a paradigmatic neo-classical work. Here, as in other instances, Schoenberg includes a waltz to no formal effect; that is, while traditional forms are otherwise employed as guarantors of comprehensibility, the waltz offers no such guarantee.[25] Timothy Bowlby has remarked on the "puzzling" inclusion of a waltz at this point, and concludes that its presence forces the listener to make connections between this work and earlier ones, namely the Serenade and the waltz of Op. 25, No. 5.[26] This is an argument that can be made in general for Schoenberg's waltzes, and

---

[22]See "Serenade für Klarinette, Baßklarinette, Mandoline, Gitarre, Geige, Bratsche, Violoncell und eine tiefe Männerstimme op. 24: Sources," Arnold Schoenberg Center, http://schoenberg.at/6_archiv/music/works/op/compositions_op24_sources_e.htm#, (accessed April 18, 2008)

[23]It is tempting to argue that the Serenade forms another bridge directly to *Pierrot*, in which the lines between ironic detachment and autobiography are often blurred. It is worth noting, too, that *Pierrot's* most grotesque waltz is "Serenade," No. 19. Is it possible that *Pierrot's* "Serenade" of 1912 speaks to the Serenade of 1923, perhaps suggesting the inclusion of waltzes in the latter?

[24]Therese Muxeneder, "Quintett für Flöte, Oboe, Klarinette, Horn und Fagott op. 26: Program notes" Arnold Schoenberg Center, http://schoenberg.at/6_archiv/music/works/op/compositions_op26_notes_e.htm, (accessed July 8, 2007).

[25]See Simms, " 'My Dear Hagerl', " 263-64. Simms writes, ". . . the concerts of 1907 forced him to reassess this attitude [i.e. loosening of formal principles in favor of free expression] and to experiment with a mixed style in which Classical formal gestures could mingle with an advanced tonal language." Simms quotes Schoenberg: ". . . a form must be selected that eases understanding by a familiar sequence of events."

[26]Timothy Bowlby, "A Contextual Analysis of Arnold Schoenberg's Quintet for Woodwinds and Horn, Op. 26" (Ph.D. diss, University of Illinois at Urbana-Champaign, 1991), 162-63.

specifically for the waltzes in his chamber music: they point to each other and are connected, again building bridges between the past and present.

The slow third movement, containing the waltz, was written sometime in 1924. While the Serenade's waltzes—and, arguably, most of the waltzes that come before—were for Mathilde, this is the first waltz for Gertrud (the Wind Quintet was finished one day before Schoenberg's marriage to his second wife). While nominally dedicated to "Bubi Arnold," Schoenberg's first grandson, who was born in April of 1923, it is likely that the work, with its "puzzling" waltz fragment, was also a tacit offering to Gertrud, marking a point at which past and present meet.

The final waltzes to be considered in this essay are found in the Suite for piano, piccolo clarinet, clarinet, bass clarinet, violin, viola, and cello, Op. 29, dedicated to Gertrud Kolisch. The Suite was begun in the autumn of 1924 and completed at the beginning of May, 1926. It marks a definitive arrival at a "new life" with yet another small cluster of waltzes. The piece itself is effectively a modern Baroque dance suite, cast in four movements: Overture, Dance Steps, Theme and Variations, and Gigue. Malcolm MacDonald refers to the Suite as a belated wedding gift for Gertrud; Schoenberg began composing it only ten days after their wedding.[27] The Suite is programmatic, according to Walter Bailey, insofar as Schoenberg wove Gertrud's married initials—G and E-flat (Es)— into the beginning and endings of each movement.[28] Moreover, it can be interpreted as a personal statement in that it contains two waltzes and, like the Serenade, was meant to contain more. Schoenberg's earliest plan for the Suite included a list of movements: the third movement in this plan is labeled, in shorthand, "Fl. Kschw. Waltz" (Fräulein Kolisch Waltz).[29] So, the work was not only dedicated to Gertrud, but was originally to contain her own waltz as one of the movements; moreover, and significantly, one of the Suite's waltzes is given pride of place in the opening movement, the Overture. In this movement, the waltz appears, yet again, as a transitional passage, effectively taking the place of the development section in the movement's quasi-sonata structure, connecting the opening exposition to the recapitulation before making a return appearance in the coda. There is a second waltz to be found in the Dance Steps movement. As in the March of the Serenade, this little waltz is partly obscured, written in two but sounding in three. Allen Shawn describes it as a romantic and Straussian tune, albeit a "humorous hybrid" of twelve-tone music and waltz lilt: "[c]hange the notes and one is in the realm of Johann Strauss"[30] Here, then, in the Suite, the

---

[27]MacDonald, *Schoenberg*, 145.

[28]Bailey, *Programmatic Elements in the Works of Schoenberg*, 133.

[29]See ibid., 134. See also "Suite für Kleine Klarinette, Klarinette, Baßklarinette, Geige, Bratsche, Violoncello und Klavier op. 29," Arnold Schoenberg Center, http://schoenberg.at/6_archiv/music/works/op/compositions_op29_notes1_e.htm (accessed April 17, 2008).

[30]Shawn, *Arnold Schoenberg's Journey*, 220.

third of this triptych of works spanning the death of Mathilde and the early years of Schoenberg's second marriage, more waltzes are found and the other side of the bridge is definitively reached: from the Serenade, which reconnects with the past while paradoxically closing it off, to the Wind Quintet, which marks some tentative steps towards a new life, to the Suite, in which the despair and isolation of the past are transcended and a new life is begun.

The Suite is one of only two pieces in Schoenberg's oeuvre dedicated to a wife; the Op. 10 Quartet is the other (the Suite is rather warmly dedicated to "Meiner lieben Frau," whereas the Quartet dedication reads simply "Meiner Frau"). The Suite and Quartet are connected not only by virtue of their dedications, but also by the fact that both works include a variation movement as their respective third movements, and both works contain a quotation from a folksong: "Ach, du lieber Augustin" in the Quartet, and "Ännchen von Tharau" in the Suite. The latter, really a quasi-folksong, is a Prussian wedding poem from the seventeenth century, written by Simon Dach; the tune set by Schoenberg was composed by Friedrich Silcher in the early nineteenth century.[31] In the text of "Ännchen von Tharau," Ännchen is described by the poet as follows:

> Ännchen von Tharau ist die mir gefällt,
> Sie ist mein Leben, mein Gut und mein Geld.

> Annie of Tharau pleases me,
> She is my life, my goods and my gold.

This is like the negative image of the scenario in "Augustin," in which "all is lost," including the poet's girl and his money:

> Geld ist hin, Mädl ist hin,
> Alles ist hin, Augustin!

> Gold is gone, girl is gone,
> All is gone, Augustin!

---

[31]Renate Johne, writing about the representation of women in literature and the timeless themes of "the 'reward' of true love and two people becoming one," offers "Ännchen von Tharau" as an example; she also cites the text of the poem in full. See Johne, "Women in the Ancient Novel," in *The Novel in the Ancient World*, ed. Gareth Schmeling (Leiden: Brill, 1996), 173. According to Johne, the poem, originally written in dialect by Dach as "Anke von Tharaw" in 1637, was rendered into High German by Johann Gottfried Herder in 1778, and was set by music by Silcher in 1825. For the German text and H.W. Longfellow's translation, see Bailey, *Programmatic Elements in the Works of Schoenberg*, 134.

It is possible that these two folksong quotations, separated by more than fifteen years, were connected in Schoenberg's mind, and perhaps by offering the celebratory "Ännchen" to Gertrud he was closing the door on the past and the desolate "Augustin."

It is also worth noting that the triple-timing of the "Ännchen" tune seems to impel the occasional, fragmentary waltz lilt in Schoenberg's variations, especially in the 3/4 opening statement of the theme. This movement was intended for Gertrud: in the sketches, it corresponds musically to a plan for a piece Schoenberg entitled "Fr AS Adagio," meaning, presumably, "Frau Arnold Schoenberg Adagio." If "Ännchen von Tharau" hints, at least in passing, to a waltz, then it is one of three waltzes in the Suite Schoenberg wrote for and dedicated to his new wife. Like the Serenade, the Suite can thus be understood as another very personal testament in Schoenberg's oeuvre—yet another work that employs waltzes in the context of a musical reflection on love and marriage.

Waltzes are meaningful personal gestures for Schoenberg, perhaps as important as his signature key of D minor. In his chamber music, waltzes function as markers of crisis and change and function metaphorically as a means of transition from an unhappy past to a new and better life. If there is some doubt as to whether Schoenberg's waltzes are really connected in this way to self-reflection, self-expression, and ultimately to memory, consider that a waltz makes a later and very significant appearance in the eschatological String Trio, Op. 45, composed in the aftermath of a near-fatal heart attack and conceived as a meditation on trauma, life, death, and the act of remembering itself. Waltzes in Schoenberg's chamber music play an important role in his negotiation with the past and navigation into the future. For the composer, waltzes are intimately connected to memory and are, in a sense, ciphers of self, relating to emotional ties and emotional foment: part of "the objectification of [his] private world," they are another important key to understanding Schoenberg's music and life.

The "Popular Effect" in Schoenberg's Serenade*

Áine Heneghan

In his *Notes to Literature*, Theodor W. Adorno discussed the unusual syntax of Friedrich Hölderlin's late poetry, drawing particular attention to the poet's propensity for juxtaposing propositions without the use of a connective. This linguistic device, whereby the relationship between clauses is not indicated, is called parataxis. Although we might consider a literary style that relies on simple copulatives—such as "and" or "namely"—as primitive or inelegant, Adorno argued that "the function of language in Hölderlin qualitatively outweighs the usual function of poetic language," and cautioned that parataxis is exploited by Hölderlin for expressive purposes, mirroring, and reinforcing, in the text of "Brot und Wein," for instance, feelings of remoteness and alienation.[1]

Schoenberg, in his invocation of parataxis, undoubtedly had similar expressive concerns, yet, at the same time, it represented a way out of an impasse.[2]

---

*An earlier version of this paper was presented at the 69th Annual Meeting of the American Musicological Society in Houston, Texas. Facsimiles and transcriptions are used here with kind permission of Lawrence Schoenberg and Belmont Publishers.

[1]Adorno described the device using language appropriate to music: for instance, he observed "the rondo-like associative linking of the sentences" in "Der Einzige," designating the effect as "music-like." See Theodor W. Adorno, "Parataxis: On Hölderlin's Late Poetry," in *Notes to Literature*, vol. 2, ed. Rolf Tiedemann, trans. Shierry Weber Nicholsen (New York: Columbia University Press, 1992), 109–49 and 339–40 (note 135).

[2]For descriptions of parataxis, see Eric A. Blackall, *The Emergence of German as a Literary Language, 1700–1775*, 2nd ed. (Ithaca and London: Cornell University Press, 1978), 150; Michael Patrick O'Connor, "Parataxis and Hypotaxis," in *The New Princeton Encyclopedia of Poetry and Poetics*, ed. Alex Preminger and T.V.F. Brogan (Princeton: Princeton University Press, 1993), 879–80. Harald Kaufmann provided an overview of parataxis in the works of various Austrian composers; see "Versuch über das Österreichische in der Musik," in Harald Kaufmann, (cont.)

Áine Heneghan is an Assistant Professor of Music Theory at the University of Washington in Seattle. She completed her Ph.D. at the University of Dublin, Trinity College ("Tradition as Muse: Schoenberg's Musical Morphology and Nascent Dodecaphony," 2006), receiving research grants from the Irish Research Council for Humanities and Social Sciences, the Austrian and German Academic Exchange Services, and the Avenir Foundation. She has published in the *Journal of the Arnold Schönberg Center*, *Music Analysis*, the *Journal of the Society for Musicology in Ireland*, and *Notes: Quarterly Journal of the Music Library Association*. Her current projects include a monograph exploring the interrelationship of Schoenberg's theoretical writings and compositional practice as well as a volume entitled *Schoenberg on Form*, which will be published by Oxford University Press in the series *Schoenberg in Words*.

In his 1925 essay "Tonality and Form," a tirade against his fellow-composers, he likened the structure of contemporary composition to the "primitive art of presenting thoughts" in prose ("And then I said ... and then he said ... and then we laughed ... and ... and so on"), contending that the paratactic organization of the art work via an orderly succession of ideas was markedly different from the "complex structure and treatment" and "clearly woven threads" of a novel by Dickens.[3] A similar distinction was drawn in his essay "Folkloristic Symphonies" of 1947 between the musical analogues of parataxis and its antithesis, hypotaxis. In relation to the former he wrote:

> Structurally, there never remains in popular tunes an unsolved problem, the consequences of which will show up only later. The segments of which it consists do not need much of a connective; they can be added by juxtaposition, because of the absence of variance in them. There is nothing in them that asks for expansion. The small form holds the contents firmly, constituting thus a small expansion but an independent structure.[4]

Given Adorno's description of the parataxes in Hölderlin's poetry as "artificial disturbances that evade the logical hierarchy of a subordinating syntax,"[5] the kinship between the formal structure of a popular tune and parataxis in literature is suggested not only by the accretion of segments without the use of a connective or copula, but also by the absence of a hierarchy between individual segments.

By contrast, Schoenberg's conception of "developing variation" can be understood in relation to hypotaxis (the subordination in prose or verse of one clause to another). The basic criterion of "developing variation"—the generation of new motives by variation—was articulated as early as 1917 in the *Zusammenhang, Kontrapunkt, Instrumentation, Formenlehre* notebooks, where it was explained in the context of the first movement of Mozart's String Quartet in C major, K. 465 ("Dissonant").[6] Schoenberg's understanding of this type of motivic presentation

---

Fingerübungen: Musikgesellschaft und Wertungsforschung (Vienna: Elisabeth Lafite, 1970), 24–43. More recently a number of scholars have invoked parataxis in interpretations of works of various composers. See, for example, Su Yin Mak, "Schubert's Sonata Forms and the Poetics of the Lyric," *Journal of Musicology* 23/2 (Spring 2006): 263–306; and Michael Spitzer, *Music as Philosophy: Adorno and Beethoven's Late Style* (Bloomington: Indiana University Press, 2006).

[3]Schoenberg, "Tonality and Form," in *Style and Idea: Selected Writings of Arnold Schoenberg*, ed. Leonard Stein, trans. Leo Black (London and Boston: Faber and Faber, 1975), 256. As Severine Neff has noted, Schoenberg frequently referred to literary forms in his discussions of musical forms. See Severine Neff, "Reinventing the Organic Artwork: Schoenberg's Changing Images of Tonal Form," in *Schoenberg and Words: The Modernist Years*, ed. Charlotte M. Cross and Russell A. Berman (New York and London: Garland, 2000), 279–80.

[4]Schoenberg, "Folkloristic Symphonies," in *Style and Idea,* 164.

[5]Adorno, "Parataxis: On Hölderlin's Late Poetry," 131.

[6]Arnold Schoenberg, *Zusammenhang, Kontrapunkt, Instrumentation, Formenlehre (Coherence, Counterpoint, Instrumentation, Instruction in Form)*, ed. Severine Neff, trans. Charlotte M. Cross and Severine Neff (Lincoln and London: University of Nebraska Press, 1994), 38–43.

remained unchanged, as confirmed by his reference in "Folkloristic Symphonies" to the first movement of Beethoven's Fifth Symphony (see Example 1).

Example 1. Schoenberg's illustration of "developing variation" with reference to the first movement of Beethoven's Fifth Symphony.

The hierarchy here arises because the motive of the so-called transition (Schoenberg's Example 2) is "derived from a reinterpretation" of the notes E flat and F of Example 1, while the so-called subordinate theme (Schoenberg's Example 3) is "related to" the opening motive via that of the transition. The organic interrelationship of motives that Schoenberg perceived as characterizing "developing variation" is analogous to his description of the "clearly woven threads" in a novel by Dickens.[7]

Consideration of Schoenberg's distinction between the construction of popular tunes and sonata-form structures in terms of parataxis or hypotaxis provides a lens through which we can read his comments on the "popular effect" as well as a context for the examination of his music from the early 1920s, when he was evidently seeking to re-access large-scale instrumental homophonic forms. Exemplified by the compositions of the *Wiener Klassik* (Haydn, Mozart, and Beethoven), such forms were, for Schoenberg, predicated on contrast and formal differentiation ("large forms develop through the generating power of contrasts" and "contrast in mood, character, dynamics, rhythm, harmony, motive-forms and construction should distinguish main themes from subordinate, and subordinate themes from each other"),[8] and inextricably linked with what Schoenberg regarded as "the technique of homophonic [art] music since Haydn," namely, "development" or "developing variation" [*Entwicklung* or *entwickelnde Variation*].[9] Indeed the two factors were interdependent

---

[7]Schoenberg, "Folkloristic Symphonies," in *Style and Idea,* 164. Schoenberg's musical example is catalogued at T29.04 in the Arnold Schönberg Center Privatstiftung, Vienna.

[8]Arnold Schoenberg, *Fundamentals of Musical Composition,* ed. Gerald Strang with the collaboration of Leonard Stein (London and Boston: Faber and Faber, 1967), 178 and 183.

[9]Schoenberg, "Der musikalische Gedanke, seine Darstellung und Durchführung" (July 6, 1925), catalogued at T37.08 in the Arnold Schönberg Center Privatstiftung, Vienna, paragraph 17. The title of the manuscript is given on T37.07.

in Schoenberg's conception of large-scale homophony, insofar as "developing variation" was predicated not only on a particular type of motivic manipulation but on the organization of those motives into stable and loose formation, stable and loose being Schoenberg's own translations for the terms *fest* and *locker/los* respectively.

Yet Schoenberg's homophonic structures of the early 1920s, especially those from 1920 and 1921, did not arise from "developing variation," nor did they exhibit the form-building distinction between stable and loose organization. Instead, in the quest for large-scale instrumental forms, he employed alternative strategies for replicating the formal differentiation previously furnished by tonality, resorting to linkage techniques he associated with "primitive" presentation. Specifically, he invoked "stringing-together" [*Aneinander-Reihung*], a method he assimilated from his study of the canon, as a way of neutralizing the issue of large-scale form. By taking as my point of departure the writings of Schoenberg and his inner circle, my aim here is to examine Schoenberg's method of "stringing-together," exploring its function and significance in his compositions of the early 1920s, particularly in the Serenade, Op. 24 (composed intermittently between 1920 and 1923), and identifying in his additive motivic and phrase construction an organization akin to parataxis. In so doing, I suggest that popular forms, as Schoenberg understood them, played an important role in the evolution of dodecaphony.

That Schoenberg revered the organic structures of the *Wiener Klassik* is well known, yet he also considered popular music as a legitimate, albeit primitive, mode of presentation. Indeed he expressed his admiration for the music of Johann Strauss on a number of occasions:

> Who can say how arrogantly generations of musicians would speak of [that] light music, had Brahms not been able and sufficiently educated to recognize its purely musical substance and the value of that; had he not had the respect for achievement possessed only by those who know at first hand what achievement is; and had he not added: "Not, alas, by Johannes Brahms" after the first bars of the *Blue Danube Waltz?* Light music could not entertain me unless something interested me about its musical substance and its working-out. And I do not see why, when other people are entertained, I too should not sometimes be entertained; I know indeed that I really ought at every single moment to behave like my own monument; but it would be hypocritical of me to conceal the fact that I occasionally step down from my pedestal and enjoy light music.[10]

While it was Strauss who embodied "real popularity [or] lasting popularity,"[11] Schoenberg believed that many other composers successfully wrote in a popular style. Thus, in his extensive *Gedanke* manuscript of 1934, he

---

[10] Schoenberg, "Why No Great American Music?" in *Style and Idea*, 178.
[11] Schoenberg, "Brahms the Progressive," in Ibid., 415.

Figure 1. "Popular Melodies" in Schoenberg's *Gedanke* manuscript of 1934.

highlighted with brackets the rhythmic recurrences in a number of "popular melodies" [*populären Melodien*] by Beethoven, Brahms, Schubert, and Strauss—the first of two pages of analytical excerpts is given as Figure 1.[12] Clearly, these observations, and hence his classification of the melodies as "popular," rest on "motivic transformations" that are "in no way extensively varied."[13] To that extent, the examples exhibit "extremely slow and sparing development" and, thus, perfectly illustrate, for Schoenberg, one of the most important attributes of melody. Further, they serve as examples of the primitive melodic constructions described in his 1909 aphorism published in *Die Musik* and his 1913 essay "Why new melodies are difficult to understand" [*Warum neue Melodien schwerverständlich sind*].[14] Schoenberg was still of this opinion in 1946, when he claimed that "Schubert's melodic construction—his juxtaposition of motives, which are only melodically varied, but rhythmically very similar—accommodated, probably instinctively, to the popular feeling."[15]

Schoenberg's plans to include texts exploring the interrelationship of both "higher and lower forms" and "primitivism and art music" in his treatise of 1934 further attest to his interest in popular music.[16] Yet it was as early as 1925, in a *Gedanke* manuscript coeval with the above-mentioned "Tonality and Form," that he offered his exposition of the primitive mode of presentation alongside more "artful" methods. "Stringing-together" [*Aneinander-Reihung*] was identified as one of the "main methods of connecting small parts with each other," the others being "unfolding" [*Abwicklung*] and "development" [*Entwicklung*].[17] Whereas "unfolding" was found only in contrapuntal compositions such as fugues, homophony embraced the "development" or "developing variation" associated with sonata forms as well as the more primitive or popular presentational method of "stringing-together."

[12]The examples have been transcribed and identified in Arnold Schoenberg, *The Musical Idea and the Logic, Technique, and Art of Its Presentation*, ed., trans. and with a commentary by Patricia Carpenter and Severine Neff (New York: Columbia University Press, 1995), 180–87. The examples are as follows: (1) Beethoven, Violin Sonata, No. 9, in A major, Op. 47 ("Kreutzer"), second movement, mm. 1–8; (2) Schubert, *Moments Musicaux*, Op. 94, No. 3, mm. 1–10; (3) Strauss, *On the Beautiful Blue Danube*, Op. 314, mm. 1–24; and (4) Beethoven, Symphony No. 9, Op. 125, third movement, mm. 25–32. Examples from Brahms's *A German Requiem* and Symphony No. 3 are given on the subsequent page of the manuscript (T65.03, Arnold Schönberg Center Privatstiftung, Vienna).

[13]Ibid., 182–83.

[14]Ibid., 180–81. For transcriptions and translations of the 1909 and 1913 documents, see Joseph Auner, *A Schoenberg Reader: Documents of a Life* (New Haven and London: Yale University Press, 2003), 64; and Bryan R. Simms, "New Documents in the Schoenberg-Schenker Polemic," *Perspectives of New Music* 16/1 (Autumn-Winter 1977): 115–16.

[15]Schoenberg, "Criteria for the Evaluation of Music," in *Style and Idea*, 128.

[16]Schoenberg, *The Musical Idea*, 94–95.

[17]Schoenberg, *Gedanke* manuscript (July 6, 1925), T37.08 (see note 9), paragraph 13. For a detailed account of Schoenberg's three forms of presentation, see Severine Neff, "Schoenberg as Theorist: Three Forms of Presentation," in *Schoenberg and His World*, ed. Walter Frisch (Princeton: Princeton University Press, 1999), 55–84.

The principles of comprehensibility [*Fasslichkeit*] and diversity [*Mannigfaltigkeit*], mentioned in the opening paragraph of the 1925 manuscript, govern the presentation of the musical idea:

> The more primitive a musical idea and the piece that is based on it, the greater is the regard for comprehensibility, the slower the tempo in which it is presented, the fewer the shapes and the fewer the more remote shapes that can be made use of in this context.[18]

Accordingly, "stringing-together" had the merit of immediate intelligibility but, as indicated in the same manuscript, it was not precluded in higher art forms and could potentially be used alongside more "artful [*kunstvoll*] treatments":

> *Stringing-together* is in itself the most primitive of the three methods, but it can nevertheless be used with more artful treatments. Its presupposition is a certain unproblematic or relaxed quality, *a certain rest between the constituent parts* of the components which just barely allows continuation without demanding it. Even where contrast is apparently great, connection is based on the repetition of numerous components.[19]

Nine years later, in his extended *Gedanke* manuscript, he espoused the same view, claiming that "the popular effect [*populäre Wirkung*] of popular music is based on its broad understandability" [*breite Verständlichkeit*].[20] Though separated by almost a decade, the two texts adumbrate the same criteria for the primitive or popular mode of presentation—that immediate intelligibility could be assured by small- and large-scale repetition, by the presence of a small number of shapes [*Gestalten*], and by the recurrence of rhythmic figures to coincide with variation of melodic content:

> Broad understandability is mainly achieved through an extremely slow "tempo of presentation." This means:
>
> I the *Grundgestalten* 1) themselves usually contain only a very few
> motivic forms; 2) are very often repeated in nearly unvaried forms;
> and 3) if after several (2–5 or more) such repetitions a more
> developed variation appears, it often changes so much that it could be
> hard to comprehend, were not the entire section repeated again and
> again, or, if it is varied more in pitch, the rhythm remains (almost)
> unchanged.

---

[18]Schoenberg, *Gedanke* manuscript (July 6, 1925), T37.08, paragraph 2. This passage is translated in Carl Dahlhaus, "What is Developing Variation?" in *Schoenberg and the New Music*, trans. Derrick Puffett and Alfred Clayton (Cambridge: Cambridge University Press, 1987), 128.

[19]Schoenberg, *Gedanke* manuscript (July 6, 1925), T37.08, paragraph 15. This passage is translated by Charlotte Cross in Schoenberg, *The Musical Idea*, 379–80.

[20]Schoenberg, *The Musical Idea*, 300–01.

II   1) In general, on the one hand, changes whose content is hard to comprehend will scarcely ever be used; 2) on the other hand, the logic is usually not very profound if "larger leaps" are taken.

III   As already mentioned above, the frequent repetitions of each part play a large role, and in spite of that it does happen that a popular piece was not popular from the beginning, not immediately recognized, understood.[21]

Implicit in Schoenberg's writings on popular music is the notion that simplicity of texture guarantees a greater degree of comprehensibility: he wrote that "density of texture is certainly an obstacle to popularity" and, in relation to Johann Strauss, that "the popular element is apparent in the fact that everything that happens is concentrated in the melody."[22]

Schoenberg's arrangements of compositions by Strauss, Schubert, Denza, and Sioly provide further evidence of his engagement with popular forms during the early 1920s (see Table 1).

Luigi Denza	"Funiculì, funiculà"	voice, clarinet, mandolin, guitar, string trio
Franz Schubert	"Ständchen," D. 889	voice, clarinet, bassoon, mandolin, guitar, string quartet
Johann Sioly	"Weil i a alter Drahrer bin"	clarinet, mandolin, guitar, string trio
Johann Strauss	*Rosen aus dem Süden,* Op. 388	harmonium, piano, string quartet
Johann Strauss	*Lagunenwalzer,* Op. 411	harmonium, piano, string quartet

Table 1. Schoenberg's arrangements in 1921 (select list).

Rather than dismissing these arrangements as "minor/casual works" [*Gelegenheitsarbeiten*],[23] or as transcriptions for pedagogical purposes,[24] they could

---

[21]Ibid., 300–01. Similar points are made in *Gedanke* manuscript (July 6, 1925), T37.08, paragraphs 1, 2, 6, and 15.

[22]Schoenberg, "Brahms the Progressive," in *Style and Idea*, 415. See also Schoenberg, "New Music/My Music," trans. Leo Black, transcribed by Selma Rosenfeld, *Journal of the Arnold Schoenberg Institute* 1/2 (1977): 102–03.

[23]Rudolf Stephan, "Schönberg und der Klassizismus, " in *Vom Musikalischen Denken: Gesammelte Vorträge*, ed. Rainer Damm and Andreas Traub (Mainz: Schott, 1985), 149.

[24]Leonard Stein, "Schoenberg: Kaiserwalzer and Other Transcriptions," sleeve notes for CD Elatus 0927 49552-2 (2003).

be considered indicative of Schoenberg's broader compositional concerns at that time, something intimated by Ernst Hilmar in his brief discussion of Schubert and the Viennese School.[25] Furthermore, the instrumentation of the compositions by Schubert, Denza, and Sioly approaches the sound-world of Schoenberg's Serenade, Op. 24 (scored for clarinet, bass clarinet, mandolin, guitar, violin, viola, cello, and voice),[26] a fact that was not lost on members of the Viennese School at the time: Hanns Eisler suggested that Schoenberg drew on the Serenades of Mozart and Haydn as well as on Viennese folk music ("Schrammelmusik"),[27] while Paul Amadeus Pisk remarked that the mandolin and guitar endow Schoenberg's composition with a serenade-like and playful character such that *Leichtigkeit* or the quality of light music prevails.[28]

Moreover, Schoenberg alludes to the popular idiom by his inclusion in the Serenade of a March, which, in accordance with the serenading tradition of the eighteenth century, frames the inner movements, as well as a Waltz and "Ländler" that make up the fifth-movement Dance Scene [*Tanzscene*]. That the choice of forms is significant is suggested by Schoenberg's statement in the *Gedanke* manuscript of 1934: "The *dance forms* are among the simplest forms."[29] Erwin Stein, arguably the foremost prose advocate for the Viennese School during the early 1920s, similarly wrote that "the first movement is a march, its form accordingly transparent."[30] Despite Schoenberg's principle of "never repeating without varying,"[31] and his claim that the absence of repetition presents a "difficulty" to understanding his compositions,[32] he employs a repeat sign to indicate large-scale repetition in the March, a feature he described as "the most primitive coherence-producing form of repetition."[33] Stein's remark of 1924

---

[25]Ernst Hilmar, "Schubert und die Zweite Wiener Schule, " in *Schubert durch die Brille: The Oxford Bicentenary Symposium 1997*, ed. Elizabeth Norman McKay and Nicolas Rast (Internationales Franz Schubert Institut, Mitteilungen, 21; Tutzing: Hans Schneider, 1998), 77–88.

[26]Perhaps the association of Serenade and mandolin in this work, and in the arrangement of Schubert's "Ständchen" (or Serenade), recalls Don Giovanni's serenading of Donna Elvira's maid in "Deh vieni alla finestra." Another possible influence for the sonority may be the second "Nachtstück" of Mahler's Seventh Symphony, which includes both guitar and mandolin.

[27]Hanns Eisler, "Über Schönbergs Serenade op. 24," in *Musik und Politik, Schriften 1924–1928*, ed. Günter Mayer (Gesammelte Werke, III/1; Leipzig: VEB Deutscher Verlag für Musik, 1973), 454.

[28]Paul A. Pisk, "Arnold Schönbergs Serenade," *Musikblätter des Anbruch* 6/5 (May 1924): 201.

[29]Schoenberg, *The Musical Idea*, 142–43.

[30]Erwin Stein, "Neue Formprinzipien," *Arnold Schönberg zum fünfzigsten Geburtstage, 13. September 1924, Sonderheft der Musikblätter des Anbruch* 6/7-8 (September 1924): 297; Erwin Stein, "New Formal Principles," in *Orpheus in New Guises*, trans. Hans Keller (London: Rockliff, 1953), 69–70.

[31]Schoenberg, "Krenek's *Sprung über den Schatten*," in *Style and Idea*, 480.

[32]Schoenberg, "New Music/My Music," 96–97.

[33]Schoenberg, *The Musical Idea*, 156–57.

that the Serenade is characterized by "simpler formal means . . . where we even encounter repeats"[34] highlights such a feature as atypical of Schoenberg's practice hitherto: the two discrete units forming the opening section of the March (mm. 1–48) are subject to repetition and only minor variation (although variation is predominantly executed by means of inversion, consistency in articulation and, above all, preservation of rhythm ensure the audibility of connections); the middle section (mm. 49–95) is repeated exactly. Berg, who, in his annotated copy of the score, recorded these interrelationships, implying a taxonomy *a b a' b' b b'*, where *a* and *b* are defined by themes in the low strings and the clarinets

Divisions	Annotations *(translations)*
mm. 1–8	
mm. 9–16	
mm. 17–24	U von 1–8 *inversion of 1–8*
mm. 25–32	25–32 = U von 9–16. Das Ganze! *25–32 = inversion of 9–16. The whole thing!*
mm. 33–40	33–40. Wörtlich wie 9–16 *33–40. Literally like 9–16*
mm. 41–48	41–47/8. Wörtlich wie 25–31/2 und [U] von 9–15/6 *41–47/8. Literally like 25–31/2 and [inversion] of 9–15/6*

respectively, was clearly surprised by the degree of literal repetition, as his comments in Table 2 reveal.[35]

Table 2. Berg's division of, and annotations in, the opening section (mm. 1-48) of the March from Schoenberg's Serenade.

Berg's annotations also serve to highlight the sectionalized nature of the passage, characterized as it is by the juxtaposition of successive eight-measure units, the only semblance of a connective tissue being the triplet rhythms that signal the end of each unit. That this additive phrase structure can be understood in terms of "stringing-together" [*Aneinanderreihung*] is corroborated by Pisk's

---

[34]Stein, "Neue Formprinzipien," 297; "New Formal Principles," 69.

[35]Berg's score of the Serenade is catalogued at F 21 Berg 170/II in the Music Collection of the Austrian National Library, Vienna.

use of the verb "anreihen an" (meaning "to add to") in his description of this opening section.[36]

Such paratactic organization also governs the structure of the fifth movement, Dance Scene. Berg's inscription at the head of the movement suggests structural simplicity: "Rondo, ohne kunstvolle Kadenz / Binnenwiederholung," which roughly translates as "Rondo without artful cadence [or] internal repetition." Given that much of the *Gedanke* manuscript of 1925 is concerned with the distinction between the popular [*populär*] and the artful [*kunstvoll*] style, the latter displaying a faster pace of presentation and, thus, placing greater demands on the listener,[37] Berg's annotation implies a simple repetition, rather than the artful, which is akin, perhaps, to the way in which, according to Schoenberg's analytical comments, Franz Lehár's "Love Unspoken" from *The Merry Widow* achieves coherence by dint of the repetition alone.[38] As if to compensate for the fact that, in Stein's words, "the first section abounds in motivic shapes,"[39] it is repeated exactly.

The trio of the Dance Scene, in the tempo of a "Ländler," better exemplifies Schoenberg's conception of the popular mode.[40] Stein astutely observed that it comprises "a loose sequence of dance tunes" [*lose aneinandergereihter Perioden*], which give the movement its "loose build" [*lockere Bau*],[41] terminology which is also found in Berg's 1929 lecture on *Wozzeck*: "The forms of the outer acts are much freer [*lockerere*]"; "They consist of five loosely connected pieces of music corresponding to the five loosely related scenes of the act [*lose aneinandergereihten Szenen*]."[42] He continued by describing Act I as "five character pieces that are strung together [*fünf aneinandergereihte Charakterstücke*]."[43] The accumulation of musical segments to form a composition—or, in the case of Berg's *Wozzeck*, the building of an Act by means of a collection of character

[36]Pisk, "Arnold Schönbergs Serenade," 202.

[37]Schoenberg, *Gedanke* manuscript (July 6, 1925), T37.08, paragraphs 3, 4, and 12.

[38]Schoenberg, *The Musical Idea*, 306–07.

[39]Stein, "Neue Formprinzipien," 299; "New Formal Principles," 73.

[40]Schoenberg noted that in higher art music only individual sections are composed using the principle of "stringing-together." See Schoenberg, *Gedanke* manuscript (July 6, 1925), T37.08, paragraph 15.

[41]Stein, "Neue Formprinzipien," 299–300; "New Formal Principles," 73. See also Erwin Stein, "Arnold Schönbergs Serenade," *Musikblätter des Anbruch* 7/7 (August-September 1925): 422. In a later unpublished essay on the Serenade, Stein wrote that the Dance Scene is "the merriest piece of the lot," containing "a chain of happily invented tunes among which a Viennese landler [sic] stands out." The short typescript is found among Stein's papers; I am grateful to Mrs. Marion Thorpe for kindly allowing me to examine and quote from this material.

[42]Alban Berg, "'Wozzeck'-Vortrag von 1929," in Hans Ferdinand Redlich, *Alban Berg: Versuch einer Würdigung* (Vienna: Universal Edition, 1957), 314; "A Lecture on 'Wozzeck,'" in Douglas Jarman, *Alban Berg: Wozzeck* (Cambridge: Cambridge University Press, 1989), 157.

[43]Berg, "'Wozzeck'-Vortrag von 1929," 314. My translation.

pieces—was identified by Stein as a way of addressing what he called "the problems of form raised by modern music."[44] The multipartite Trio of the Dance Scene, which comprises a series of closed musical segments, conforms to Schoenberg's later definition of loose organization, typified as it is by "direct and immediate repetition of segments [and] juxtaposition of contrasting segments."[45] Its structure bears more than a passing resemblance to the sequence of Waltzes in Strauss's *Roses from the South* and *On the Beautiful Blue Danube* as well as to the third of Schubert's *Moments musicaux*, pieces that appear in the *Gedanke* manuscript of 1934.[46]

Stein also argued in 1922 that symmetry played a crucial role in the articulation of musical form after the collapse of tonality.[47] Likewise, Schoenberg associated formal symmetry and the divisibility [*Teilbarkeit*] of the constituent elements of a composition with the popular form of disposition.[48] The divisibility of the opening section of the March into eight-measure groups, which effects a greater degree of comprehensibility, and the symmetrical structure of the overall form of the Dance Scene substantiate his assertion that "much of the organization of classic music reveals, by its regularity, symmetry and simple harmony, its relation with, if not derivation from, popular and dance music."[49]

Like the Dance Scene, the contemporaneously composed Waltz from the Five Piano Pieces, Op. 23, exhibits a symmetrical structure (ABCBA), with the addition of a Coda. A closer look at the technique of motivic presentation similarly reveals aspects of popular presentation as Schoenberg conceived it.[50] The melody of the Waltz is distinguished by repetitions of rhythmic motives, something which Stein perceives as contributing to its "lighter character."[51] Example 2 illustrates the rhythmic patterns of the second section (or B-section) of the Waltz. Initially, the rhythmic profile of the treble in measures 29–31 is repeated exactly in measures 32–34; the repetition in measures 35–37, now articulated in the bass, is varied in that the two dotted-quarters are replaced by three quarters; the three-quarter motive is retained in measures 38–39, although subdivided, whereas the dotted figure of measures 31, 34, and 37 is augmented in measures 40–41.

---

[44]Erwin Stein, "Alban Berg and Anton Webern," *The Chesterian* 26 (1922): 33.

[45]Schoenberg, *Fundamentals of Musical Composition*, 204.

[46]Schoenberg, *The Musical Idea*, 182–85 and 302–03.

[47]Stein, "Berg and Webern," 33.

[48]Schoenberg, *Gedanke* manuscript (July 6, 1925), T37.08, paragraphs 6, 7, and 8.

[49]Schoenberg, "Brahms the Progressive," in *Style and Idea*, 409.

[50]Different readings of this piece are given in Ethan Haimo, *Schoenberg's Serial Odyssey: The Evolution of his Twelve-Tone Method, 1914–1928* (Oxford and London: Clarendon Press, 1990), esp. 75 and 97–98; and Kathryn Bailey, *"Composing with Tones": A Musical Analysis of Schoenberg's Op. 23 Pieces for Piano* (Royal Musical Association Monographs, 10; London: Royal Musical Association, 2001), esp. 104.

[51]Stein, "Neue Formprinzipien," 297; "New Formal Principles," 69.

Example 2. Rhythmic motives in measures 29–41 of the Waltz from Schoenberg's Five Piano Pieces, Op. 23.

The simple repetition and variation of rhythmic motives recalls Schoenberg's analytical remarks on the melodies of Strauss, Verdi, Mozart, Brahms among others,[52] and his comment that "constant repetition of a rhythmic figure, as in popular music, lends a popular touch to many Schubertian melodies."[53] Bearing in mind that the simple form of presentation can be used alongside more artful treatments, the Waltz does indeed demonstrate aspects of popular presentation that are, by their nature, more sophisticated compared with those outlined in the March and the Dance Scene. However, they do not accord with Schoenberg's description of "developing variation" since, unlike the example from Beethoven's Fifth Symphony, they neither demand continuation nor create consequences in the course of the composition. Instead this passage is followed almost immediately by section C of the Waltz, which is distinct from preceding or subsequent sections (and which Martina Sichardt has appositely identified as exhibiting a relationship with Hauer's second canonic technique).[54] We can infer, therefore, that, while individual sections may contain local variation, the overall organization of the composition is paratactic.

The conception of form as one that results from the concatenation of individual units, as distinct from the teleological thread of interconnected themes defining "developing variation," was apparent in Schoenberg's sketches from that period. His designation "potpourri" for the title of the Serenade's Finale calls to mind his response to the labelling of Mahler's symphonies as "gigantic symphonic potpourris":

> The characteristic of the potpourri is the unpretentiousness of the formal connectives. The individual sections are simply juxtaposed, without always being connected and without their relationships (which may also be entirely absent) being more than mere accidents in the form. But this is contradicted by the term "symphonic" [*symphonisch*],

---

[52]Schoenberg, *The Musical Idea*, 182–95 and 302–07.

[53]Schoenberg, *Fundamentals of Musical Composition*, 27.

[54]Martina Sichardt, *Die Entstehung der Zwölftonmethode Arnold Schönbergs* (Mainz: Schott, 1990), 173.

which means the opposite. It means that the individual sections are organic components of a living being, born of a creative impulse and conceived as a whole.[55]

Elsewhere, he described "potpourris" as "forms of looser construction,"[56] a description which befits the Finale of the Serenade in its seemingly capricious combination of motives and fragments from earlier movements. Crucially, the use of the word "loose" by Schoenberg, Berg, Stein, and others in relation to the Serenade implied a musical form based on the principles of "stringing-together" and juxtaposition. However, the contrast between stable and loose formation, something that was vital to "developing variation" and its concomitant thematic differentiation, was not a defining feature in the Serenade, or in other pieces composed before the spring of 1923.

With this in mind, we could surmise that the "popular effect," characterized primarily through the accretion or "stringing-together" of closed musical units, could be seen as a way of solving what might then have appeared as a compositional conundrum. In "Opinion or Insight?" Schoenberg noted the absence of tonality as an obstruction to large-scale composition; hence, in the period leading up to 1920, he resorted to text-based pieces, where "the words represent the cohesive element."[57] By late spring of 1923, however, the four-movement classical sonata cycle, associated in Schoenberg's mind with developing variation, was regained, after an absence of fifteen years, in the Wind Quintet, Op. 26.[58] Yet, as late as 1922, Schoenberg unequivocally stated that modern music was turning towards polyphony,[59] a style exemplified by the Prelude from the Suite for Piano, Op. 25, composed in 1921, in which coherence is achieved by the manipulation of contrapuntal combinations ("unfolding").[60] In notes for his 1932-33 lectures on Schoenberg, Berg presents Op. 26 as the realization of the potential of dodecaphony to effect the large-scale structures of the sonata cycle, categorizing the preceding works and their respective technical procedures as "various attempts" [*Verschied. Versuche*] to this end.[61] Co-existing

[55]Schoenberg, "Gustav Mahler," in *Style and Idea*, 462. The original German is given in Arnold Schönberg, *Stil und Gedanke: Aufsätze zur Musik*, ed. Ivan Vojtech (Arnold Schönberg: Gesammelte Schriften, 1; Frankfurt am Main: S. Fischer, 1976), 17. The designation "potpourri" appears on Sk500 of sketchbook V (Arnold Schönberg Center Privatstiftung, Vienna).

[56]See Schoenberg, "'Folkloristic Symphonies," in *Style and Idea*, 163.

[57]Schoenberg, "Opinion or Insight," in *Style and Idea*, 262.

[58]See Erwin Stein, "Schönbergs Bläserquintett," *Pult und Taktstock* 3/5-6 (May-June 1926): 103.

[59]Schoenberg, *Theory of Harmony*, trans. Roy E. Carter (London: Faber and Faber, 1978), 389.

[60]See John Brackett, "Schoenberg, Unfolding, and 'Composing with Twelve Tones': A Case Study (Op. 25/1)," *International Journal of Musicology* 11 (forthcoming); and Áine Heneghan, "An Affinity with Bach: Form and Function in Schoenberg's 'New Polyphony,'" *Journal of the Arnold Schönberg Center* 7 (2006): 99–123.

[61]Berg, F 21 Berg 101/VII, fol. 8; transcription in Werner Grünzweig, *Ahnung und Wissen, Geist und Form: Alban Berg als Musikschriftsteller und Analytiker der Musik Arnold Schönbergs* (Vienna: Universal Edition, 2000), 281.

with the contrapuntal forms of the early 1920s, the simpler and more popular mode of presentation could, in its recapturing of homophony (albeit a primitive as opposed to a more artful homophony), be understood as one such "attempt."

Equally plausibly, we might construe the incorporation of manifold symmetries and repetitions as an attempt on Schoenberg's part to maximize intelligibility: "in higher art music," the popular mode of presentation occurs "mostly in favor of a particular circumstance, for example, because comprehensibility is impeded by the significant newness of a style."[62] In either case, what seems unmistakable is that the choice of titles (March, Dance Scene, Waltz, etc.) represents a deliberate evocation of the popular idiom, where the predilection for simpler forms evinces a quest for greater transparency. In this respect, the Serenade could be regarded as something of an oxymoron in its paradoxical fusion of the "popular effect" and nascent dodecaphonic practice.[63]

---

[62]Schoenberg, *Gedanke* manuscript (July 6, 1925), T37.08, paragraph 15. My translation.

[63]On the topic of the new and the popular in art, see "Avant Garde and Popularity," in Dahlhaus, *Schoenberg and the New Music*, 23–31. For a different interpretation of Schoenberg's "light music," see Rudolf Stephan, "Überlegungen zum Thema 'Schönberg und Mozart,'" in *Mozart in der Musik des 20. Jahrhunderts: Formen ästhetischer und kompositionstechnischer Rezeption*, ed. Wolfgang Gratzer and Siegfried Mauser (Schriften zur Musikalischen Hermeneutik, 2; Laaber: Laaber-Verlag, 1992), 105–16.

ANALYTICAL PERSPECTIVES

Schoenberg as Webern: The Three Pieces for Chamber Orchestra, III (1910)

Allen Forte

Schoenberg composed what are now known as his Three Pieces for Chamber Orchestra in 1910, following the extraordinary music he composed in 1909: the expressionist monodrama, *Erwartung*, Op. 17 and *Die glückliche Hand*, Op. 18. The eminent Danish scholar Jan Maegaard gives the dates of composition of the first two of the brief chamber orchestra pieces as 8/2 1910.[1] The date of the third movement—the topic of the present essay—and its grouping with the first two movements—is somewhat more problematic. Maegaard writes as follows:

> The 8-bar complete fragment of the third piece is found on folio 2, p. 1; p. 2 has instrumental indications but no clef and no noteheads. Although the fragment is undated and although it was obviously not written with the same pen as Pieces I and II, and therefore probably not on the same day, there are two features that substantiate membership with the first two pieces. The first and most decisive is the pagination. The continuous pagination 1-4 on the first and second of the two leaves permits the third piece to appear as a continuation of I and II. Further, the tempo indications are similar: I: Rapid Quarters; II: Moderate Quarters . . . . [2]

[1] Jan Maegaard, *Studien zur Entwicklung des dodekaphonen Satzes bei Arnold Schönberg* I (Copenhagen: Wilhelm Hansen, 1972), 65.

[2] Ibid., 66 (my translation). Das 8 T. umfassende Fragment des dritten Stückes befindet sich auf Bl. 2 p. 1; p. 2 hat Instrumentenangaben, aber keine Schlüssel und keine Noten. Obwohl das Fragment undatiert ist und obwohl es offensichtlich nicht mit derselben Feder wie Stücke I (cont.)

Allen Forte is Battell Professor of Music Theory Emeritus in the Department of Music, Yale University, where he was instrumental in initiating the Ph.D. program in music theory. His publications include some twelve books and eighty articles, published in *Journal of Music Theory, Music Theory Spectrum, Music Analysis, Perspectives of New Music,* and *Journal of the American Musicological Society,* reflecting his interest in pitch-class set theory, the study of avant-garde music of the twentieth century, principally that of the Second Viennese School and the music of Olivier Messiaen, Schenkerian analysis, and other aspects of music theory. In addition, he has written about and recorded music of the classic American popular song repertoire. His 1958 monograph on the development of diminutions in American jazz was the first detailed analytical study of that repertoire. Professor Forte was founding President of the Society for Music Theory and is a Fellow of the American Academy of Arts and Sciences. During his tenure at Yale, Professor Forte advised seventy-eight Ph.D. dissertations. In 2000 Yale established an endowed professorship in his name, the Allen Forte Professorship of Music Theory. He resides in Hamden, Connecticut with his wife, concert pianist Madeleine Forte.

Why did Schoenberg compose these short orchestral pieces? The older Schoenberg literature, which either pays little attention to these works or ignores them altogether, does not provide significant clues to an answer to this question. For example, in his standard catalogue, Josef Rufer cites Three Short Pieces for Chamber Orchestra (the third incomplete) (1910).[3] This listing confirms the dates of these intriguing works, but does not interpret their significance within Schoenberg's *oeuvre*, the primary concern of the present paper.

Recent discussions of the Three Short Pieces are relatively brief. Of these, I will comment on only two. The first appears in an editorial comment by Joseph Auner: ". . . the posthumously published Three Pieces for Chamber Orchestra, from February 1910, were left as fragments."[4] This gloss is only partially accurate. Only the third piece was not completed, or, more likely, the completion was lost. The facsimile published along with the edition of the Three Short Pieces by Belmont Music Publishers shows that the fragment breaks off exactly at the end of a manuscript page, strongly suggesting that the continuation is missing. Thus, the notation of the third movement may convincingly be regarded as a fragment, albeit a substantial one. The detailed account of the source documents in Jan Maegaard's *Studien zur Entwicklung des dodekaphonen Satzes bei Arnold Schönberg*, cited above, does not, however, interpret their significance with respect to Schoenberg's compositional *oeuvre* as a whole.

I direct my second comment to Bryan Simms's recently published study.[5] This publication contains six references to the Three Pieces for Chamber Orchestra.[6] Relevant to the present discussion is Simms's comment that " . . . in the third piece . . . the initial five-note chord returns persistently as a motto."[7] I ask the reader to keep this observation in mind; I will return to it later in my paper.

In an article I wrote some thirty years ago titled "Schoenberg's Creative Evolution,"[8] I observed that the movement discussed by Simms is canonical throughout, with the *dux* a linear presentation of his "five-note" chord (5-z17),

---

und II geschrieben, wurde und daher wahrscheinlich nicht am selben Tag entstanden ist, gibt es doch zwei Merkmale, die eine Zugehörigkeit zu den beiden ersten Stücken belegen. Das erste und entscheidende ist die Paginierung. Die fortlaufende Paginierung 1-4 auf den beiden ersten und zweiten Seiten der beiden Blätter lässt das dritte Stück als eine Fortsetzung von I und II erscheinen. Ferner sind die Tempoangaben ähnlich: I: *Rasche Viertel*; II: mässige Viertel . . . .

[3]Josef Rufer, *The Works of Arnold Schoenberg* (Kassel, Bärenreiter, 1959).

[4]Joseph Auner, *A Schoenberg Reader* (New Haven: Yale University Press, 2003), 101.

[5]Bryan Simms, *The Atonal Music of Arnold Schoenberg 1908-1923* (Oxford University Press, 2000).

[6]Ibid., 38, 60, 82-84, 104, 116, 119.

[7]Ibid., 38.

[8]"Schoenberg's Creative Evolution: The Path to Atonality," *The Musical Quarterly* 64/2 (April 1978): 133-76.

whose Z-correspondent, 5-z37, is, not coincidentally, a subset of Schoenberg's hexachord, 6-z44.[9] Thus, the "five-note chord" not only "returns persistently," as Simms observes, but it is constantly represented in the music either literally or by its complement. Both are components of the canonical thread. Thus, *all* the "vertical" harmonies in the movement are created by the unfolding canon—an extraordinary structure, coordinating vertical and horizon dimensions such that the pentad 5-z17 is constantly present.

Following his mention of Schoenberg's predilection for a "sustained motto-like chord,"[10] Simms cites examples, among them the short work under discussion in this article: "The third of the Three Pieces for Chamber Orchestra (1910) is based likewise upon a sustained six-note chord in the organ."[11] This observation also invites amplification.[12] This chord is an instance of set-class 6-z43, a sonority often heard in Webern's atonal music. For example, it occurs as the harmony at the beginning of his Op. 10, No. 3, composed 8 September 1913.[13] Is Schoenberg's use of a form of this sonority therefore to be construed as a "borrowing" from Webern? If true (and I believe it is), this would be still another instance of the concealed irony that is sometimes evident in the music and personal relations within the Schoenberg circle. On the other hand, Schoenberg seems (little wonder) to have been wholly unaware of the musical references to his persona in Berg's monumental opera, *Wozzeck*.[14]

In his retrospective essay, "Composition with Twelve Tones (1)," Schoenberg writes: "The first compositions in this new [atonal] style were written by me around 1908 and, soon afterwards, by my pupils Anton von Webern and Alban Berg."[15] But the major Schoenberg work "around 1908" is his *Fünfzehn Gedichte aus Das Buch der Hängenden Gärten von Stefan George*, Op. 15, composed

---

[9]Readers are reminded that pitch class sets having identical cardinality and the same interval content, but different prime forms, are said to be Z-related; see Forte, *The Structure of Atonal Music* (New Haven: Yale University Press, 1973; reprint 2006).

[10]Simms, *The Atonal Music of Arnold Schoenberg*, 38.

[11]Ibid.

[12]I would like to mention that the first three characters of my Connecticut automobile license plate are 537, a subset of Simms's motto-like chord, and a mystical symbol quite in keeping with the occult orientation of the Second Viennese School, as well as representative of my own music-theoretical work and the interest of the State of Connecticut Department of Motor Vehicles in twentieth-century avant-garde music!

[13]See Allen Forte, *The Atonal Music of Anton Webern* (New Haven: Yale University Press, 1998), 213-17.

[14]See Allen Forte, "The Mask of Tonality: Alban Berg's Symphonic Epilogue to *Wozzeck*," in David Gable and Robert P. Morgan, eds., *Alban Berg: Historical and Analytical Perspectives* (Oxford, Clarendon Press, 1991), 151-200 (especially Table 4, p. 161).

[15]Schoenberg, "Composition with Twelve Tones I [1941]," in *Style and Idea: Selected Writings of Arnold Schoenberg*, ed. Leonard Stein, trans. Leo Black (Berkeley: University of California Press, 1975), 217.

[16]Maegaard, *Studien zur Entwicklung I*, 65. The exact chronology within that period, according to Jan Maegaard, remains uncertain: "The chronology of only seven of the fifteen Lieder (cont.)

between March 1908 and March 1909.[16] Are these songs "the first compositions in this new style"? Probably not, since only the last of these, No. 15 (dated by Schoenberg as having been completed on 2 February 1909), can be regarded as fully atonal. The remaining songs are, to use a descriptive term I have adopted before, "hybrid tonal-atonal." It seems likely, however, that Schoenberg was influenced by Webern's "experimental" music along the path to the new atonal style, and that these short works exemplify that influence.

Maegaard specifies 1910 as the date of composition of Schoenberg's Three Pieces for Chamber Orchestra.[17] Here the question of historical priority rears its controversial head, since Webern's 1905 String Quartet exhibits very strong atonal characteristics, thus providing very strong evidence that pupil preceded master in this instance (and no doubt others) and suggesting that Webern, not Schoenberg, was the innovator with respect to the non-tonal music of the Second Viennese School.

The question of whether Schoenberg was willing to let the issue rest (namely the question of priority with respect to the pioneering efforts in atonality), remains unsettled. In a 1924 essay on Webern's *Bagatelles*, Schoenberg makes interesting comments on these brief compositions, beginning with the rather abstruse observation that "While the brevity of these pieces is their eloquent advocate, such brevity stands equally in need of advocacy. . . . These pieces will be understood only by someone who has faith in music as the expression of something that can be said only musically."[18] Surprisingly, Schoenberg makes no reference to his own miniature Three Pieces for Chamber Orchestra, perhaps wishing to avoid any undesirable association with the music of his student, Anton Webern, or perhaps not wishing to place himself in the position of master following pupil!

Additional encounters with Webern are apparent in the posthumously published collection of Schoenberg's writings, *Style and Idea*, which contains significant material of historical importance. For instance, in his essay "Twelve-Tone Composition," he offers an explication of the term "emancipation of the dissonance," highlighting the following declamation:

> What distinguishes dissonances from consonances is not a greater or lesser degree of *beauty*, but a greater or lesser degree of *comprehensibility*. In my *Harmonielehre*, I

---

can be specified, namely: IV, V, III, VIII, XIII, and XV, the composition of which extends from March 15, 1908 to February 28, 1909." This dating also appears in the opening paragraph of Theo Hirsbrunner, "*Fünfzehn Gedichte aus Das Buch der Hängenden Gärten von Stefan George,*" in ed. Gerold Gruber, *Arnold Schönberg: Interpretationen seiner Werke I* (Laaber: Laaber-Verlag, 2002), 196.

[17]See Maegaard, *Studien zur Entwicklung I*, 65.

[18]Arnold Schoenberg (trans. Leo Black), "Anton Webern: Foreword to his *Six Bagatelles for String Quartet*, Op. 9 (1911 and 1913)."

presented the theory that dissonant tones appear later among the overtones, for which reason the ear is less intimately acquainted with them.[19]

Whether Schoenberg was aware of the historical origin of this thesis (in the writings of Rameau, for example), is moot, although we have Schoenberg's famous disclaimer "Ich bin kein Leser."[20] The specific reference to Webern, which I mentioned earlier, occurs implicitly at the end of the 1911 edition of his *Harmonielehre*, where he inserts an excerpt from Webern's *Fünf Sätze für Streichquartett*, Op. 5, in the section entitled *Ästhetische Bewertung sechs- und mehrtöniger Klänge* [Aesthetic Evaluation of Chords of Six or More Tones].[21] The excerpt is presented as an example of dissonant harmonies without resolution to consonances, thus placing Webern in the compositional avant garde. Schoenberg takes care, however, to identify the composer of the excerpt and his subordinate relation to the master, preceding the excerpt with: "Und in einem Streichquartett meines Schülers Anton von Webern steht folgende Stelle" [And the following passage occurs in a string quartet by my pupil Anton von Webern].

In Schoenberg's retrospective writings it is clear that he wished to maintain both Webern and Berg in positions subservient to that of the master, ranks that neither disputed. However, toward the end of his life, in a radio interview with Halsey Stevens,[22] Schoenberg complained that Webern followed too closely in his footsteps, even though one of his own best known piano works is the set of miniatures for piano, the Op. 19 of 1911, the brevity and general style of which are certainly Webernian. Similarly, only two months before his death in 1951, a somewhat bitter-sounding Schoenberg reflects on his on-going competition with Webern in a short essay on the future compositional use of *Klangfarbenmelodien*, where he takes issue with his onetime pupil Frederic Dorian-Deutsch regarding Webern's priority as follows:

> Dorian-Deutsch studied with Webern, and recently, when he visited me, he told how Webern was the first to write *Klangfarbenmelodien*, and that I then used this at the end of *Harmonielehre*. Anyone who knows me at all knows that this is not true. It is known that I should not have hesitated to name Webern, had his music stimulated me to invent this expression. One thing is certain: even had it been Webern's idea, he would not have told it to me. He kept secret everything 'new' he

---

[19]Schoenberg, "Composition with Twelve Tones I [1941]," in *Style and Idea*, 216.

[20]In a letter to Hugo Leichtentritt of 3 December 1938 (Archive of the Arnold Schoenberg Center, Vienna)

[21]Arnold Schoenberg, *Harmonielehre* (Leipzig and Vienna: Universal-Edition, 1911), 500.

[22]This short interview ("Schoenberg as a Painter: Interview with Halsey Stevens") can be heard on *The Music of Arnold Schoenberg*, Vol. 3, Columbia M2S 709 (LP), 1965, and *Schoenberg: the Expressionist Years, 1908-1920*, Sony Classical SMK 62020 (CD), 1995 (Track 24).

had tried in his compositions. I, on the other hand, immediately and exhaustively explained to him each of my ideas—with the exception of the method of composition with twelve tones—that I long kept secret, because, as I said to Erwin Stein, Webern immediately uses everything I do, plan, or say, so that—I remember my words—'By now, I haven't the slightest idea who I am.' On each of these occasions I then had the pleasure of finding him highly enthusiastic, but failed to realize that he would write music of this kind sooner than I would.[23]

As far as is known, Schoenberg was unaware of the extent of Webern's obsequious attachment to him, concealed in the (transformed) statements of Schoenberg's signature hexachord, Es-C-H-B-E-G, which reduces to set-class 6-44 [012569], in Webern's music. Neither was he aware of Webern's use of high A-flat as the climactic pitch in his quartets. A-flat in German is represented by AS, Schoenberg's initials. That this musical cipher has remained hidden is evident from the lack or references to it in the Schoenberg literature. Also Schoenberg did not respond to Webern's problematic position following the German *Anschluss* of Austria in 1938. At the time, Webern moved himself to a small village to the south, and thus escaped the allied bombing of Vienna in 1944.

Another example of hidden musical tributes to Schoenberg within the Viennese Triumvirate is Berg's concealed quotation in *Wozzeck*, at the beginning of Act I, Scene 2 (Wozzeck and Andres). This consists of Schoenberg's pentad 5-z17 from the "Farben" movement of Op. 16, the first of the succession of three chords, which reads, from the bass up: C-E-C♯-E♭-A♭. Another instance is provided by Schoenberg's references in the first movement of Opus 15 to Alma Mahler and to his nemesis, Richard Gerstl, with whom his first wife had a secret love affair. The third of Schoenberg's Three Pieces for Chamber Orchestra also contains personal musical references—in this case to the composer himself. The hexachord 6-z43 (prime form: 012589), stated at the very beginning of this movement of Webern's piece for piano and violin under discussion and sustained throughout is not only a sonic reference to Webern, as a sonority, but also contains all the alphabetic notes A, B, and E, derived from Schoenberg's name which have correspondents in Webern's (i.e., Arnold schoenBErg, Anton wEBErn). The A, E, and B (B♭) in the upper 3-5 [016] trichord, is replicated by F, C, G♭ in the lower, a transposition (up 8 semitones or down 4) of the upper trichord.

Again, an example of the mystical use of pitch-names to represent persona, in this case Webern's deity—associated with the Christ figure, a religious emblem, as I have discussed in my book on Webern.[24]

Webern himself does not hesitate to "sign" his music, as in the opening double stop in the violin part of his Four Pieces for Piano and Violin, Op. 7,

[23]Schoenberg, "Anton Webern: *Klangfarbenmelodie* [1951]," in *Style and Idea*, 484.
[24]See Forte, *The Atonal Music of Anton Webern*, 347-48.

No. 2: A-E , which may be regarded as a hidden tribute to his teacher, since A and E are the only two vowels shared by their names (again, an example of the Viennese penchant for musical numerology).

While these cabalistic references are part and parcel of the "mystique" of the Second Viennese School's music, to be understood only by a select few in the musical elite (one wonders how large its contemporary constituency was, or is!), the practice has a long history in European art music, going back to the Renaissance and exemplified periodically in classical music, throughout the nineteenth century.

To return to the predominant hexachord at the beginning of Schoenberg's music, why does he compose these sonorities, which comprise the transformations of 6-z43, apart from the pitch symbols they contain and their putative connection with Webern? I have listed two major possibilities below.

First, they are non-tonal. That is, they are not part of the harmonic vocabulary of traditional tonal music—or, for that matter, are they prominent constituents of other non-traditional music of the earlier twentieth century (Bartók, Debussy, Strauss, et al). For aesthetic and "historical" reasons (the creation of "new" music), Schoenberg and his two prominent pupils, Berg and Webern, were deeply involved in the discovery of new sonorities, even though in the final chapter of his 1911 *Harmonielehre* on chords of six and more tones, Schoenberg began with a caveat directed to students, one that reflects his own conservative approach to teaching as well as his apprehension concerning the possible imitation of his compositional technique: "I do not recommend that the pupil use the harmonies shown here, in connection with compositional endeavors, unless they also appear in other, more conservative, textbooks."[25]

Second, the interval content of Schoenberg's own signature, 6-z44/z19, can be succinctly represented in vector format as [313431], in which the leftmost number gives the number of intervals of class 1 (e.g., minor seconds), the second gives the number of major seconds, and so forth. Most strikingly, Schoenberg's signature vector records the maximum number of interval-class 4 (e.g., major thirds) with respect to all the hexachordal classes in the 12-note system. It also displays certain sonically important correspondences: minor seconds, minor thirds, perfect fourths are all present in the same number (3 of each). Thus 6-z44 and its complement, 6-z19, are special sonorities in the atonal harmonic universe, no doubt selected by the composer for their non-traditional sound as well as their uniqueness.

Schoenberg's concern for sonorities with unusual characteristics in the new "atonal" music is evident everywhere in his atonal repertoire, often with specific musical references to persons associated with the Viennese Circle. For example,

---

[25]Schoenberg, *Harmonilehre*, 458 (my translation). Ich empfehle dem Schüler nicht, sich bei Kompositionsversuchen der hier aufgezeigten Harmonien zu bedienen, soweit sie nicht auch in anderen, konservativeren Lehrbüchern vorkommen.

tetrachord 4-19 [0148] is maximally represented (under inversion) as a subset of 6-z19 [013478] and its complement, Schoenberg's emblematic 6-z44 [012589]. As I have stated elsewhere, tetrachord 4-19 [0148] may be regarded as the sonic emblem of music of the Second Viennese School because of its prevalence and its multiple strategic functions.[26]

Schoenberg's mastery of orchestrational technique is beautifully and concisely evident in the work under consideration here. For the convenience of the reader, I have provided a condensed score (see Example 1).[27]

As noted above, the music used for this article is clearly a truncated version of the original, the complete form of which is missing or lost. Nevertheless, it is possible to comment upon some of its basic features, beginning with orchestration, a musical universe in which Schoenberg was not only completely at home, but one that encouraged his musical creativity. The fragment cannot be said to realize Schoenberg's concept of "Klangfarbenmelodien," described at the end of his *Harmonielehre*:

> I cannot agree unquestioningly with the distinction customarily made between tone color and pitch. I find that pitch is made evident through tone-color, which is a dimension of pitch . . . . Tone-color melodies! What highly developed senses, which can discriminate and which can find delight in such subtle things![28]

However, the orchestral texture does come close to the *Klangfarben* concept. Against the hexachord 6-z43—a favorite of Webern, as the reader will recall— played by harmonium, different instruments present short figures in their home registers, perhaps the most salient of which occur in the flute and contrabass parts at the registral extremes. And, once again, the Schoenberg autograph pitches are apparent here: the high G in flute, measure 3, the contrabass D-flat in measure 4 (G as in schoenberG, D-flat, German Des, as in arnolD ESchönberg, linking the first and last names of the composer.

With respect to other registral issues, the analyst (and conductor) confront difficult choices. It seems possible that the contrabass D-flat is not to be transposed down an octave, which would be at the extreme lower end of the instrument's register. On the other hand, the celesta clearly sounds as notated, not transposing down an octave. Moreover, each melodic component has not only its own

---

[26]See Forte, *The Structure of Atonal Music*, 217.

[27]I have condensed this fragment to six staves (without changes in notes or notation). All the other notational features are in the original manuscript (slurring, articulations, instrumentation, and so on).

[28]Schoenberg, *Harmonilehre*, 471 (my translation). Ich kann den Unterschied zwischen Klangfarbe und Klanghöhe, wie er gewöhnlich ausgedruckt wird, nicht so unbedingt zugeben. Ich finde, der Ton macht sich bemerkbar durch die Klangfarbe, deren eine Dimension die Klanghöhe ist ... Klangfarbernmelodien! Welche feinen Sinne, die hier unterscheiden, welcher hochentwickelte Geist, der an so subtilen Dingen Vergnügen finden mag!

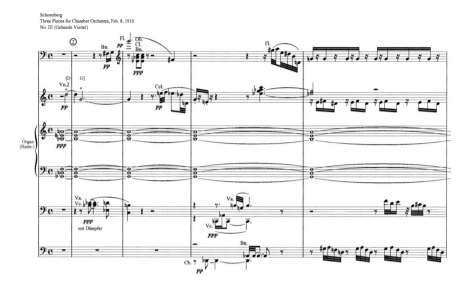

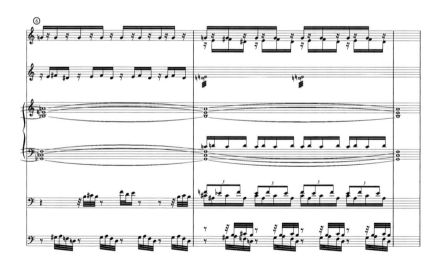

Example 1: Schoenberg, Three Pieces for Chamber Orchestra, III, mm. 1-8. (condensed score)

register but also its own rhythm, thus creating (again) a Webernian texture. Of more immediate interest, this feature distinguishes the first four bars from the last four (as noted above?). What this would imply for an imaginary continuation is of course moot. A large-scale binary form?

Yet another Webern connection is suggested by the extreme dynamic levels so characteristic of Webern's atonal music. Unfortunately, these are left incomplete in the fragment. However, the central sonority, Webern's 6-z43, cited above, is played by the harmonium at a constant pianissimo level throughout.

I have focused in this essay on pitch-relations, with a near total disregard for matters of rhythm. I refer the reader to other published analytical discussions of rhythm in atonal music, generally, and Webern's music in particular.[29] Furthermore, in my reading of this music I have not included an inventory of the total, twelve pitch-class chromatic, since, unlike the atonal music of Webern, it seems not to be essential to the unfolding music of the fragment. For the record, however, cello A-flat in measure 4 completes the twelve pitch-classes and is doubled an octave lower by the bassoon's A-flat in the same measure. To the analyst this strategic placement of the Schoenberg dyad AS is a golden moment. More important to an effective analysis is the identification of the fragment's pitch-class set constituents. On another occasion, as they say, I will present and discuss a pitch-class set analysis of the third movement of the Three Pieces for Chamber Orchestra.

---

[29]See, for example, Allen Forte, "Aspects of Rhythm in Webern's Atonal Music," *Music Theory Spectrum* 2 (Spring 1980): 90-109; and Allen Forte, "Foreground Rhythm in Early Twentieth-Century Music," *Music Analysis* 2/3 (October 1983): 239-68.

Juxtaposing Popular Music in Schoenberg's Second String Quartet, Op. 10

Severine Neff

Arnold Schoenberg's infamous quotation of the old Austrian tune, "Ach, du lieber Augustin," in the Scherzo of the Second String Quartet, Op. 10, marks the occasion in which he first used pre-existing and popular materials in a mature work (Example 1).[1] He knew that this crossover into a vernacular language would catch his listeners' attention; any Viennese audience, too, would have been familiar with the apocryphal tale of Augustin, the alcoholic musician (a bagpiper in some versions) who became so stupefied while doing the rounds of the inns during the 1681 plague that he was taken for dead and thrown into a pit for victims having succumbed to the epidemic. According to some accounts, Augustin awoke from his stupor the next day, climbed out of the pit, and composed the folk tune with its text "O, dear Augustin, all is undone"—an ironic ode to life.[2]

---

[1]Schoenberg's other compositions quoting folk material include the Suite, Op. 29 ("Ännchen von Tharau") and *Kol Nidre*, Op. 39.

[2]For a history of the folksong, see James J. Fuld, *The World Famous Book of Music: Classical, Popular, and Folk*, 4th ed. (New York: Dover, 1995), 399-401. The fin-de-siècle Viennese audiences had heard the other references to "Augustin" in the works of Ferruccio Busoni and Max Reger; see Ferruccio Busoni, *Fuge über das Volkslied, "O, du lieber Augustin"* [*Fugue on the Folksong "O Dear Augustin"*]; and Max Reger, *Sechs Burlesken*, Op. 58. For a brief discussion of "Augustin" in Viennese culture, see Jutta Theurich, "Preface to Ferruccio Busoni's *Fuge über das Volkslied, "O, du lieber Augustin"* (Leipzig: Breitkopf und Härtel, 1987), 1-2. However, there is no documentary evidence to indicate that Schoenberg recognized these earlier works as precursors.

Severine Neff is Eugene Falk Distinguished Professor in the Arts and Humanities at the University of North Carolina at Chapel Hill. She has received research awards from The Andrew W. Mellon Foundation, The Newberry Library, The National Endowment for the Humanities, and was a Senior Fulbright Scholar at Moscow State Conservatory and a Faculty Fellow of The Mannes Institute in New York. Professor Neff has published in numerous journals including *Music Theory Spectrum* and has edited books on Schoenberg's theoretical writings: Arnold Schoenberg, *Coherence, Counterpoint, Instrumentation, Instruction in Form* (with Charlotte M. Cross), Arnold Schoenberg, *The Musical Idea and the Logic, Technique, and Art of its Presentation* (with Schoenberg's student, the late Patricia Carpenter), and a Norton Score of the Second String Quartet, Op. 10, by Arnold Schoenberg. She is General Editor (with Sabine Feisst) of *Schoenberg in Words*, a nine-volume collection of Schoenberg's writings to be published by Oxford University Press.

Example 1. The quotation of "Augustin" in Schoenberg's Second String Quartet, Op. 10.

Virtually every commentator on the Quartet since 1909 has been captivated by "Augustin" and seems to have a different interpretation of its words. Musicologist Philip Friedheim and composer-theorist Ethan Haimo, for instance, consider the tune and the text to be a joke—they cite Schoenberg's own description of the passage as combining themes in a "tragicomic manner."[3] Whereas Reinhold Brinkmann, Elmar Budde, and Walter Frisch see "Augustin" as an entirely serious matter—a metaphor pointing to Schoenberg's awareness of the fact that he had pushed tonality to its limits.[4] Michael Graubart, Rudolf Kolisch,

[3]See Ethan Haimo, *Schoenberg's Transformation of Musical Language* (Cambridge: Cambridge University Press, 2006), 230; Philip Friedheim, "Tonality and Structure in the Early Works of Schoenberg" (Ph.D. diss., New York University, 1963), 385.

[4]See Reinhold Brinkmann, *Arnold Schönberg, Drei Klavierstücke Op. 11: Studien zur frühen Atonalität bei Schönberg* (Wiesbaden: F. Steiner, 2000), 19-20; Elmar Budde, "Zitat, Collage, Montage," in *Die Musik der sechziger Jahre*, ed. Rudolf Stephan, *Veröffentlichungen des Instituts für neue Musik* (cont.)

Dika Newlin, Bryan Simms, and Hans Heinz Stuckenschmidt claim that the text comments on the tension in Schoenberg's marriage.[5]

The strong historical and extra-musical interest in "Augustin" is indubitably predicated on Schoenberg's desire to shock his audience by the juxtaposition of a popular melody within the context of a contrapuntally dense, extended tonal work. I will argue that Schoenberg's notion of musical juxtaposition in vernacular music—a topic he pursued in many compositions, arrangements, analyses, and commentaries—intersects with his understanding of purely classical works, thus capturing compelling and novel conceptions of musical form. After a general scrutiny of Schoenberg's theoretical, historical, and extra-musical involvement with popular music in his own works and others, I shall turn to ideas of juxtaposition in the classical form of the Scherzo from Brahms's Fourth Symphony and the "crossover form" as exemplified by the intrusion of "Augustin" in the Second String Quartet.

Presenting Musical Ideas in Popular Forms

In his theoretical texts, Schoenberg analyzed Johann Strauss's "On the Beautiful Blue Danube" more than any other work.[6] The incomplete draft of the theoretical treatise, *The Musical Idea and the Logic, Technique and Art of Its Presentation*, contains detailed analyses not only of "On the Beautiful Blue Danube," but also of Strauss's "Laguna Waltzes," "Roses from the South," Johann Strauss Sr.'s *Radetsky March*, and Franz Lehár's "Love Unspoken" from *The Merry Widow*. Moreover, the unpublished manuscript of 1925 entitled "Johann Strauss" and later essays in the collection *Style and Idea* address aesthetic, theoretical, and philosophical issues related to vernacular forms (Figure 1).

---

und Musikerziehung Darmstadt, 12 (Mainz: B. Schott's Söhne, 1972), 26-38; Walter Frisch, *The Early Works of Arnold Schoenberg, 1893-1908* (Berkeley: University of California Press, 1993), 266.

[5] In January 1909, Schoenberg underlined Kraus's aphorism about familial relations, having an ironic message and tone akin to "Augustin:" "Family life carries with it a *caveat*—that of its invasion of one's private, personal life"; see *Die Fackel* 275-81 (1909): 32. See also Michael Graubart, "Hans Heinz Stuckenschmidt's *Schönberg: Leben—Umwelt—Werk*," in *Tempo* 111 (1974): 48; Rudolf Kolisch, "On Schoenberg's String Quartet No. 2, Op. 10," The Rudolf Kolisch Collection, Harvard University, *86-M99; Dika Newlin, "Arnold Schoenberg's Debt to Mahler," *Chord and Dischord* 2/5 (1948): 21-28; Bryan Simms, "'My dear Hagerl:' Self-Representation in Schoenberg's String Quartet No. 2," *19th-Century Music* 26/3 (Spring 2003): 258-77; H[ans] H[einz] Stuckenschmidt, *Arnold Schoenberg: His Life, World, and Work*, trans. Humphrey Searle (New York: Schirmer Books, 1977), 96.

[6] E.g., Arnold Schoenberg, *Style and Idea: The Selected Writings of Arnold Schoenberg*, ed. Leonard Stein, trans. Leo Black (Berkeley: University of California Press, 1984), 124, 134-35, 138-39, 148, 164, 176-77, 178, 256, 268, 311, 336, 395, 415; Arnold Schoenberg, *The Musical Idea and the Logic, Technique and Art of Its Presentation*, ed. and trans. Patricia Carpenter and Severine Neff (New York: Columbia University Press, 1995), 136-37, 201.

Figure 1. Schoenberg and popular music.

COMPOSITIONS:

(after 1882)	*Alliance-Walzer* [*Alliance Waltz*] for 2 violins
(after 1882)	*Sonnenschein-Polka* [*Sunshine Polka*] for 2 violins
(fall to winter, 1897)	*11 Walzer für Streichorchester* [*11 Waltzes for String Orchestra*]
1901	*6 Brettl Lieder* [*6 Cabaret Songs*]
1916	*Der deutsche Michel* [*German Michael* (i.e. common man of German peasantry)]
1916	*Die eiserne Brigade* [*The Iron Brigade*]
1921	Untitled music for a family Christmas celebration

ARRANGEMENTS:

1918	*Lagunenwalzer* [*Laguna Waltzes*], Op. 411, *Rosen aus dem Süden*, [*Roses from the South*], Op. 388, Johann Strauss
1921	*Santa Lucia* and 2 smaller works for violin, viola, cello, mandolin, guitar, and clarinet
1922	*Gerpa*, theme and variations for horn, piano, two violins, harmonium
1929	4 untitled folksongs for voice and piano
1929	4 Folksongs for *a cappella* mixed chorus
1935	"My Horses Ain't Hungry" (Appalachian folk song) for *a cappella* mixed chorus (incomplete)
1948	4 Folksongs for voice and piano, Op. 49
1948	4 Folksongs for *a cappella* mixed chorus

ORCHESTRATIONS:

1916	*Austrian Grenadiers' March* of Neipperg (incomplete)
1916	*Imperial Grenadiers' March* of Neipperg (incomplete)

QUOTATIONS IN WORKS:

1907-08	"Ach, du lieber Augustin" in Scherzo of Second String Quartet, Op. 10
1925	"Ännchen von Tharau" in Theme and Variations of Suite, Op. 29

PROSE WRITINGS:

1911/1922	*Harmonielehre* [compare *Theory of Harmony*, Roy E. Carter, trans. (Berkeley: University of California Press, 1978), 131].
1925	*Der musikalische Gedanke, seine Darstellung und Durchführung* (manuscript T 37. 04, 07-8, Arnold Schoenberg Center), 4-5.
1925	"Johann Strauss" (unpublished manuscript T 35.04, Arnold Schoenberg Center), 1.

1934	"The Laws of Musical Coherence," "Melody," "Popular Music and Melody" in *The Musical Idea and the Logic, Technique, and Art of Its Presentation*, Patricia Carpenter and Severine Neff, ed. and trans. (Bloomington: Indiana University Press, 2006).
1938-42	*Fundamentals of Musical Composition*, Gerald Strang and Leonard Stein, ed. (London: Faber and Faber, 1967), 102.
1946-47	"Criteria for the Evaluation of Music, " "Folklorist Symphonies" in *Style and Idea: The Selected Writings of Arnold Schoenberg*, Leonard Stein, ed., Leo Black, trans. (Berkeley: University of California Press, 1984).

Why did this creator of some of the densest, most complex European art music take such an interest in popular works? Schoenberg himself provides a direct response to this question:

[I] do not see why, when other people are entertained, I, too, should not sometimes be entertained; I know indeed that I really ought at every single moment to behave like my own monument; but it would be hypocritical of me to conceal the fact that I occasionally step down from my pedestal and enjoy light music. . . . [But] light music could not entertain me unless something interested me about its substance and its working out.[7]

Schoenberg's intellectual interest in popular music manifested itself in his very earliest attempts at composition. He grew up on Taborstrasse in Vienna's Second District. The neighborhood is part of an island bordered by the Danube River on the north and the Danube Canal on the south. Large parks in the district— the Prater and the Augarten—were favorite gathering places, teeming with crowds attending concerts, festivals, and parades, as well as an amusement center called "Venice in Vienna" (complete with mock palaces and artificial canals). Schoenberg's friend, the journalist David Joseph Bach, recalls:

It was in front of the *Erstes Kaffeehaus* on the main avenue of Vienna's Prater Park; among the other onlookers there stood a young fellow in a short, light yellow overcoat, speaking loudly about music in general and about the music resounding from the park pavilion. That is my first memory of Arnold Schönberg, and that initial image has not blurred over the years to this very day. There we were, all of us . . . standing there at the fence, listening to the music free of charge.[8]

---

[7]Schoenberg, *Style and Idea*, 178.
[8]David Josef Bach, "Aus der Jugendzeit," in *Arnold Schönberg zum 50. Geburtstage, 13. September 1924* (Vienna: Universal Edition, 1934), 31-32, (translation by Grant Chorley).

Example 2. The opening juxtaposition of the March and Waltz in Schoenberg's *Alliance Waltz*.

Plate 1. Arnold Schoenberg with his mother Pauline and sister Ottile ca. 1879.

Plate 2. Schirmer's collection of folk songs given to Schoenberg by Carl Engel.

Schoenberg's earliest surviving compositions imitate the pieces he heard in the park. These include the *Alliance Waltz*, part of which is pictured in Example 2. Schoenberg's undated piece was clearly written after he began violin lessons as an eight-year-old in 1882 (Plate 1). The boy Schoenberg scored his waltz for two violins, so that he and his friends could play the work. When writing this waltz, he did not have the compositional skill to contrast long-term structures through modulation; thus he juxtaposed an introductory German march in 2/4 with a lilting Viennese waltz in 3/4 instead, representing his main theme in both— hence the title, *Alliance Waltz*.

Figure 1 shows that the mature Schoenberg's involvement with composing, arranging, orchestrating, and writing about popular music continued throughout his life. One of his last and very unique ventures into vernacular forms occurred in 1935, two years after his arrival in America. At this time Schoenberg began the arrangement of an Appalachian folksong.[9] The mention of this piece first arises in an exchange of letters in the spring of 1935 with his publisher at G. Schirmer, Carl Engel, in which Schoenberg told Engel that he would provide him a short choral number sung *a cappella*—that is, if he found himself in 'the right mood for such a piece."[10] Schoenberg also asked his publisher to send "materials for something of that kind (songbooks or hymnals or the like)." Engel honored Schoenberg's request with a collection of folk tunes entitled *Songs of the Hill Folk, 12 Ballads from Kentucky, Virginia, and North Carolina*, edited in 1934 by the renowned collector, composer, and Kentucky balladeer John Jacob Niles (Plate 2).[11] Schoenberg chose "My Horses Ain't Hungry" for his arrangement (Plate 3**)**.

This folk tune has a complex history; its text relates to a group of songs connected with the Appalachian tune, "On Top of Old Smoky," its melody to a drinking song of the white South, "Rye Whisky," and amusingly, to the African-American melody called the "Temperance Rhyme."[12] However, all such rich

---

[9]I discovered the sketches and draft for the work several years ago at the Arnold Schoenberg Center; composer Allen Anderson has reconstructed the work for Belmont Edition; see Arnold Schoenberg, *My Horses Ain't Hungry* (arr. 1935), reconstruction by Allen Anderson (Pacific Palisades: Belmont Music Publishers, 2007).

[10]Letters to Engel, dated March 1935, are on the website of the Arnold Schoenberg Center; see also Severine Neff with Sabine Feisst, "Foreward," in Schoenberg, *Horses*.

[11]See Schirmer's American Folk-Song Series, Set 14: *Songs of the Hill Folk, 12 Ballads from Kentucky, Virginia and North Carolina*, collected and simply arranged with accompaniment for piano by John Jacob Niles (New York: G. Schirmer, 1934). John Jacob Niles (1892-1980) collected and set folk songs from his native Appalachia as well as composing his own. In his collection, Niles claims that "My Horses Ain't Hungry" originated in Pulaski County, Kentucky— perhaps he first heard the song there.

[12]Certain published scores of the "My Horses Ain't Hungry" printed in Chicago in the 1930s, are more strongly related to the tune of "Rye Whiskey" than Niles's transcription: compare *Tiny Texan, World's Greatest Collection of Cowboy and Mountain Ballads* (1930), 32; *Play and Sing: America's Greatest Collection of Old-Time Songs and Mountain Ballads* (1930), 30; *Blue Grass Roy, The* (cont.)

Plate 3. John Jacob Niles's published score of "My Horses Ain't Hungry" (retrograde indicated with arrows).

Example 3. The folk tune accompanying itself in *My Horses Ain't Hungry.*

Hamlin's Korn Kracker (1930), 32; see also Carson J. Robison's *World's Greatest Collection of Mountain Ballads and Old Time Songs* (1930), 32; *KFBI Songs of the Plains* (Radio Station KFBI: Abilene, Kansas, 1933), 30, and the booklet of *Old-Fashioned Hymns and Mountain Ballads As Sung by Asher Sizemore and Little Jimmie* (New York: Decca Records, 1933), 27. In these versions, phrases one, two, and four (i.e., "eat your hay," "right away," and "from your door") end on repeated tonic pitches, thus allowing harmonization with plagal ("Amen") cadences, used in Protestant church hymnals. Fermatas appear on the introductory pitch of each line of text, capturing the lilt of a Southern American dialect. See also *Thomas Talley's Negro Folk Rhymes: A New, Expanded Edition*, with Music edited with an Introduction and Notes by Charles K. Wolfe (Knoxville: University of Tennessee Press, 1991), 174.

historical facts were undoubtedly irrelevant to Schoenberg, who had no knowledge of American folk culture, and in 1935, only a rudimentary knowledge of English. Taking Niles's transcription as the definitive rendition of the folk tune, he most likely chose the melody for its contrapuntal possibilities (Example 3). The beginning of the tune can be combined with its own augmentation: compare C-sharp-A-F-sharp-E in the tenor (m. 1) and in the soprano (mm. 1-2); the melody itself can be reproduced canonically at the octave, and most remarkably, the third phrase of the tune is its own retrograde (marked with arrows in Plate 3). All of these intricate relations are worked out in his sketches and score for the arrangement.[13]

Schoenberg understood limitations on development to be a necessity when dealing with popular materials. In an essay written in 1947, he compares his approach to vernacular materials to Bach's designs in chorale preludes:

> [Because] Bach often derives the voices, which contrapuntally accompany the main theme in his chorale preludes from the chorale melody itself, there is no possibility or necessity of a development [or] growth.[14]

Unlike a typical popular work, the arrangement of "Horses" has a setting of the second verse in the remote key of C-sharp major and is sated with variations of motives from its first phrase. Perhaps "Horses" became too developed for Schoenberg, for he abandoned the work soon after beginning it.

In 1935, six months before beginning the "Horses" project, Schoenberg had written his most extended theoretical discussion of popular works. He asserts:

> The popular effect of popular music is based on its broad understandability . . . [which] is mainly achieved through an extremely slow 'tempo of presentation.' This means: 1) the *Grundgestalten* themselves usually contain only a very few motivic forms; 2) are very often repeated in nearly unvaried form; and 3) if after several (2-5 or more) such repetitions a more developed variation appears, it often changes so much that it could be hard to comprehend, were not the entire section repeated again and again, or, if it is varied more in pitch, the rhythm remains (almost) unchanged.[15]

And, he further explains, "segments do not need much of a connective; they can be added by juxtaposition, because of the absence of variation in them. There is nothing that asks for expansion."[16]

Schoenberg demonstrated his criteria in several analyses of popular works. Here I will particularly emphasize the juxtaposition of segments, a technique,

---

[13]See Schoenberg, *Horses*, "Foreword," 4, 10-11.
[14]Schoenberg, *Style and Idea*, 165.
[15]Schoenberg, *The Musical Idea*, 300-01.
[16]Schoenberg, *Style and Idea*, 164.

which contrasts with that of developing variation. And indeed, the physical layout of Schoenberg's analyses of popular music emphasizes this very point. For instance, Example 4—his analysis of "Love Unspoken" from *The Merry Widow*—contains an initial column of *Gestalten* that, to his ear, are distinct in contour, rhythm, and intervallic succession from those in the second column; for example, the opening D-G-A-B is, in these senses, unrelated to its consequent C-B-A.[17] There is no intermediary form between these *Gestalten* to diminish the distinctions—a second intrudes on a first. For this reason Schoenberg terms their succession as "not very logical"—that is, not varied and joined through connectives in the organic sense of "developing variation" but rather merely juxtaposed. In his words, the *Gestalten* are "set next to each other . . . like columns of items that are to be added together and indeed are added up at the end."[18] Thus Schoenberg sees the popular form not as more than the sum of its parts, but as the ordered sum of its parts—a form that always exists in the present with no future implication, aesthetically realizing only a secure reliving of the past.

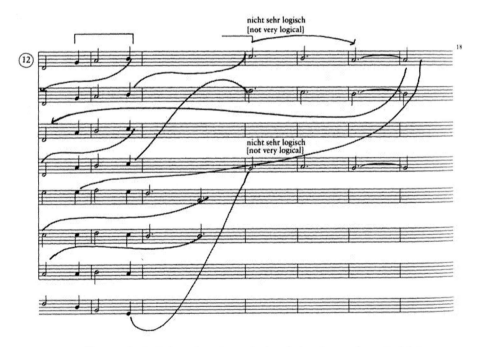

Example 4. Schoenberg's analysis of the theme from Lehár's "Love Unspoken."

[17]Schoenberg, *The Musical Idea*, 306.
[18]Ibid., 158-59.

This lack of continuous development between parts gives the work "a certain unproblematic or relaxed quality, a certain rest between the constituent parts of the components which just barely allows continuation without demanding it."[19] Schoenberg writes:

> Structurally, there never remains in popular tunes an unsolved problem, the consequences of which will show up only later. The segments do not need much of a connective; they can be added by juxtaposition, because of the absence of variation in them. There is nothing that asks for expansion. The small form holds the contents firmly, constituting thus a small expansion but independent structure.[20]

Schoenberg further likens this "problem-less" presentation of popular music to a literary form:

> [The] vernacular art of presenting thoughts belongs wholly to [those], who can only relate an orderly succession to things just as they happen, who have no grasp of the whole, who can therefore neither anticipate nor go back nor connect one sentence with another except by means of the copula 'and' . . . 'And then I said . . . and then he said and then we laughed . . . and . . . and so on.' The narrative goes on only because the story that is being told goes on, because a continuous action drives the storyteller on. The climax is then only dynamic.[21]

Juxtaposition in a Scherzo of Brahms

This concrete aspect of simple presentation—its technique of juxtaposition—interested Schoenberg in part because he thought it had implication in "more artful treatments," treatments in which simple juxtaposition would appear along with tonal problems and developing variations.

In his main manuscript on the "musical idea," Schoenberg speaks of a hypothetical situation in an artwork in which the juxtaposition of materials is so cryptic and intrusive that a composer can explain its presence only by returning to it and varying it so as to connect with more central thematic materials. He writes:

> A very high degree of remoteness from the initial *Gestalt* is to be found in those variations that introduce a subordinate idea. Often their connection to the *Grundgestalt* (frequently an indirect one) becomes clear very late. As a rule these *Gestalten* develop forward hardly at all, but rather backward: they approach the initial *Gestalt*.[22]

---

[19]Ibid., 378-79.
[20]Ibid., 164.
[21]Ibid., 256.
[22]Ibid., 158-59.

Here, I take Schoenberg to be discussing relations so distant from an initial *Gestalt* as to act as intruders—blatant juxtapositions comparable to those of popular music. But, as the work unfolds forward in time, these unrelated *Gestalten* develop "backward"—revealing their connection to the initial *Gestalt*.

I understand the paradoxical notion of "backward development" as occurring in one of Schoenberg's favorite works—the Scherzo of Brahms's Fourth Symphony. Its opening theme consists of several phrases of sharply contrasting character and tonality, juxtaposed with a brutal frankness (compare Example 5a): a vigorous four-bar opening melody, a single fortissimo chord at the fifth measure (marked "X" in Example 5a) followed by a striking idea with a repeated sixteenth-note rhythm; and finally a seemingly unrelated theme in the flat mediant, leading back to V of the tonic. The chord at measure 5 (a subdominant chord, but without the fifth) is heard simultaneously as a continuation of the vigorous opening, as the beginning of the sixteenth-note idea, and also as a harmony paradoxically isolated in register, dynamic, and articulation from its surroundings.

This curious, single chord proves to be perhaps the single most powerful and decisive component in the Scherzo's form, precisely because of the emphasis, which results from its immediate context—it functions as an abrupt, foreign element demanding resolution and thus continuation, what Schoenberg would call a "tonal problem." At each structural juncture of the Scherzo—transition, development, and coda—this cryptic chord returns and eventually initiates progressions of similar chords, which ultimately prefigure the main theme of the Symphony's fourth movement (compare harmonies and rising lines marked with "X" in Example 5b-d).

Thus Brahms's "backward development" of the cryptic F major chord into an initial theme miraculously transcends the traditional boundaries of the major junctures of his sonata-allegro schema—thus allowing its different juxtaposed parts to develop independently. In the Coda, all three portions of the theme follow a long dominant pedal, but they appear in keys which are tonally distant and virtually irreconcilable—F major (mm. 311-18), A major (mm. 331-37), and finally the tonic C major (mm. 337-46), which enters *without* a dominant (see Examples 6a-c). For Brahms's confidant, Elisabeth von Herzogenberg, the penultimate return to tonic C-major in this context was a shocking juxtaposition. She writes in a letter to Brahms:

> And now for my one grief with respect to this movement: all that beauty, all that rich tenderness, and then the rapid—almost brutally rapid—return to C major! Believe me, it is as if you had played us some glorious thing on the piano, and then, to ward off all emotion and show your natural coarseness, snort into your beard:

Example 5. Juxtaposition and backward development in Brahms's Fourth Symphony, Op. 98, III and IV. a) Initial juxtapositions in the First Theme.

Example 5. b) The Development's rising line prefiguring
the fourth movement's theme.

Example 5. c) The Coda's rising line prefiguring
the fourth movement's theme.

Example 5. d) Main theme of the fourth movement.

F major

Examples 6a-c. The abrupt return to the tonic in the Coda.

Example 6a.

Example 6b.

Example 6c.

'All rot, all rot, you know!' It hurts so, this forcible C major; it is no modulation, but an operation—at least, so I feel it, Heaven forgive me![23]

From the perspective of Schoenberg's understanding of the possibilities of juxtaposition, we might speculate that it was precisely Brahms's use of juxtaposition in this return to the tonic and its consequences for form and tonality that proved too radical for this astute German musician.

Yet there are more consequences of the "rapid return" to the tonic in the Coda of the Scherzo. Could it be that the intrusion of the tonic is an aid in pushing the symphony forward to the main theme of the fourth movement— the very theme prefigured by the backward development of the Scherzo's initial juxtaposition, the F major chord? Interestingly, the tonics within main key areas prolonged in the coda—F (mm. 311-18), A (mm. 331-37), and C (mm. 337-46)—spell out this very chord. Moreover, the voicing and scoring of the first A-minor chord in the fourth movement de-emphasizes the root A and highlighting C and E—thus singling out the pitches shared with the tonic triad at the Scherzo's penultimate cadence. Schoenberg poses the question in *Harmonielehre*, [Is] "the ceremonious way in which the close of a composition used to be tied up, bolted, nailed down, and sealed . . . , too ponderous for present-day sense of form to use it?"[24]

Juxtaposition in Schoenberg's Scherzo

Several decades after the composition of Brahms's radical Scherzo movement, Schoenberg would push the ideas of juxtaposition to their limits with a "crossover form"—the intrusion of "Augustin" in his own Scherzo. Schoenberg articulates his Scherzo as an ABA schema in an unusual duple meter (see Figure 2). He states its main theme in a sentence form presenting his first theme or *Grundgestalt* in the form of a contrapuntal combination restated in invertible counterpoint at the octave (Examples 7a-c). Although the lines of the combination and its inversion articulate the diatonic harmonies of D minor, they are in themselves not triadic, featuring instead "problematic" chromatic functions analogous to those in the first movement: sharp-4, G-sharp, and flat-5, A-flat. The Scherzo's lightning tempo gives weight to the linear repetition of these chromatic pitches and obscures their fleeting triadic accompaniment. And indeed, at the liquidation (mm. 11-12), 025 trichords replace triads as the prevalent harmonies (see Example 7d). The sentence-form closes on a single chord [02579] (m. 13), anchored by the cello's flat-1 and flat-5, both pitches remaining unresolved. At the ensuing fermata (m. 13), the movement "grinds to a halt."

[23]Johannes Brahms, *The Herzogenberg Correspondence*, ed. Max Kalbeck, trans. Hannah Bryant (New York: Da Capo Press, 1987), 263.

[24]Arnold Schoenberg, *Theory of Harmony*, trans. Roy E. Carter (Berkeley: University of California Press, 1978), 128.

The utter lack of forward motion gives added weight to the low D-flat, flat-1, a radical function, which will be repeated at later climaxes.

A-Section

Exposition of 3 Themes

mm. 1-13	Theme 1 (in invertible counterpoint)	D minor
mm. 14-17	Theme 2	"roving"
mm. 17-19	Theme 3	"roving"

Their Development

mm. 20-34	Theme 1	D minor, "roving"
mm. 35-62	Theme 2	D minor, "roving"
mm. 62-80	Theme 3	D minor, "roving"

Transition

mm. 80-84	Theme 1 (augmented)	"roving"

Reprise

mm. 85-97	Theme 1	D minor

Section B: Trio

mm. 98-122	Theme 4	F♯ major/minor, C major, "roving"
mm. 123-50	Theme 4	C major, "roving"
mm. 151-64	Theme 4	E♭ minor, "roving"
mm. 165-94	"Augustin"	D major, "roving"

Figure 2: The Form of Schoenberg's Scherzo.

A-Section (return)

mm. 195-203	Theme 1	F# minor, D minor
mm. 204-14	Theme 2	F major, "roving"
mm. 215-18	Theme 3 (augmented)	"roving"
mm. 219-37	Theme 3 (augmented)	D minor
mm. 238-49	Theme 1	D minor
mm. 250-58	Theme 1, Theme 3 (augmented)	D minor,
	"Augustin"	D major/minor

Coda

mm. 259-75	Theme 1	D major/minor

a) Statement

b) Variation in invertible counterpoint

Example 7. The Scherzo's main theme as a sentence-form.

c) Reduction

d) Liquidation/Cadence

Example 7. (cont.)

This cadence is the harbinger of a momentous event. Entering alone in stark octaves (mm. 14-15), the second theme appears at the tempo *etwas langsamer*—one slower than anything in the movement so far (see Example 8). Here, vertical harmonies, the mainstay of triadic tonality, are absent. Theme 2 has no chance to develop—Theme 3 follows "on its heels." Thus, in terms of phrase structure, the second theme also functions ambiguously—that is, neither as the statement of a sentence or the antecedent of a period. Theme 3 goes on to introduce the fastest motion at the softest dynamic thus far in the movement. Moving forward, its phrases could be analyzed as the antecedent of a period structure, its consequent curtailed by an abrupt fermata (mm. 17-18, first violin). Thus Themes 2 and 3 (mm. 14-19) share no characteristics of surface rhythm or intervallic contour but are virtually juxtaposed. Their one common feature is the stop on a sustained C (both mm. 15-16 and m. 19), quelling any expectation of a return to the tonic D minor. It is difficult to imagine a more disjointed, unbalanced exposition of themes.

Example 8. The juxtaposition of Themes 2 and 3.

In the Quartet, the strangely foreign juxtaposition created by the combination of Themes 2 and 3 "sets the stage" for the most memorable intrusion in the movement, the introduction of the folk song "Augustin." Schoenberg makes their role clear by creating surface parallelisms between two climactic points, one in Section A, the other in the Trio—both highlighting juxtapositions. The A-section builds to a climax through the development of Theme 2; then at the climax, repeated tetrachords take on a liquidating function and abruptly break off into silence (m. 62) (Example 9). There, Theme 3 reappears (m. 62), recreating a striking juxtaposition of register and character. Before Theme 3 can clearly define itself as the statement of a sentence or period, motives composed of fourths combine with it (m. 63), and together they liquidate to a cadence on the tritone D-A-flat.

The climax of the Trio is higher, longer, and more dramatic than that of the A-section. It features a high tremolo, D-G-sharp (mm. 160-64) stated fortissimo in the violins (Example 10). Ultimately, the violin line stops in midstream as if to herald the outset of a momentous event. But instead, the

Example 9. A second juxtaposition at measures 62-65.

three-note climactic violin figure sets up a 3/4 meter in the best manner of an operetta-waltz before the refrain. "Augustin" follows in harmonically ambiguous counterpoint with a varied form of its functional counterpart, Theme 3. This is surely the movement's most stunning surprise and its consummate juxtaposition of material and emotion.

Strong measures are clearly needed to pull the popular and pre-existent materials of "Augustin" back into the extended tonal sound world of the Scherzo. The process is very deliberate and developmental. It occurs over the course of twenty measures (mm. 171-94), in great contrast to the rapid counterpoint and

Example 10. Juxtaposition of the climax with "Augustin" and Theme 3.

quicksilver juxtapositions typical of the Scherzo as a whole. Schoenberg specifically varies and develops the features of "Augustin" into the second theme of the first movement (see Examples 11a-b)—the first thematic interconnection of materials from several movements of the Quartet. Thus through its intrusion at a climactic point and unique immediate development, Schoenberg has made "Augustin" the compositional centerpiece of the movement[25]

[25]Ernst Waeltner's essay also traces the crucial significance of the "Augustin" rhythm and its variation throughout the Scherzo. See Ernst Ludwig Waeltner, "'O du lieber Augustin' des Scherzo-Satzes im II. Streichquartett von Arnold Schönberg," in *Bericht über den 2. Kongreß der Internationalen Schönberg-Gesellschaft,* ed. Rudolf Stephan (Vienna: Elisabeth Lafite, 1974), 246-61.

Example 11. The transformation of "Augustin" into Theme 2a

a) Theme 2a, Movement One, mm. 43-46.

Example 11. b) The transformation.

I contend that the intrusion of the folk song "Augustin" is not only crucial to the Scherzo's "crossover" form but also essential to understanding the vocal-instrumental form of the Quartet as a whole. During the fall of 1907 when he began composing the Scherzo, Schoenberg was intensely concerned about his friend, benefactor, and mentor Gustav Mahler, whose departure from Vienna was imminent. It is tempting to connect the verbal message of "Augustin"—*alles ist hin*, all is undone—to Mahler's departure. But it is more crucial to note that on 24 November 1907, Mahler conducted his Symphony No. 2— intriguingly, his first work to juxtapose instrumental and vocal movements. Schoenberg wrote that hearing this performance "moved him to the utmost."[26] Perhaps the scoring of Mahler's symphony helped inspire the ultimate vocal-instrumental combination of the Quartet.

And indeed, the intrusion of the folk song "Augustin" holds a special place in the Quartet's vocal-instrumental layout. The assumption of all scholars has been that no Austro-German audience hears "Augustin" without its words. And perhaps the marked folk-song character of "Augustin" would suggest the possibility of a text to any audience, even if they would not know that particular text.[27] The instrumental-yet-verbal quality of "Augustin" subliminally bridges the gap from the instrumental first movement to the vocal third and fourth movements—paradoxically binding the work into a unity, despite its arrival as a stark inorganic juxtaposition. In this way, the very presence of "Augustin" epitomizes the brilliant wedding of classical and popular form in Schoenberg's compositional thought. Only a very popular song known by virtually every Austrian could assure that a text would always be associated with a tune, whether or not the words were sung. Thus "Augustin" creates a highly individualized compositional scenario. Schoenberg's Quartet, an extended tonal work of art, *needs* the text of a popular tune to exist as an organic whole. This is the consummate use of juxtaposition in a "crossover" technique—and for Schoenberg one that unfortunately remained unique to the Quartet.

He would not include a popular form in any of his own music for the next twenty-two years.

---

[26]Henri de La Grange, *Gustav Mahler: Vienna, The Years of Challenge, 1897-1904* (New York: Oxford University Press, 1995), 769.

[27]Compare the remarks of Albrecht Dümling in Konrad Boehmer, ed., *Schoenberg and Kandinsky: An Historic Encounter* (London: Harwood Academic Publishers, 1997), 113.

A Chronology of Intros, an Enthrallogy of Codas: The Case of Schoenberg's Chamber Symphony, Op. 9

Don McLean

In the twilight zone of fin-de-siècle tonality, composers faced new challenges in finding the right vocabulary and syntax with which to begin and end works. How does one convincingly construct the affirmation of tonality within a work when tonality itself is systemically disintegrating around it? How does one compellingly assemble the thematic components of a work in the changed form-functional environment of extended tonal or atonal pitch relations? Through a "chronology of intros" I briefly review a variety of exemplary opening gambits in selected symphonic works by Bruckner, Strauss, Mahler, Debussy, Schoenberg, and Berg. Similarly, the challenge of balancing strategies for peroration or dissipation in closure leads through a parallel consideration of what has been aptly termed an "enthrallogy of codas." In the case of Schoenberg's Chamber Symphony, a chamber work in richly symphonic guise, the renowned introductory quartal gesture and subsequent thematic materials set up their own chronology of form-functional expectation. And the closing sections of the first movement exposition and the work as a whole create their own enthrallogy of ecstasy-inducing codas.

Enthrallogy, Chronology, Bangs and Whimpers

Beginning with the end in mind, let us first examine the "Enthrallogy of Codas" shown in Figure 1. This list, as well as the neologism itself, was first introduced to me by Robert Falck in a seminar on Impressionism and Expressionism at the University of Toronto in the late 1970s. Falck's selections

Don McLean is Dean of the Schulich School of Music of McGill University and Chair of the Board of the Centre for Interdisciplinary Research in Music Media and Technology (CIRMMT). A music theorist specializing in Schenkerian theory and analysis and the music of Alban Berg, his recent research publications and projects include: studies of Wolf and Berg songs, structural framing in nineteenth-century music (with Brian Alegant), Schoenberg's *Formenlehre* applied to the music of Second Viennese School, Bruckner and Heavy Metal, and Musical Frisson (with Sandy Pearlman), and a survey of Canadian University Music Schools (with Dean Jobin-Bevans). Dr. McLean also works with various university institutions and international organizations as a consultant, speaker, and conference organizer on future directions in music, the music industry, new media, higher education, and cultural policy.

might easily be augmented of course, and many of us will have our own favorites both on and off his list. But his "enthrallogy" provides an idiosyncratic yet intriguing anthology of Austro-German and French repertoire (with one Puccini example for operatic good measure). Each work or movement on the list— whether orchestral, chamber, or solo keyboard—possesses a particularly beautiful, awesome, enthralling, transfiguring, splendid close.[1]

1. Brahms, String Quintet, Op. 88 (1882), II
2. Franck, Symphony in D-minor (1888), I
3. Bruckner, Symphony No. 3 (1873), III
4. D'Indy, *Istar* Variations (1896), end
5. Bruckner, Symphony No. 4 (1874), I
6. Chausson, Symphony in B-flat major (1890), I
7. Reger, String Trio, Op. 77b (1904), II
8. Puccini, *Manon Lescaut*, Intermezzo to Act III (1893)
9. Mahler, Symphony No. 5 (1902), I
10. Debussy, String Quartet (1893), II
11. Schoenberg, *Verklärte Nacht* (1899), end
12. Debussy, *La Mer* (1905), end
13. Schoenberg, String Quartet, Op. 10 (1908), IV
14. Ravel, *Daphnis et Chloé* (1912), end
15. Berg, String Quartet, Op. 3 (1910), end
16. Debussy, *Brouillards, Preludes*, Book II (1913), last page
17. Webern, *Orchesterstücke*, Op. 6 (1909), I, complete

Figure 1. Robert Falck's "Enthrallogy of Codas."[2]

I will not elaborate further on Falck's list in this paper. Rather, with apologies to T. S. Eliot, I will ask: "Which is the way tonality ends? With a bang or with a whimper?" That is, a work or movement may invoke a tonal closure that is compelling, affirming, ecstatic, and anti-entropic. Alternatively, it may seek an end that is dissipating, resigned, cathartic, that winds-up only to wind-down. The same options obtain in the introductions of works: they may "start with a bang," or find their way forth gradually. Fully aware of the risk that such whimsical ideation on my part may run, the reader is nonetheless directed to Figure 2.

[1]The reader will note that Schoenberg's Chamber Symphony is not on Falck's shortlist, though I know it to be one of his personal favorites. *Transfigured Night, Pelleas and Melisande*, the First and Second String Quartets, and the Chamber Symphony were always central Schoenbergian members of Falck's wider enthrallogy canon.

[2]Some additional comments on Figure 1. The listener's experience of the coda of the third movement of Bruckner's Third Symphony is dependent on which of at least three versions (1873, 1876, 1889/90) is played: the most straightforward yet splendid coda is found in the 1889 version, where the final measures of the Scherzo near-reiterate in ecstatic hypermetric extension. The Ottawa conference took as its title the vocal conclusion of Schoenberg's Second String Quartet ("I feel the air of another planet"), a choice that provided as near a conceptual rendering, and rending, of the experiential threshold between tonality and atonality as (cont.)

	Beginning Intro	Middle Climax	End Coda
1.	Bang	Bang	Bang
2.	Bang	Bang	Whimper
3.	Bang	Whimper	Bang
4.	Bang	Whimper	Whimper
5.	Whimper	Bang	Bang
6.	Whimper	Bang	Whimper
7.	Whimper	Whimper	Bang
8.	Whimper	Whimper	Whimper

Figure 2. Bangs and Whimpers.

Given the opportunity for a work to "start with a bang" and/or "end with a bang," and possibly to direct itself to one or more significant climactic bang(s) in between; alternatively, for a work to start or end with a tentative "whimper," some form of dissolution of tonal and thematic elements, with an alternative determinant in between—Figure 2 produces the available beginning-middle-end triplets. Of course the reality of the middle is routinely more complex than this, particularly in longer works with several climaxes and moments of quietude in play.[3] Variants 1—bang, bang, bang—and 2—bang, bang, whimper, as well as 5—whimper, bang, bang—and 6—whimper, bang, whimper—are intuitively more typical, since "mid-whimper" options are generally bleak, in violation of what Roger Sessions called the "principle of cumulation."[4] Variants 3—bang, whimper, bang—and 4—bang, whimper, whimper—are centrally or fully "entropic" (dissipative) respectively; they and the "anti-entropic" (or

---

anyone might conceive. Falck's Franck, Ravel, and Debussy orchestral examples, and, from across the atonal boundary, the Berg Op. 3 String Quartet, all illustrate the ecstatic mode of coda enthrall. (Stravinsky's *Firebird* and *Rite* extend this practice.) Webern's first piece from Op. 6 is found on Falck's "coda" list in its aphoristic entirety: the argument is that the piece is framed by static post-cadential gestures in invertible contrapuntal relation with intermediate preparations for same; its position as the first of the set of pieces is therefore ironically un-introductory.

[3]Some additional comments on Figure 2. It is important to note that loudness or quietness alone do not a bang or whimper make. The challenge of creating strong endings in an extended tonal context requires more form- and harmonic-functional ordering than can be clinched by volume alone. Similarly, the constructive, or rather deconstructive, art of the dissipating whimper requires refined handling of thematic and functional components than go well beyond mere diminuendo.

[4]Roger Sessions, *The Musical Experience of Composer, Performer, and Listener* (New York: Atheneum, 1965), 60. Sessions references three principles: progression or cumulation, association, and contrast.

ultimately cumulative) 7—whimper, whimper, bang—are rather too "postmodern" for fin-de-siècle aesthetics, and 8—whimper, whimper, whimper—is too artistically suicidal for any but Webern's shorter aphorisms. Focusing on beginnings and endings, intros and codas, in fin-de-siècle works, where do such schemata occur?

As any historian knows, chronology makes for strange bedfellows. Without the hindsight of interpretive ordering, what are we to make of the juxtapositions in Figure 3? For example, that Schoenberg's Second String Quartet, Op. 10, cohabits the atonality-establishing pivotal year 1908 not only with Mahler's tonally unraveling *Song of the Earth*, and Berg's very extended-tonal Piano Sonata, Op. 1, but also with Scriabin's mystical extended-tonal Fourth Symphony and Elgar's ambitious but still quite tonally-grounded First? That Mahler's visionary Ninth Symphony of 1909 (first performed posthumously in 1912) is written three years *after* Schoenberg's Chamber Symphony (which Mahler declared himself unable to comprehend), but in the same year as Schoenberg's Op. 11 atonal Piano Pieces and Webern's massively aphoristic Op. 6 Orchestra Pieces, as well as Rachmaninoff's hyper-romantic Third Piano Concerto, and Strauss's hyper-expressionist opera *Elektra*? The columns in Figure 3 show the "inner circles" of influence in and on the New Viennese School through the Bruckner, Strauss, Mahler pedigree, with others in the Franco-Russian and other schools considered "outer circles"; the "opera" column provides a stylistically variable counterpoint from that genre. I now move to a consideration of some of the salient features of introductions (openings) and codas—in either "bang" or "whimper" state. Items in boldface on Figure 3 are woven into the discussion as selective illustrations.

Introductions may find their way into being by starting from a state of *Ungrund* or formlessness (e.g., Bruckner's Ninth Symphony, Berg's Op. 6 *Präludium*), moving *ex nihilo* from *prima materia* to thematic materialization by tentative stages.[5] Themes may thus not present themselves fully formed but emerge through an assemblage of fragments—recall the Schoenberg School's description of Mahler "shuffling his themes like a pack of cards" (e.g., Mahler's Adagietto from the Fifth Symphony, the opening of the Ninth).[6] Alternatively, the appearance of

---

[5]*Ungrund* or unformedness should not be confused with *Urgrund* or fundamental form. To posit a Schenkerian parallel, we speak not of *Ursatz* but of "*Unsatz*." Bruckner's aesthetic position was grounded in a coupling of his understanding of the mystical philosophical tradition of Jakob Böhme and the nineteenth-century scientific obsession with thermodynamics and entropy. The classical reference for *Ungrund* is the opening of Haydn's *Creation*; the nineteenth-century reference is the opening of Beethoven's Ninth, which Bruckner variously revisited in many of his works, notably the Third and Ninth Symphonies, both also in D minor.

[6]Mahler's pack of cards: the attribution is sometimes made to Schoenberg, but documented usage is by Erwin Stein in his introduction to the Universal Edition study score of Mahler's Fourth Symphony.

Year	Inner Circles	Outer Circles	Opera
1885	Bruckner *Te Deum*	Brahms S4	*Zigneuerbaron,*
1886		d'Indy S...*montagnard*	*Mikado*
1887	**Bruckner S9**		*Otello*
1888	J. Strauss II, *Kaiser-Walzer*	Tchaikovsky S5, Franck, Dvorak S8	
1889	Mahler S1, **Strauss *Don Juan***		
1890	Strauss *Tod und Verklärung*	Chausson Symphony	*Pique Dame*
1891	J. Strauss II, *Gross-Wien*		
1892	**Bruckner S8**		*Pagliacci*
1893		Tchaikovsky S6	*Hansel, Manon,*
1894	Mahler S2	Dvorak S9, **Debussy *Faune***	*Jenufa Falstaff*
1895	Mahler S3 (02)[FN], Strauss *Till*		
1896	**Strauss *Zarathustra***	d'Indy *Istar*	*Bohème*
1897	Strauss *Don Quixote*	Sousa *Stars & Stripes*	
1898	Strauss *Heldenleben*		
1899	**Schoenberg Op. 4** (02)	Sibelius *Finlandia*	
1900	Mahler S4 (01)	Elgar *Gerontius*	*Tosca, Louise*
1901	Schoenberg *Gurrelieder* (13)	Debussy *Nocturnes*, Fauré *Pelléas*	
1902	**Mahler S5** (04)	Sibelius S2, Ives S2	
1903	Schoenberg *Pelleas* Op.5 (05)		
1904	Mahler S6 (06), Strauss *Domestica*	Ravel SQ, Sibelius VnC, Ives S3	
1905	**Schoenberg Op. 7** (07), Mahler S7 (08)	**Debussy *La Mer***	*Salome*
1906	**Sch. Chamber Symphony Op. 9** (07)		
1907	Mahler S8 (10)	Stravinsky S1, Sibelius S3	
1908	Sch. Op. 10, Mahler *Lied*, **Berg Op. 1**	Scriabin S4, Elgar S1	
1909	**Mahler S9** (12), Web. Op. 6, Sch. Op. 11	Rachmaninoff PC3	*Elektra*
1910	Berg SQ Op. 3, Sch. Op. 15	Stravinsky *Firebird*, Debussy *Iberia*	*Fanciulla*
1911		Scriabin S5, Sibelius S4, Elgar S2	*Rosenkavalier*
1912	Schoenberg Op. 16, *Pierrot*	Stravinsky *Petrushka*, Ravel *Daphnis*	
1913		Stravinsky *Rite*, RVW *London S*	
1914	**Berg Op. 6**		

Figure 3. Selective chronology of works with interesting Intro-Coda considerations.[7]

the principal thematic elements may be delayed in deference to tentative dramatic or scenic gestures (e.g., Debussy's *La Mer,* Schoenberg's *Transfigured Night*), or thematic materials may be evident but ambiguously supported (e.g., Debussy's *Faune,* Mahler's Ninth—really underway only after the big cadence in m. 46). The tonic scale-step or some alternative "referential sonority"—superficially omnipresent (e.g., Wagner's *Tristan* chord) or posited as a tonic-substituting structural referent (e.g., Schoenberg's *Farben,* Berg's Op. 6 fourth-chord)—may be deliberately constructed or ushered in through incomplete cadential progression (e.g., Berg's Piano Sonata, Schoenberg's Chamber Symphony, modern variants of the off-tonic opening). Referential (including tonic-triadic)

---

[7]Figure 3. Parenthetic numbers (02) indicate the year of first performance (1902) for some pieces where the gap from date of composition is significant. Short titles are often given, but the works should be easily identifiable; also S abbreviates Symphony, PC Piano Concerto, VnC Violin Concerto.

sonorities may display deliberate spatialization or space-staking span, often with awe-inspiring effect (e.g., Bruckner's Ninth, Strauss's *Zarathustra,* Schoenberg's Chamber Symphony, Berg's Op. 6 *Präludium*). The true opening "bang" can stride forth with energetic pell-mell (e.g., Strauss's *Don Juan,* the Finale of Bruckner's Eighth Symphony, Schoenberg's First String Quartet), a drive challenging for any composer to sustain without careful plan to step back at some point to construct a process that will eventually regain or surpass such initial momentum.

In the case of codas, pitch (or pitch-class) centricity of course remains the key element of tonal closure. However, intentional failure to close, or positing ellipsis in closure, becomes a fin-de-siècle expressive ploy of the whimper type (e.g., the abandoned "unresolved" pizzicati bass C♮ in the context of sustained B major in Strauss's *Zarathustra,* the registral lifts supplying $\hat{1}$ in the "wrong" register to close the hyperventilate oboe $\hat{3}$-$\hat{2}$ motion at the end of the first movement of Mahler's Ninth, the registral effervescence in the final $\hat{1}$-$\hat{6}$-$\hat{1}$ embellishing motion in Debussy's *Faune*). Cadential motions that gain the tonic scale-step forcibly, and "post-cadential" motions that affirm it, remain typically triumphant signifiers of big bang conclusions (e.g., Strauss's *Don Juan* with its return of the main theme at the cadential point, Bruckner's Ninth Symphony post-cadential Neapolitan decoration over tonic pedal point). The combinational stacking of thematic elements into a single contrapuntal complex is an entropy-defying variant (e.g., Finale of Bruckner's Eighth, Debussy's *La Mer* "chorale tune," Schoenberg's Chamber Symphony). Such conclusions are often associated with hypermetric manipulations where motivic materials recur in iterative and successive compressions until they converge on the closing point (e.g., Bruckner's Ninth, Schoenberg's Chamber Symphony).[8]

Post-cadential gestures associated with codettas and (ends of) codas are normally reiterative and redundant, eschewing new thematic development, which would be form-functionally misleading for the listener, for short-breathed recessive iteration, often in "counts" of three (or four)—statement, restatement, final statement (with possible fourth stopping iteration, a final sounded or silent ictus).[9] Alternatively, thematic dissipation can liquidate and devolve into a motivic "remnant" (e.g., Debussy's *Faune,* Mahler's Adagietto from the Fifth Symphony,

---

[8]The precision of Bruckner's hypermetric compressions in cadential (or, more accurately, post-cadential) circumstances is seldom acknowledged in the literature, despite considerable interest shown in his sketch-evident measure-counting obsessions. The technique typically consists of the progressive clipping of the length of a principal motive: 4, 2, 1, one-half measures, with a final truncated concluding statement. The end of the first and final movements of the Third Symphony may be considered referential. This technique shares sizing features with "fragmentation" (the breaking of the idea into smaller units), a typical "continuational" phenomenon, but does not usually have the associated acceleration of harmonic rhythm (since there is often no harmonic motion) or "liquidation" of motive (since the characteristic features of the motive do not evaporate into cadential formula, but rather become fractal, and crystallize in the final gesture).

Berg's Piano Sonata and Op. 6 *Präludium*, Schoenberg's *Transfigured Night* and the end of the Adagio movement/section in the Chamber Symphony).[10] The undermining of a cadential nexus through harmonic substitution, or rhythmic "scumbling" becomes a typical way of turning a potential bang into a whimper (e.g., the post-cadential-signaling D-natural in the harp near the end of *Faune*, the un-cadential composed-out rather than dropping bass motion near the end of the Adagietto of Mahler's Fifth).[11]

Finally, two important and widespread (though seldom cited) formal-motivic associations of ending functions need to be acknowledged: "structural framing"—the reference at the end of a formal unit to materials associated with its beginning; and "closing parallelism"—the reference at the end of a formal unit to materials associated with the end of a similar previous passage.[12] Examples of structural framing from my selections in Figure 3 include the thematic fragments that open up at the beginning and return to close down the end of the first movement of Mahler's Ninth, the attenuated major-mode return of the main theme near the end of Schoenberg's First Quartet, and the dissipating head-motive tags in the coda of Berg's Piano Sonata.

Closing parallelisms are most easily appreciated in "binary" baroque suites, where the non-tonic concluding materials of the first section recur as the tonic concluding passage of the whole. The impression on the listener is that materials that earlier signified ending function return to "end again." The concept carries forward historically in sonata form to become the return in the recapitulation in

---

[9]My use of terms such as "presentation," "continuation," "cadential," "expanded cadential progression (ECP)," and "post-cadential" is based on William Caplin's far-reaching development of Schoenberg's writings on *Formenlehre*; see William E. Caplin, *Classical Form: A Theory of Formal Function for the Instrumental Music of Haydn, Mozart, and Beethoven* (Oxford: Oxford University Press, 1998). Schoenberg's writings on form post-date the Chamber Symphony. His most explicit account is found in *Models for Beginners in Composition*, rev. ed. Leonard Stein (Los Angeles: Belmont Music, 1972; New York: Schirmer, 1943), expanded in the posthumously published *Fundamentals of Musical Composition*, ed. Gerald Strang and Leonard Stein (London: Faber, 1970), as well as *Structural Functions of Harmony*, rev. ed. Leonard Stein (New York: W. W. Norton, 1969; London: Williams and Norgate, 1954). That formal theory was a part of Schoenberg's teaching and theoretical thought from earlier periods is evidenced by the publication of his draft notebook *Coherence, Counterpoint, Instrumentation, Instruction in Form* [*Zusammenhang, Kontrapunkt, Instrumentation, Formenlehre*], ed. Severine Neff, trans. Charlotte M. Cross and Severine Neff (Lincoln: University of Nebraska Press, 1994), sometimes abbreviated ZKIF.

[10]"Remnant" refers to what Adorno called "*ein Rest*" in describing Berg's predilection for such meticulous liquidation processes. Theodor W. Adorno, *Alban Berg: Master of the Smallest Link* (Cambridge: Cambridge University Press, 1991), 3.

[11]"Scumbling" is a visual art technique whereby the linear elements of a charcoal drawing are rubbed to blur their contour. The opportunity to develop an "anatomy of musical scumbling" is suggested in Donald R. McLean, "A Documentary and Analytical Study of Alban Berg's Three Pieces for Orchestra" (Ph.D. diss., University of Toronto, 1997), 164, 210n7, and 524.

[12]On "structural framing" and "closing parallels" see Brian Alegant and Don McLean, "On the Nature of Structural Framing," *Nineteenth-Century Music Review* 4/1 (2007): 3-29.

the tonic key of the codetta materials that ended the off-tonic exposition, as well of course as the preceding subordinate theme materials—which are less a recapitulation ("starting over") than they are a "coming home." A fascinatingly skewed example from the list is the recurrence at the end of the piece of the exquisite subordinate-theme-like transfiguration music in *Transfigured Night*: in its first occurrence, Schoenberg's theme gives the impression of potential coda function, though in F-sharp major with string harmonics and high violin tune, yet it soon becomes sequentially continuational; the theme returns in "corrected" form as a true closing parallelism in the D-major home key of the coda. Both structural framing and closing parallelism are formal procedures that characterize Schoenberg's Chamber Symphony, to which I now turn.

In the examples that follow, I first establish the principal components of Schoenberg's "intro" and "main theme" sections. Next I separate out the "intro" elements to explore their redistribution and transformation as the piece unfolds— its "chronology of intros." I then explore the conclusive character of the codetta of "Part I of the Symphony" (First Movement/Exposition), as well as the nature of its changed recurrence in the "Recapitulation (quasi Finale)." Finally, I explain how these codetta-cum-coda materials are combined with ideas from the main theme and intro to create the work's series of supercharged concluding sections—its "enthrallogy of codas."

The Case of Schoenberg's Chamber Symphony— A "Chronology of Intros"

Berg's thematic analysis of Schoenberg's Chamber Symphony remains the best introductory synoptic guide to the work (now available in parallel German-English translation by Mark DeVoto), though it needs to be supplemented by the more detailed documentary and analytical studies by Walter Frisch and Catherine Dale.[13] Since I will employ Berg's enumerated thematic identifiers throughout the discussion, readers—particularly those less familiar with the work—will find it useful to have Berg's *Thementafel* at hand. For convenience, Example 1 reproduces themes 1-7 of Berg's Table: materials for the Main Theme (*Hauptsatz*) section of the "First Part" of the Symphony. My analysis will reveal that the chronology of intros is formed from the distributed recurrence of Berg's introductory thematic items 1, 2, and 3, as well as the displaced or false returns of main theme 4, and the relocation of cadential idea 7.

---

[13] *Arnold Schönberg Kammersymphonie Op. 9. Thematische Analyse von Alban Berg* (Leipzig-Wien: Universal-Edition, 1921). Edition and Complete English translation by Mark DeVoto in *Journal of the Arnold Schoenberg Institute* 16/1-2 (1993): 236-68. Walter Frisch, *The Early Works of Arnold Schoenberg 1893-1908* (Berkeley: University of California Press, 1993), 220-47. Catherine Dale, *Schoenberg's Chamber Symphonies: The Crystallization and Rediscovery of a Style* (Aldershot: Ashgate, 2000), 20-108.

Example 1. Berg's thematic table, main section, themes 1-7.

Example 2 shows the beginning of the work in more complete texture: in order to balance the need for greater detail with ease of reading, Schoenberg's reduction of the score for piano four-hands is used.[14] Three important ideas precede the main theme in the bipartite "intro" (*Langsam*, mm. 1-4; and *Sehr rasch*, mm. 5-9):

---

[14] *Arnold Schoenberg, Chamber Symphony, Op. 9,* arranged for piano four-hands (Los Angeles: Belmont Publications, 1975). Used with permission. Also available in *Arnold Schönberg: Sämtliche Werke, Complete Edition,* Series A, Vol. 5 (Mainz: Schott Musik International und Wien: Universal Edition, 1973). Full score: *Arnold Schönberg: Sämtliche Werke, Complete Edition,* Series A, Vol. 11 (1976). The full instrumentation of the Chamber Symphony is for fifteen solo instruments: (cont.)

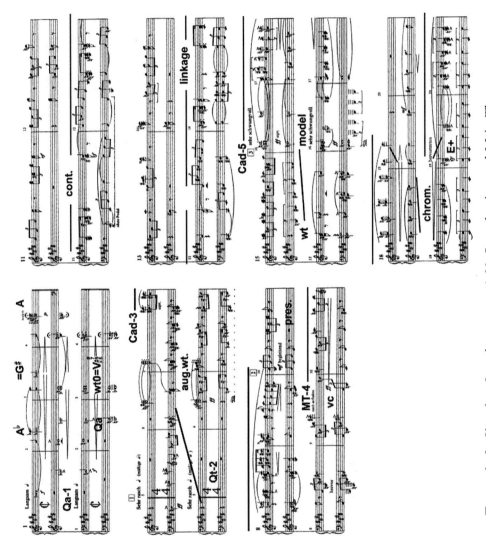

Example 2. Chamber Symphony, mm. 1-20, Introduction and Main Theme.

1. "Qa-1" is the *Einleitender Quarten-akkord*, Berg's thematic idea number 1 (a fourth-chord, here G-F-C-B♭-E♭-A♭, fully stated by m. 2) and its associated harmonic progression (mm. 2-4)

2. "Qt-2" is the *Quarten-thema*, thematic idea number 2 (here, D-G-C-F-B♭-E♭/D♯, mm. 5-6, a modern "bang-up" variant of the classical "rocket" theme)

3. "Cad-3" is the *kadenzierende Thema*, thematic idea number 3, a screaming cadential marker that begins on the leading-tone (D♯) and twice lands on flat $\hat{6}$-(C), before cascading to fifth-degree (B), an octave lower, at the beginning of the Main Theme proper (*Hauptthema*, "MT-4," m. 10, in the cello [vc]).

Other important elements of the introduction are the melodic progression from A-flat/G-sharp to A in measure 4 and its associated harmonic progression from Qa-1 through a six-note whole-tone chord (m. 3), effectively a "dominant-ninth chord with raised and lowered fifth" (C-E-G♭-G♯-B♭-D), to a fermata F major chord (m. 4), itself eventually understood as the Neapolitan of home-key E major. Qt-2 and Cad-3 are accompanied by arpeggiated augmented triads descending by whole-tones ("aug. wt.": wt 0), and MT-4 is anticipated by two statements of its triplet head motive (A2-D2-D3-G♯3).[15]

The main theme itself, MT-4, is a pell-mell figure of the *Don Juan* thematic type. From a form-functional perspective, the "presentation" of the basic idea

---

flute (also piccolo), oboe, English horn, clarinet in D (also E-flat), clarinet in A (also B-flat), bass clarinet in A (also B-flat), bassoon, contrabassoon, 2 horns in F, 2 violins, viola, cello, and double bass. My use of Schoenberg's piano score results in the unfortunate impression of undervaluing the work's extraordinary timbral character. However, in view of the necessity to limit the focus and scope of my analysis, and not to further overburden the examples and commentary with descriptions of instrumentation, I have set aside most timbral considerations in the present study.

[15]The abbreviation "wt 0" refers to the one of two available whole-tone hexachordal collections that includes pitch-class 0 (or C), the other being "wt 1." Pitch-classes are identified as all enharmonic equivalents of C=0, C♯/D♭=1, D=2 etc., with B♭ and B♮ represented by modulo 12 letters A and B. Where required, register identification uses C4 for middle C, the octave above being C5, below C3, etc. with C as the register change point. What I have described functionally as a "dominant ninth chord with raised and lowered fifth" or "whole-tone dominant" can also be considered a "doubly augmented sixth" after Daniel Harrison, "Supplement to the Theory of Augmented-Sixth Chords," *Music Theory Spectrum* 17/2 (Autumn 1995): 186, 188. The generative relation between the voice leading of the opening chords and the omnibus progression is discussed by Peter Schubert, "'A New Epoch of Polyphonic Style': Schoenberg on Chords and Lines," *Music Analysis* 12/3 (October 1993): 299, 302. An effort to catalogue the chordal and scalar vocabulary of the opening using procedures from Anthony Pople's *Tonalities* Project is found in Michael Russ, "'Fishing in the Right Place': Analytical Examples from the Tonalities Project," *Music Analysis* 23/2-3 (July 2004): 210-13.

Example 3. Chamber Symphony, mm. 50-58, "cadential stride" to "counter-exposition feint"/transition.

(mm. 10-11, "pres.") is not immediately repeated, but is rather subjected to a more "loose-knit," syncopated and sequential "continuation" (m. 11) though still recognizable from its dotted-figure end-tag. The end-tag, kicked forward via "linkage technique," then leads through a whole-tone wedge to an E-major tonic "cadence" (m. 16), somewhat "scumbled" by the appoggiatura character of "Cad-5," an idea that initially appears cadential (or even post-cadential) given the strong E pedal point. Cad-5, which subsequently arrives at an F-minor cadence (m. 32, not shown) via imitative entries and model-sequence technique (moving from E to G), becomes the locus of the famous "second main theme." (The theme is "famous" because Schoenberg discussed its intuitive motivic derivation from MT-4 on several occasions.) I will call it "Middle-theme 6," or "Mid-6" (see Berg's item 6 in Example 1).[16]

The main-theme section announces impending closure with a whole-tone-based "cadential stride" figure ("Cad-stride-7," Berg's item 7; see Example 3). The progression is a variant on the classical "expanded cadential progression" ("ECP," mm. 50-52, bass rising whole-tone motions from A♭, B♭, and C) that soon reaches "dominant arrival" (m. 53); the scale-step is marked harmonically by the extended dominant minor ninth (V♭9/7), but also motivically by a "structural framing" reference to MT-4 in fragmentary form (MT-4 frag). The Cad-3 marker (mm. 56-57) then ushers in a return of MT-4 proper, as if to begin a "counter-exposition."[17] This proves a feint, however, as elements of MT-4 (m. 58) and Cad-5 (m. 62) are chained together one more time (not shown), whereupon a brief harmonic recollection of Cad-7 (m. 66)—see Example 4—leads to a perfect

[16]F-minor theme references: see in particular *Style and Idea: Selected Writings of Arnold Schoenberg*, ed. Leonard Stein, trans. Leo Black (London: Faber & Faber, 1975): "Heart and Brain in Music (1946)," 58-63; and "Composition with Twelve Tones (1) (1941)," 222-23. Schoenberg's analysis of the relation between the themes is often considered "far-fetched" (Frisch, *Schoenberg's Early Works* [1993], 243), but a persuasively supportive argument is made by Mark Doran, "The 'True Relationship': Schoenberg's Analysis of 'Unity' in the Op. 9 *Kammersymphonie*," Tempo 219 (January 2002): 13-21.

My use of the term "middle theme" (Mid-6) for the F minor tune stems from a desire to recognize its initial character as non-tonic contrasting material to MT-4. We might expect a Main Theme section with small ternary design with MT-4 returning after Mid-6 finds the dominant, but the reality is more complex. Instead, Mid-6 yields to the "Cadential Stride" Cad-7 a quasi-ECP (expanded cadential progression) that produces the "return" of MT-4 only over dominant arrival and counter-expositional feint, then closes out with a cadential idea (m. 66) that effectively takes up where the initial point of the ECP began (compare m. 50 and m. 66) this time finally bringing the Main Theme section to a close with a tonic cadence into the start of the Transition (m. 68).

[17]Frisch (*Schoenberg's Early Works* [1993], 222) argues that the return of MT-4 at m. 58 actually begins a real "double exposition"; he contends (227-29) there is a "double recapitulation" as well (m. 435 and m. 497, which Berg calls the Coda), and a double Coda (m. 555 and m. 576, the latter Berg's "End-Coda"). I am arguing for a more conventional but expansive form in the First Movement, with the return at m. 58 acting as a structural-framing "counter-expositional feint," the Main Theme section not actually over until the cadence at the beginning of the Transition (m. 68). The form-functional complexities of Recapitulation (quasi Finale) and Coda are addressed later on.

Example 4. Chamber Symphony, mm. 65-69, cadence of Main Theme into Transition section.

authentic cadence (PAC) in the home key (m. 68), at which point the Transition section begins (mm. 68-83; Berg's theme 8). It is remarkable that, despite the advanced chromatic vocabulary, all materials to this point have been well grounded in the home key of E major, with the exception of the F-minor theme (Mid-6) and the introductory motion to F major (Qa-1).[18]

---

[18]Both Frisch (*Schoenberg's Early Works* [1993], 222-23 and 244-46) and Dale (*Schoenberg's Chamber Symphonies* [2000], 20, 35-36, and 49) comment on the F-E conflict and its Neapolitan pedigree. Another remarkable instance of F minor/E major conflict is the first movement of Tchaikovsky's Fourth Symphony, which Schoenberg certainly knew.

Themes of the Transition (8-10)

Subordinate Theme

Themes of the Closing Section / Codetta (12-14)

Example 5. Berg's thematic table, main section, themes 8-14.

For the reader's convenience items 8-14 from Berg's Thematic Table are reproduced in Example 5. The remainder of the First Movement section of the Chamber Symphony includes three Transition ideas (Berg 8, 9, and 10), the exquisite Subordinate Theme (ST-11, in A major), and three closing/codetta ideas (12 [derived from 11], 13, and 14). Later, I will examine in more detail the role these codetta ideas play in establishing closure of the First Movement, as well as their reworked recurrence in the Finale/Recapitulation and Coda. But first, I return to the opening materials (Qa-1, Qt-2, and Cad-3) to explore their distribution across the work as a "chronology of intros." Figure 4 provides a summary.

From Figure 4 it can be seen that the three introductory ideas—together the Qa-1, Qt-2, and Cad-3 complex—which I call original instance 0, develop a chronology of reappearance that distributes them as a "compositional matrix" across the work. Following the original occurrence, I identify seven further instances for consideration.

Cad-3 can be independently split off from the Qa-Qt complex and recurs first at measure 58 and, similarly, at measure 133—the two together deemed instance 1. In both cases, Cad-3 ushers in the main theme (MT-4), as it did in the opening, but both MT-4 statements initiate "counter-expositional" feints. In the first instance, MT-4 returns (m. 58) as if to begin a counter-exposition (as noted above) but reveals itself instead to be a structural framing cadential statement that helps close out the Main Theme section (m. 68). In the second instance, Cad-3 (mm. 134-35) appears at the end of the First Movement section (mm. 130-32) and sets up a statement of MT-4 (m. 133) that might, in a conventional single-movement form, indicate the beginning of the development section, in the familiar manner where an apparent composed-out exposition-repeat deviates to reveal itself retrospectively as the opening of the development. In the present case, however, the passage instead soon elaborates a two-part transition (m. 142 and m. 148) that sets up the Scherzo movement (m. 160). When Cad-3 occurs again (second instance, m. 281) it is in transposed form—in F minor and in association with the header of Mid-6 (also normally in that Neapolitan minor key)—and follows on more loosely than it normally does from the Qt marker (m. 279, here descending) at the end of Scherzo II. In this instance, Cad-3 establishes the introduction ("pre-core") of a long tripartite Development Section (m. 284 based mostly on ST-11, m. 312 based on Trans-8, m. 334 based on MT-4 as well as Trans-8 and culminating in the climax based on Qt-2, mm. 354-67).

Cad-3 has two further appearances (end of instances 6 and 7), both in augmentation. The first bridges the return of MT-4 (m. 476) in the second part of the Recapitulation (Finale). The second is a stunning structural framing gesture at the very end of the work (mm. 589-93). Overall, it is evident that Cad-3 always has the "annunciating marker role," normally preparing the entrance (or return) of the main theme, MT-4. It is notable, however, that subsequent to its

Formal location:

Intro	Expo...	Scherzo I...II	Dev	Adagio... climax 'moonrise' end	Finale/Recap. Episode MT	Coda

Measures:

1	5	7	10	58	133	193-7	200	279	354-64	368-377	378-407	410	435	473-480	574	577	589-93	Instance #
Qa	Qt	Cad																0
	Cad	Cad																1
			Qt	Qt	Cad(F-)													2
					Qt-Qa													3
						Qt-Qa	Qa											4
								Qt-Qa										5
														Qt(Qa)Cad(aug)				6
															Qt(Qa) Cad(aug)			7

Figure 4. "Chronology of Intros": distributed compositional matrix of opening ideas.

original introductory role, Cad-3 is always associated with altered, even formally "misleading," versions of MT-4: two false "counter-expositions" (m. 58 and m. 136), a transposed F-minor variant (m. 281) that associates with Mid-6 (and eventually ST-11) rather with than MT-4, one breached recapitulation (via augmentation), and a final framing statement that ends post-cadentially rather than introducing anything at all. Though Cad-3 is inherently cadential, the trajectory I have just outlined reveals its chronological narrative of "functional drift"—from introductory to transitional to post-cadential roles.

Schoenberg himself recognized the distributional nature of the handling of the opening quartal sonorities in his Chamber Symphony. In *Harmonielehre*, he examines *Quarten-Akkorde*, initially in theoretical terms as a "filling out of the tertian system," noting their first appearance in the literature "largely as superimposed fourths" as "an impressionistic means of expression," but eventually goes on to consider voice-leading details of quartal progressions in four, five, and six parts and their generative potential to "lead to a chord that contains all the twelve tones of the chromatic scale." In citing the fourth chords of his Chamber Symphony, Schoenberg recognizes the "bang" (versus impressionistic "whimper") character of the opening horn theme and its architectonically distributed role in the compositional matrix:

> Here the fourths, springing from an entirely different expressive urge (stormy jubilation), shape themselves into a definite horn theme [Schoenberg's musical example provides the opening horn rocket theme, mm. 5-6], spread themselves out architectonically over the whole piece, and place their stamp on everything that happens. Thus it turns out that they do not appear here merely as melody or as purely impressionistic chord effect; their character permeates the total harmonic structure, and they are chords like all others.[19]

Quartal sonorities, by Schoenberg's own reckoning, "can be substitutes for a dominant," and ideas Qa and Qt are distributed in several locations across the Chamber Symphony with this harmonic-formal function, albeit with some built-in tonal ambiguities. Descending variants of Qt-2 appear twice associated with enharmonic ambiguities around E/F-flat (m. 193 and m. 274): the first instance, a quasi-V arrival (m. 196, marked with Qt ascending in an E-F span)

---

[19]Arnold Schoenberg, *Theory of Harmony*, trans. Roy E. Carter (Berkeley: University of California Press, 1978) 403-04; based on *Harmonielehre*, 3rd ed. (Vienna: Universal Edition, 1922). The location of other references: "filling out the tertian system" (399), "impressionistic" usage (399 and 402), dominant substitution (405), voice leading to and from whole-tone chords (406), all twelve tones (407). Schoenberg also observes: "The six-note quartal chord contains [i.e., spans] a minor ninth (from the bass note), and is thus the first "rather sharp" dissonance among the fourth chords [i.e., in the interval cycle segment of fourths]. One will therefore tend first to dispose of this ninth, to resolve it in some way or other" (405-06). He then gives several examples that handle the ninth. In this context, it is worth noting that the G-A-flat referential quartal span that opens the Chamber Symphony behaves in the opposite fashion: the "ninth" A-flat is retained, enharmonically revalued as G-sharp (sharp-$\hat{5}$ of V), and resolves upward to A.

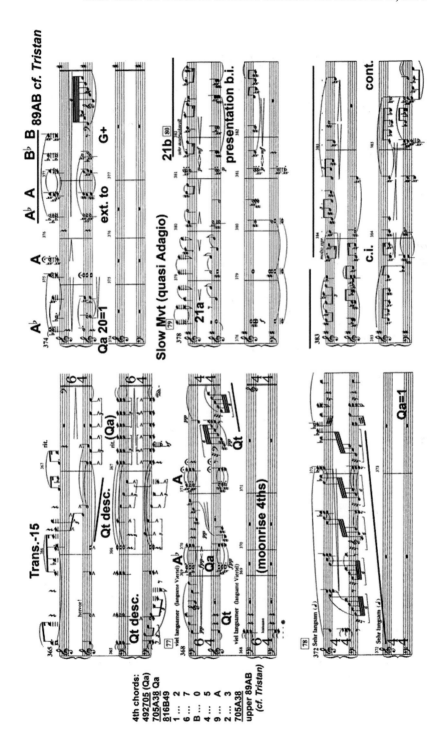

Example 6. Chamber Symphony, mm. 365–85, climax, "moonrise" 4ths, Adagio opening.

that eventually "resolves" (as flat-$\hat{6}$) to the A-flat minor key of the Scherzo II (m. 200); the second, a quasi-$\hat{3}$ (melodic scale-degree) emphasis (again, with E/F-flat ambiguities, m. 274) culminates in a descending variant of Qt (D-C♯/D♭ span) that results in a "bitonal" collision of E-flat minor and F minor chords (m. 280), the latter key bridged by its associated Mid-6 theme header and emerging as the temporary tonal winner (F♭/E becoming $\hat{7}$ to F) with the help of transposed Cad-3. A third instance employs multiple descending and ascending arpeggiations of Qt to encompass a corrective shift from descending G♭-F to F-E spans, and lands in climactic "quasi-V arrival" on a robust Qa (with E-F span, m. 364) with ascending and descending Qt riffs—an arrival which then dissolves in a rhythmic ebb of broad triplets accompanied by motivic residue from Scherzo Transition theme 15, thus structurally framing the entire Scherzo movement (from its foreshadowing transition in m. 148 to this climax at m. 364).[20]

The immediately subsequent instance of the Qt-Qa complex (instance 4) warrants a separate discussion (see Example 6). The quasi-V arrival function of the quartal chord in measure 364 (E-F span) quickly liquidates its climactic function, returning us to the introductory "waiting function" of the work's opening in a mysterious winds and flageolet string harmonics variant of Qt that I like to dub the "moonrise fourths."[21] The quartal-chord span shifts from E-F (pcs 492705) to G-A-flat (pcs 705A38) eventually regaining Qa at its original pitch level (G-A-flat span). The annotations on the left of Example 6 show the subtle way the fourth arpeggiations are chained together: 492<u>705</u> moves to <u>705</u>A38 (with three members linked), then to <u>8</u>16B49 (with only pc 8 linked, but all twelve tones now invoked), and finally to "enlarged" statements on *each* of pcs 8...1...6...B...4...9...2...7, which end with the return of the original 705A38 span. An extension of the Qa introductory progression results in the original upper voice motion of A-flat/G-sharp-A being continued through B-flat to B—a motion no doubt familiar enough to readers and listeners as the upper voice slide (G♯-A-A♯-B) from the opening of Wagner's *Tristan* Prelude! It is as if Schoenberg wished, consciously or unconsciously, to capture the melodic element of that emblematic moment of nineteenth-century chromatic crisis within the changed context of twentieth-century extended harmonic vocabulary (here, quartal harmony, Qa). The progression thus moves the Qa original beyond

---

[20]In commenting on the climactic "quasi-V" arrival (m. 364), Catherine Dale (*Schoenberg's Chamber Symphonies* [2000], 25) notes: "Closure is effected at this point by the reiteration of the [quartal] referential harmony and the *ritenuto* tempo direction in bar 367 rather than by functional progression, thus permitting Schoenberg to 'cadence' without tonal commitment." The chord stands in place of conventional "dominant arrival" rather than closure, but the idea of "cadence without commitment" is very apt, a feeling that the subsequent "moon-rise" fourths uncannily confirm.

[21]"Moonrise" fourths: in anticipation of the blood-red moonrise in Act III, Scene 2 of Berg's *Wozzeck*.

its first F major (♭II, Neapolitan) cadential goal to G major (♭III), the referential scale-step of the Adagio movement that follows (m. 317).[22]

At the end of the Adagio (m. 407, instance 5, see Example 7), a fragmentary residue of Qt (G♯-C♯-F♯) within a larger tetrachordal span (G♯-C♯-F♯-B) shifts down to the original pitch level (G-C-F-B♭), soon returning the full hexachordal Qt and Qa span (G-C-F-B♭-E♭-A♭) (see Example 7). This time Qa, again with its *Tristan*-like upper line, is further extended in a progression leading to B major (V); an expansive pre-recapitulatory "Closing Episode" ensues (m. 415; Berg's thematic idea 23).[23] Thus, overall, the initial Qa progression has moved from distributed cadential points on F major (♭II, m. 4, m. 375, m. 412), to G major (♭III, m. 377) setting up the Adagio, to B major (V, m. 415) setting up this celebratory Closing Episode (Berg's 23). The Closing Episode leads to a bipartite Finale/Recapitulation (m. 435 and m. 477)—bipartite because its first part (m. 435) recapitulates Transition-8 (in counterpoint with Episode theme 23), leading further to Transitional Ideas 9 (juxtaposed with Adagio theme 21b) and 10, and follows these with the normative home-key recapitulation of Subordinate Theme ST-11 (m. 449), before its second part brings back the Main Theme MT-4 (m. 477).

Overall, the "dual-form" of the Chamber Symphony—its four movements-in-one continuous form—creates a different sort of Finale/Recapitulation need, one that redistributes and shifts recapitulatory to concluding functions. I

[22]This apparent *Tristan* reference does not seem to be cited in the literature. Space does not permit a properly extensive elaboration of the large-scale unfolding of the voice-leading argument. However, in brief, one should note that the initial G♯/A♭-A motion to the F major goal (m. 4), becomes A♭-A-B♭ in the main theme of the Scherzo (in C minor, mm. 160-62, returning at m. 249), continues as Ab-A-B♭-B to the G major goal in the Qa progression before the Adagio (mm. 376-77), the whole A♭-A-B♭/A♯-B motion more concisely summarized again and moving to the B major goal before the Closing Episode (mm. 411-14). In the Codas section of this paper, I argue that a final compression of the G♯-A-B♭-B motion provides a clinching motivic rationale for the unusual surface chordal progression in the last measures of the work (mm. 584-93).

[23]Frisch (*The Early Works* [1993], 231) and Dale (*Schoenberg's Chamber Symphonies* [2000], 71) both note that Schoenberg's autograph score (in the Pierpont Morgan Library in New York) indicates that he considered eliminating the entire "closing episode" passage from mm. 415-35, the trail of indecision revealed by "VI-DE" and "bleibt" markings. Berg refers to theme 23 as the "second main theme" of the Slow Movement though acknowledging "it already has more the character of a transition to the last part (Finale) of the Symphony" (259). Frisch and Dale argue that Schoenberg's reconsideration of the passage stems from his concern about the appropriate length of dominant preparation. It seems to me, however, that the whole Episode, which is quite splendid, is not the problem. The potential for tedium arises rather from Schoenberg's subsequent sense of the need for the extensive recapitulation of transitional (m. 435) and subordinate theme (m. 448) and scherzo materials (m. 463)—all of which, however, present the composer with opportunities for new multiple contrapuntal combinations. The patience of most listeners is certainly well tried by the time what I have called the long "parenthetic passage" gets underway (mm. 508-51), which commences with what feels like one-too-many repetitions of Adagio Theme 21b and embeds a final swell (though unresolved) recollection of Adagio opening 21a (m. 535) as well as off-tonic Mid-6 (m. 540 and m. 457) before emerging with Cad-7 (m. 552) and the parallel codetta run (m. 555).

will reflect further on this situation when I consider Schoenberg's "enthrallogy of codas" below. But the results of this functional shift mean that we have reached a "tipping point" where the final two distributions of the opening ideas (instances 6 and 7 in Figure 4) change from introductory/initiating functions (as in instances 0, 1, and partly 2), or dominant arrival (partly 2 and 3) and "waiting" functions (instances 4 and 5), to concluding functions. I will therefore consider them (6 and 7) in the context of coda.

The Case of Schoenberg's Chamber Symphony— An "Enthrallogy of Codas"

I introduce this discussion of conclusion by returning to the closing section or codetta of the First Movement. Codetta functions, as noted in the earlier discussion of selected symphonic examples, go beyond the mere need for pitch centricity to include various cadential and post-cadential functions that may involve combinatoric and hypermetric manipulation of thematic elements, coupled with a tendency toward reiterative, redundant, and recessive gesture. Formal-motivic associations such as structural framing and closing parallelism play important waypoint roles for the listener. These can be boldly confirmed or variously undermined—rhythmically or harmonically "scumbled," or subjected to registral and other forms of ellipsis. In the Chamber Symphony, the first movement codetta (mm. 113-32) shows many of these characteristic features. Recall that the Cadential Stride figure (m. 50, Cad-7, Example 3, above), takes the role of a modified classical Expanded Cadential Progression (ECP), but that its due cadential closure is delayed via a dominant arrival (m. 53) and framing return of MT-4 and Cad-5 (m. 58) such that the Main Theme section continues until a perfect tonic cadence is achieved (m. 68). Following the bipartite and three-themed Transition section (m. 68 and m. 74; Berg 8, 9, and 10), and the Subordinate Theme section (m. 84, Berg 11), Schoenberg sets up for a "codetta run" (see Example 8).

The "codetta-run" begins with an unequivocal harmonic signal—the arrival of a cadential six-four chord (m. 113) directed towards the subordinate goal key of A major (IV). The whole codetta section (mm. 113-32) also employs more thematic redundancy, hypermetric squareness, and clear tonal focus than we have experienced thus far. As shown on Berg's thematic table (recall Example 5), there are three thematic elements: 12, a truncated version of ST-11 (m. 113); 13, a robust triplet figure (m. 123); and 14, a closing "tucket" fanfare (m. 127). They are subjected to contrapuntal combination and hypermetric compression: 12 is paired with scurrying Transition idea 9 and a staccato scalar figure in triple counterpoint; then 12 continues under 13 in double counterpoint; 13 continues under 14 with closing cadential motions; and the whole passage "compresses" from 3 measures times 3 (plus 1 connecting measure), to 2 measures times 2, to

Example 7. Chamber Symphony, mm. 406-17, end of Adagio
to Closing Episode.

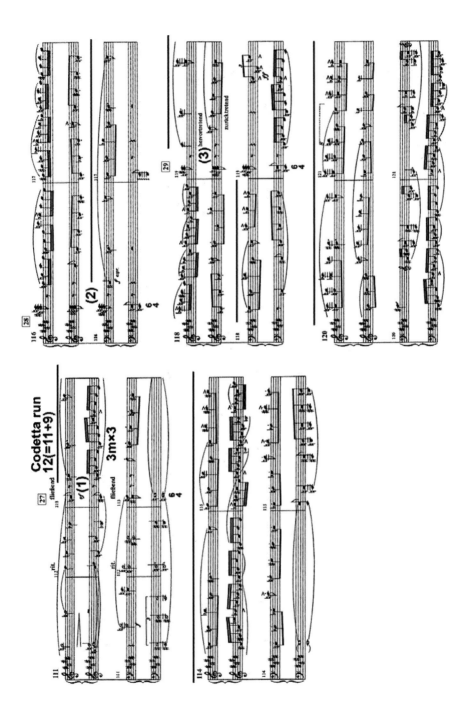

Example 8. Chamber Symphony, mm. 113–21, Exposition "codetta run."

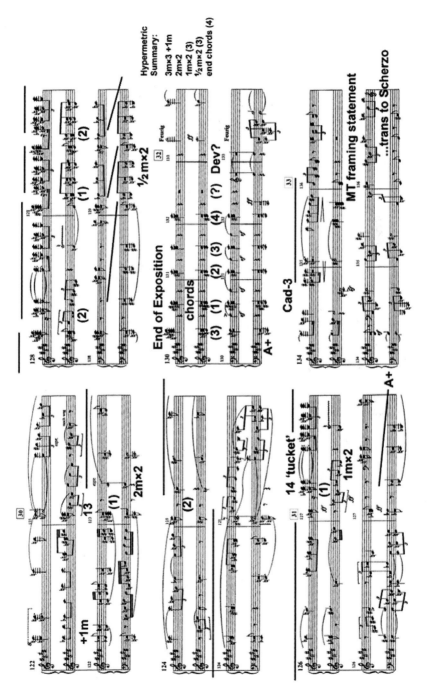

Example 8 (cont'd). Chamber Symphony, mm. 122-36, "codetta run" (cont.) to end of Exposition.

Example 9. Chamber Symphony, mm. 472-80, recapitulation of Main Theme.

1 measure times 2, to ½ measure times 3, to four stunning strokes of the goal (A major unison, juxtaposed with embellishing C-sharp major chords).[24] The hypermetric situation is summarized in the annotation to Example 8. With the help of MT-4 fragments and Cad-3 an "extra" fifth strike of A dissipates the driving forces and begins an apparent Development Section, which, as it turns out, becomes the Transition to the Scherzo movement. The whole run is a spectacular instance of codetta enthrall.

What happens when this passage returns in the Recapitulation? Closing Sections in recapitulations normally effect "closing parallelism" with their counterpart sections in the Exposition: the material that served to "close before" returns to "close again" (this time of course in the home key). In the case of the Chamber Symphony, however, the "dual-form" nature of the recapitulation results in further redistribution of compositional elements. More precisely, elements that were introductory or expository in the First Movement of the work return in the Finale with concluding function, in post-cadential and structural framing roles.

To clarify this "functional drift," I need to bring forward the final two instances of the distributed compositional matrix of the chronology of intros from Figure 4. Example 9 shows instance 6, the passage that includes the deferred recapitulation of the Main Theme (MT-4). Qt-2 emerges from the texture (with original span D-D♯, m. 473) to signal the imminent arrival of the Main Theme, but the rhythmic augmentation of Cad-3 (m. 476) ends up bridging (and thus partially scumbling) the moment of return. Moreover, MT-4 itself is given so squarely sequential a presentation—its "basic idea" ("b.i.") simply repeated up a step, at m. 477 and m. 479—and attaches itself so smoothly to variants of Cad-5 (m. 481 and m. 483, not shown) that the sense of both momentum and momentousness recedes.

The passage concludes with a direct, though slightly expanded, recollection of the brief cadential gesture that closed out the Main Theme section (and began the Transition) of the First Movement (compare m. 66, Example 4, with m. 492; see Example 10). The absence of references to the Qa-Qt-Cad marker complex at this important cadence point is significant—they are being saved for the end of the work (instance 7); instead, an extended dominant built from main-theme-associated augmented triads proceeds in contrary motion by whole-

---

[24]This stunning series of unison As with embellishing C-sharp major chords (m. 130) arises from the previous codetta progression (mm. 127-30), where the whole tone upper voice motion to A is F-G-A, over bass motion support D♭-C-B♭-A; hence, the A and C-sharp major (or D-flat major) final embellishment is a harmonic compression of the preceding progression. Furthermore, if we understand that the A unisons stand for full A major chords (not much of a stretch since they have been present as the arrival sonority on the strong beats of the last three measures), then the implied voice leading is the retention of C-sharp and the motion from E-sharp (or F) to E and G-sharp to A—precisely the motivic residue of the F-E (Neapolitan) and G♯-A upper voice motions from the beginning of the work, once again a bold structural framing effect through subtle motivic association.

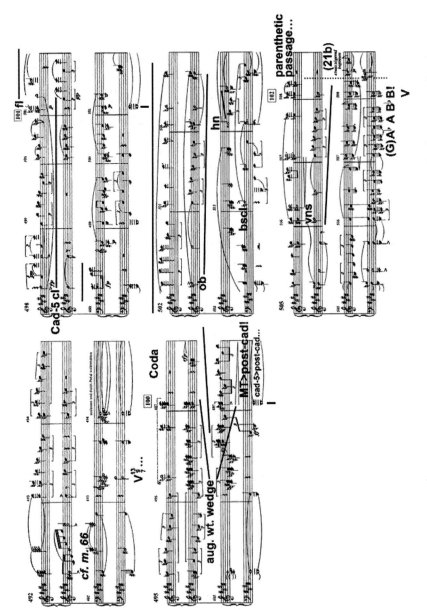

Example 10. Chamber Symphony, mm. 492–508, cadence, Coda, parenthetic passage begins.

tone "wedge" to reach what one would expect to be the final tonic of the section (m. 497). This arrival feels like "Coda," and was so identified by Berg, not merely because of the tonic scale-step, but because, with the help of recollected cadential gesture and pedal point, both MT-4 and Cad-5 are wonderfully transformed from their usual presentational and cadential roles to languid post-cadential status (mm. 492-501). However the section soon comes to a halt on a form of (minor) dominant arrival (m. 508), following which a quite extended "parenthetic passage" should be understood (mm. 508-551, not shown). The purpose of the passage is not only a final *reculer pour mieux sauter*, it also allows the derivational relationship between several thematic elements to become manifest (notably the relation between the transitional and adagio themes 8 and 21b), and numerous fresh contrapuntal combinations to be explored. The perception of potentially tedious overkill (particularly of theme 21b) is broken by a last stellar interjection of the Adagio opening (21a, m. 535). Its bass motion (normally C to G) fails to drop, and Mid-6 returns briefly centred in C minor (m. 540) and A-flat/G-sharp minor (m. 547). This thematic material suddenly yields to the return of the ECP Cadential Stride idea (Cad-stride-7, m. 552) that brings us out of the parenthetic twilight zone and signals the potential for closure parallel to that of the First Movement/Exposition. And, indeed, the "due" closing parallel of the codetta-run ensues (mm. 555-76), and the final series of enthralls is underway.

The closing parallel of the codetta run is shown in Example 11. Comparison of the two passages (mm. 113-32, Example 8 and mm. 555-76, Example 11) reveals several changes. Use of thematic idea 12 (derived from ST-11) is more truncated, and combined right away in double counterpoint with idea 13, which now takes the lead (cello, horn, violin). The hypermetric structure is also initially compressed in comparison with the codetta: two-measures-times-three plus a connecting measure, versus the three-measures-times-three in the codetta. The tucket fanfare idea 14 follows, but its one-measure-times-two design is doubled to twice one-measure-times-two through terraced registral-instrumental pairings (horns and violins). The subsequent cadential compression to one-half-measure-times-two, which in the codetta reached the stunning chordal strokes of the cadential goal in the First Movement (A major, m. 130), becomes vastly extended in the Coda; its one-half-measure units, suitably transposed to the tonic (E major, m. 566) are taken eight times over a descending whole-tone bass motion that couples a C-C octave (mm. 567-70). The hypermetric situation is summarized in the annotation on Example 11. The passage yields to a four-measure ECP (mm. 570-73) that culminates in a final *fff* descending (and overextended) Qt span (m. 574, D♭-A♭-E♭-B♭-F-C-G, with original Qa embedded) that takes place as a powerful structural framing marker *within* a V-I bass progression (mm. 573-76), only slightly undercut by the scurrying bass entry of MT-4 that overlaps the arrival point. This final appearance (instance 7 from Figure 4) of the Qa-Qt-Cad-3 introductory complex has lost all initiating

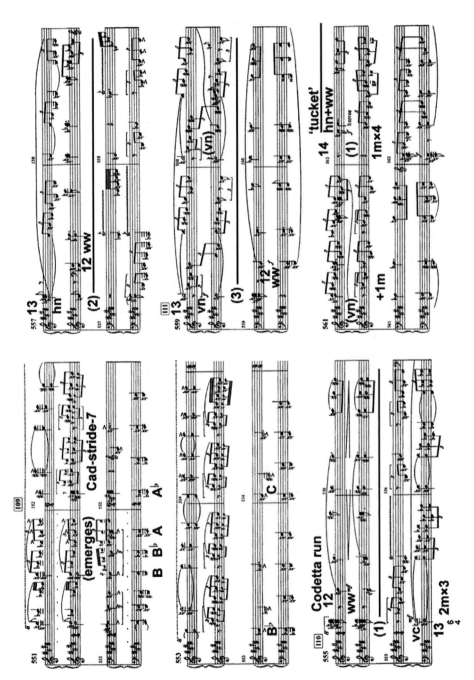

Example 11. Chamber Symphony, mm. 551-62, emerges for Finale "codetta-run."

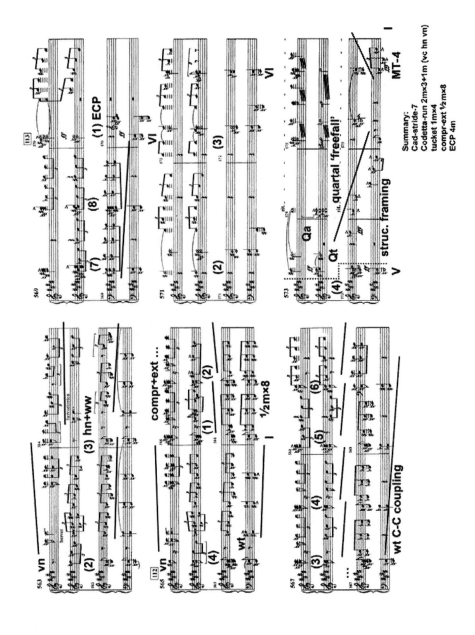

Example 11 (cont.). Chamber Symphony, mm. 563-75, "codetta run" (cont.) to Finale cadence.

First Movement/Expo... mm. 1-132	Recap/Finale 435-	476-	Coda 497	(parenthetic) (508	535-)	552 555- Cod(ett)a	574	576-593 'End-Coda'
Intro 1 2 3	.	3				2+1	4	3
MT 4 5 6 7	.	4 5	4 5		6)	7...		
Trans 8 9 10	8+23 9+21b			(21b 9-10 21a)				
ST 11	11 (+6+4)			(...				
Codetta 12 13 14						12 13 14 ECP		

Note: redistributed compositional matrix of introductory ideas and codetta ideas functional drift from introductory to recapitulatory to post-cadential functions deferred (reversed) recapitulation: Trans+Adagio, ST, MT (parenthetic insert brings out thematic parallels between Trans 8, 9, 10, ST 11, and Adagio 21b) continuity of MT 4 5 (... 6) 7 broken by parenthetic passage, emerging with 7 into codetta closing parallelism (codetta functions) and structural framing (intro-coda)

Figure 5. Comparison of First Movement/Exposition and Recapitulation/Finale passages.

values: the descending Qt within the V-I cadence is terminal. And its associated Cad-3 component is also shifted to closing function, deferred until the final measures of the work (mm. 589-93).

Figure 5 provides a comparative summary of the functional role of thematic materials in the First Movement/Exposition and their redistribution in the Recapitulation/Finale and Coda. Note the "functional drift" of the introductory materials to recapitulatory and post-cadential functions. The recapitulation is "reversed": the Transition 8 (with counterpoint from Closing Episode 23, m. 435) and ST-11 (m. 446) as well as Scherzo references (m. 463) occur *before* the MT (m. 477). The MT returns again with post-cadential function to mark the Coda (m. 497). A "parenthetic passage" follows (mm. 508-52) that breaks the continuation of the MT group (thematic ideas 4 5 ... [parenthetic gap] ... 6 7) by inserting juxtapositions of Adagio and Transition materials: 21b (m. 508), 9-10 (m. 516), 21a (m. 535). Still within the parenthetic passage, the MT group begins to reassemble with Mid-6 off-tonic (m. 540, m. 547) but emerges fully from the parentheses only with the Cadential Stride, ECP Cad-7 (m. 552). It sets up the closing parallelism of the codetta run (12, 13, 14) extended by a further ECP (mm. 555-73) culminating in the descending Qt-2 (m. 574). The intro-and-MT ideas (Berg's 2 + 1, 4 and 3) provide the final structural framing reference back to the opening of the work.

What remains of the piece consists of a pair of ecstatic passages that Berg called the "*End-Coda*" ("final coda" in DeVoto's translation; mm. 576-93), the first fundamentally in ascent, the second descending (see Example 12). Berg used the term End-Coda because he needed something that would acknowledge the multiplicity of coda-like objects that have already accrued by this point.[25] The materials that follow the cadence in m. 576 are clearly post-cadential: they show the kind of reiterative redundancy, removal of developmental complexity, and affirmative verve characteristic of such ending passages. End-Coda 1 (mm. 576-83) uses the MT-4 header in the bass in sequential fashion, explicitly composing out its augmented-triadic scaffold with whole-tone scalar motions from G-sharp, C, and E, which end with dotted-rhythm tags E-G♯, G♯-B♯(C), and C-E, respectively. Qt accompanies[26] with parallel transposition of spans D-E♭, F♯-G, and A♯-C♯—the last adjusted to end with E-A (rather than the expected F♯-B)—each of which attaches itself at the apex to a dotted "shrill tag" figure that "resolves" through colliding adjacencies to triadic goals on C (m. 578), E (m. 580), and—again the last adjusted—F (m. 582). This arrival on F finally allows an explicit "correction" within E major of the ♭II (Neapolitan) "false"

[25]Frisch (*Schoenberg's Early Works* [1993], 236-46) focuses on the Neapolitan relationship; for the "Neapolitan-plagal" aspects of the final measures, see 245-46. Dale (*Schoenberg's Chamber Symphonies* [2000], 20 and 36) discusses the prominence of the Neapolitan in relation to its remoteness in Schoenberg's chart and theory of harmonic regions.

[26]Qt accompanies: this is, in fact, the only time components of Qt-2 and MT-4 are explicitly combined, a possibility only viable when both have shifted to post-cadential function.

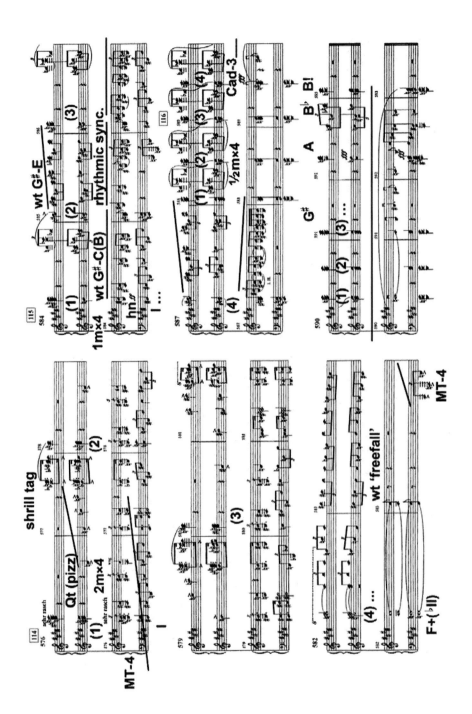

Example 12. Chamber Symphony, mm. 576–93, "End-Coda."

goals that have characterized the work since its opening measures. A "free-fall" descending whole-tone scalar flourish triplets its way into End-Coda 2.

End-Coda 2 (mm. 584-93) again leads with the header of MT-4 in the bass (further truncated so that the dotted tag is now removed), but it is the upper-voice pair of horns that seizes the listener's attention. MT-4 covers the ascending whole-tone span G-sharp up to E (imitated in the upper register in the alternate measures), the horns cover a descending span in parallel sixths from G-sharp down to B (the whole-tone motion adjusted at the end to produce the tonic triad): together they pull the whole-tone-based thematic materials into triadic conformity. The horn motive is given a fundamentally redundant yet progressively syncopated and rhythmically diminuted ululation that is definitively ecstatic. Yet even this seems outdone by the shrieking tag figure (now in triplet form) that takes over entirely as the lid of the mason jar screws down to half-measure hypermetric compressions. This process brings back a crucial closer that was missing from previous moments of Coda—the hammering chordal strokes of arrival that marked the end of the First Movement/Exposition (mm. 130-32). Such rhythmic pounding finally returns here (mm. 588-91), each flailing tonic stroke introduced by the shrieking tag (mm. 588-89). When Cad-3 returns (mm. 589-93, again in augmentation), it has nothing left to introduce. It is accompanied only by three tonic hammer strokes, tripped up in syncopated plagalism in the penultimate measure to arrive on the final note of the cadential figure and the final tonic chord via one last flourishing tag.

The "harmonic" aspects of the tag have been cause for comment: the apparent chordal progression is F-B♭-B♭-E. Talk of subdominants of Neapolitans, enharmonic ♯IV (B♭=A♯), etc., various appeals to remoteness in Schoenberg's Chart of Regions, and so on, have failed to consider a reading that would account for a large-scale motivic association.[27] As indicated earlier, the "chronology of intros" in the form of the distributed appearances of the Qt progression (mm. 1-4, mm. 368-78, mm. 410-15) constructs a large-scale upper voice motion of G♯(A♭)-A-B♭(A♯)-B, which I have related to *Tristan*. This motion is also forcibly embedded in the final tag, the G-sharp to B span

---

[27]See note 25 references to Frisch and Dale. Schoenberg's theory of harmonic regions is developed in his posthumously published *Structural Functions of Harmony* [1969 (1954)], charts on pages 20 and 30. Schoenberg positioned the Neapolitan remotely, relating it to the subdominant minor (as its VI) and the lowered submediant (as its IV). Frisch's suggested derivation of the penultimate B-flat chord as subdominant of the Neapolitan is thus comparatively economical. According to Schoenberg's Chart of the Regions, a B-flat chord could be derived from an E major tonic as the flat mediant major (B♭) of the flat mediant minor (g) via the flat mediant major (G), or as the submediant major (B♭) of the flat mediant minor's five (d) via the dominant (D) of the flat mediant (G); A-sharp, the enharmonic equivalent of B-flat, might be derived in similar fashion from the supertonic major (F♯) or submediant major (C♯ major)—one senses the derivational problem: remote indeed! In any case, these harmonic paths are not featured in the piece, whereas the linear motion from G♯ to B has been fundamental at several critical formal junctures.

supported by the E major tonic triad, the intermediate A and B♭ by the F and B♭ "harmonies" of the tag. It is a fitting allusion to find in the final measures of Schoenberg's Chamber Symphony, a work that serves, for the composer and for us all, more as the enthralling coda to nineteenth-century tonal practice than as the intro to the atonal "air of another planet" that would soon waft forth.

Schoenberg's First Chamber Symphony, Formalism, and Adorno's Critique of Twelve-Tone Composition

Murray Dineen

> Nowhere else is the secret agreement of light and progressive music more succinctly proven true than here. Late Schoenberg shares with jazz—and, incidentally, also with Stravinsky—the dissociation of musical time. Music drafts the image of a world that—for better or for worse—no longer knows history.
>
> —Theodor Adorno

I shall bring together two perspectives in this paper, one a formalist perspective growing out of my work with Schoenberg's concept of extended tonality, the other a critical perspective growing out of my work with the writings of Theodor Adorno. According to the first perspective, in his First Chamber Symphony, Op. 9, and in works like it Schoenberg explored what I shall call *tonal centrality without pitches*. By this I mean a kind of tonal orientation not centered on one, and only one, pitch or even on a central group of pitches, but instead a tonal orientation built on relationships created by intervals and patterns of intervals (which leads ultimately to an orientation built on the intervallic properties of a tone row). In works such as the First Chamber Symphony, the vehicle of tonal centrality shifts from tonic pitch orientation to tonic intervallic orientation. As a result intervals and interval patterns become the vehicles for tonal form, thus antedating Schoenberg's experiments with serialism.

Like Adorno, I find a premonition of serialism in Schoenberg's Symphony. Adorno's reading of nascent serialism differs significantly from mine, however, for mine is restricted to the framework of the introductory theme to the Symphony, while his treats the Symphony's first theme as a point of departure for a critique of the later twelve-tone technique in general. I shall begin my analysis of the opening measures to the Symphony, and turn to Adorno's critique later.

Murray Dineen is a Professor in the Department of Music at the University of Ottawa. He has written about Schoenberg and harmony, and about Adorno. He currently holds a Standard Research Grant from the Social Sciences and Humanities Council of Canada for a study of Schoenberg, Adorno, and the Left in Central Europe between the two World Wars.

Notes:

Cycle of Perfect Fifths: D   G   C   *F*   B♭   E♭   [A♭]

                             1   2   3   *4*   5   6   7

             Midpoint=F

Example 1. Schoenberg: First Chamber Symphony, cycle of fifths.

Example 1 is a short score reduction of the opening measures to the First Chamber Symphony. In the example, several pitches have been removed (E, C, and G-flat in m. 3, and A in m. 4). The pitches remaining show the prevalence of the interval of a perfect fifth (and its inversion the perfect fourth) in these measures. All the pitches in Example 1 can be seen as members of a series or cycle of fifth relations. I have sketched such a cycle as a simple listing of integers beneath the example. In this listing, each pitch is assigned an order number, 1 through 7. I have taken the French-horn call built of rising fourths as the principal instance of the cycle (as its "prime" form). It begins on the pitch D (ordered thus as 1 in the listing and the example) and rises to E-flat (ordered as 6). To the French-horn's cycle, I have added the pitch A-flat (ordered as 7) albeit parenthetically, since it is not produced by the horn, but appears prominently, nonetheless, being the first note of the work. As the work begins, in other words, the cycle seems to congeal out of thin air in "retrograde form" to the fermata of measure 4. Then and only then is a clear statement—"prime"— given to the French horn.

This cycle can be split in balanced halves around the pitch F (ordered as the fourth pitch of the cycle), which is the root of the F major triad in measure 4. In another context, the F root of that triad might serve as a tonal center. My point, however, is that the actual root of that triad is largely irrelevant; the cyclical interval of a perfect fifth is sufficient to lend this passage the coherence that we normally attribute to a single pitch as tonal center. Tonality is achieved here through an intervallic relationship not necessarily oriented to one definitive tonal center.

The centricity at work in these measures is not necessarily bound to a pitch, then, but is bound up with a musical idea, that of fifth relations. Drawing a distinction between style and idea, Schoenberg said that musical ideas take form in different ways; in essence, they are done justice to in a manner depending upon their circumstances.[1] The musical idea of fifth relation takes form in these opening measures both successively (or horizontally) and simultaneously (or vertically), in a "two-or-more-dimensional space" as Schoenberg called it.[2] I have indicated on the short score the *order numbers* of the pitches of the cycle from measure 1 onward successively, as if in a horizontal dimension. Note that order number 7 (A-flat) enters first, followed by order numbers 5 and 6 (B-flat and E-flat), 3 and 4 (C and F), and then, at the bottom of the score, order number 2 (G). After the fermata, in the French horn we hear (as noted above) the pitches or order numbers 1 (D), 2, 3, 4, 5, and 6. To reiterate, it is as if Schoenberg walked backward (or in retrograde) through the series, 7, 6, 5, 4, 3, 2, and then walked forward (or in prime), 1, 2, 3, 4, 5, 6, all this in the horizontal dimension, left to right on the score.

The musical idea of fifth relation is also expressed vertically, by scoring pitches of the cycle in descending order in the two opening measures. The highest pitch in measure 1 is A-flat, ordered pitch number 7, followed below it by E-flat, pitch 6, in measure 2, then B-flat, pitch 5, in measure 1, and so forth moving downward until pitch 2, G. The descent is reversed in the ascending French horn line after the fermata.

The very *idea* of fifth relationship is thus made tonally centric—as the principle reference point of tonal relationship and of musical form, equivalent in effect if not means to a central tonic pitch. This idea is expressed in two dimensions, as if to lend emphasis to its importance. In lieu of the pitch F, the *tonal center* of these opening measures could be said to be "perfect fifth relation," as if the piece could be said to be in the key of "perfect fifth." But while fifth-relation is the clearest vehicle for effecting tonal centrality, it is not the only one drawn upon here by Schoenberg.

[1]See Arnold Schoenberg, *Style and Idea: Selected Writings of Arnold Schoenberg*, ed. Leonard Stein, trans. Leo Black (Berkeley: University of California press, 1975), 123.
[2]Ibid., 220.

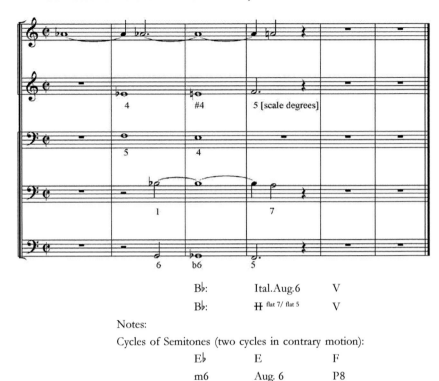

Example 2. Schoenberg: First Chamber Symphony, mm. 1-6.

Example 2 extracts pitches from the short score so as to focus on semitone relationships, these expressed as scale degrees, reckoned for purposes of this discussion in B-flat. The uppermost stave presents the rising A-flat to A (scale degrees flat 7 to the leading tone) which gives the F triad at the fermata its bright major quality. The two innermost bass clef staves present descending semitone motion from the dominant and tonic scale degrees. I shall focus, however, on the remaining staves, the second treble clef stave and the lowest bass clef stave. The two combined in measures 2-4 express the semitone cycle as two semitones in contrary motion. The intervals created between the two cycles are noted below the example: a minor sixth (G to E-flat), is followed by an augmented sixth (G-flat to E-natural), and then to octave F's in measure 4.

In much classical music the interval of an augmented sixth moving by stepwise motion to an octave is a signal, a kind of semaphore. The operant scale degrees are understood as sharp-4 and flat-6. They move customarily in contrary motion by semitone so as to double scale-degree 5. This scale-degree 5 is understood as a dominant function, and thus the preceding contrary motion semitones produce a kind of implicit tonicization of a subsequent scale degree 1 (B-flat in this instance). They can point thus to a tonic, such is the strength of the augmented interval under resolution, even if the tonic is never supplied. On this line of thought, then, the vertical interval of the augmented sixth expanding (or a diminished third contracting) by semitones in contrary motion implies motion to a scale-degree 5, a dominant.

Schoenberg's augmented sixth, G-flat to E, in measure 3, then, implies B-flat. The F major triad under the fermata is not a tonic, in this regard, but a dominant. Accordingly, I have registered measures 3 and 4 in the key of B-flat major. The upper registration follows North American practice: an "Italian" augmented sixth resolves to a simple V chord. The lower registration follows a purer Viennese tradition, which Schoenberg knew and observed: the chord with the augmented sixth is registered as an altered II chord with missing root (following Simon Sechter) and transformed by a major third, flat fifth, and flat seventh.[3]

What does this reference to a B-flat tonic have to do necessarily with tonality and interval cycles? Nothing. The resolution of the augmented sixth need be no more expressive of a tonic pitch than are the entries in the perfect fifth cycle that surrounds it. While in a host of other situations the augmented sixth would necessarily imply a tonal center as I have suggested, in Schoenberg's Symphony this implication is irrelevant, neither taken up, nor disproved. The resolution of the augmented sixth clarifies only that there are two related chords here, just as the cycle of fifths discussed above clarifies only that there are related pitches there. The relationship is drawn along the lines of altered II going to V, but only "along the lines," not necessarily and thus definitively so. "Along the lines of altered II going to V"—that is merely a postulate; it covers only a bar or two. It is no more definitive than the interval cycles of semitones and fifths that surround it. In these measures, Schoenberg does not offer a single, all-encompassing tonal perspective aligned with one pitch. Instead he offers the very idea of tonal perspective, which he then leaves hanging.

This notion of a tonal centrality without pitches relies upon ideas that I set forth in greater detail in a recent essay.[4] There I introduced Schoenberg's little known but important concept of substitution, a concept by which he accounts for chromaticism. Tonality, which Schoenberg calls *monotonality*, is made up of tonal regions—divisions or sub domains of one all-encompassing tonality. Elsewhere these regions are called *keys* and identified by pitch-letter names. But in Schoenberg's thought, they are merely segments of a grand tonality, and thus he gave them names that reflect this subordinate relation to a grand tonal center. So, for example, in a tonality with tonal center F, the key of F should be called the *tonic region*, the key of C called the *dominant region*, the key of B-flat minor

---

[3]See Schoenberg, *Theory of Harmony*, trans. Roy E. Carter (Berkeley: University of California Press, 1978), 246; Simon Sechter, *Die Grundsätze der musikalischen Komposition* (Leipzig: Breitkopf und Härtel, 1853): *Erste Abteilung: Die richtige Folge der Grundharmonien, oder vom Fundamentalbass und dessen Umkehrungen und Stellvertreten*, section 8, p. 216 [the first example therein].

[4]See Murray Dineen, "Schoenberg's Modulatory Calculations: *Wn* Fonds 21 Berg 6/III/66 and Tonality," *Music Theory Spectrum* 27/1 (Spring 2005): 97-112.

would be called the *subdominant minor region*, and so forth. These regions are set forth in Schoenberg's Chart of the Regions.[5]

In Schoenberg's theory, chromaticism is created by replacing pitches of the tonic region with pitches borrowed from other regions. The tonic region serves as a frame, and the other regions serve as sources from which pitches are borrowed so as to (as Schoenberg puts it) *substitute* for tonic region pitches. The framing tonic region, in other words, swaps its own pitches for those of other regions. In this way, modulation is attained not by changing keys but by swapping or substituting chromatic pitches for diatonic tonic region pitches. The tonic region, in other words, is made to borrow pitches from source regions related to the tonic.

Schoenberg, as we say, has his cake and eats it too. Through substitution, the tonic frame of reference is preserved, but related regions are articulated as source regions for substitutes. Thus tonal relationship is drawn and tonality created. The combination of tonic framing region and the source regions is what he calls *expanded tonality*. In essence an expanded tonality keeps a constant frame of reference—the tonic region—but expands by means of substitution to encompass the source regions. (The concept of "changing keys" implies a change of tonic frame of reference, a change of tonality, rather than the chromatic enrichment or expansion of a single tonality. Schoenberg eschews the former in preference for the latter.) My main point here is that tonality—like that in Schoenberg's Symphony—is not necessarily centric around one pitch. It depends as much upon a *relationship* between a framing region and related source regions as it does upon a definitive tonic region in and of itself.

Working temporarily with a definitive tonic region of F major, I have sketched a substitution analysis in Example 3. Assuming temporarily F major as its tonic region, then, the opening pitch A-flat might be borrowed from the tonic minor region (the region of F minor). I have indicated this in the commentary below Example 3: on these lines, the A-flat is borrowed from the tonic minor, F minor, to substitute for the A natural of the tonic major region, F major. Where this happens, the tonality expands to encompass both the tonic major frame (F major) and the tonic minor region (F minor).

The two remaining substitute pitches here, G-flat and E-flat, are obtained likewise by substitution. In Example 3, I say "G-flat might be borrowed" from the region of the subdominant minor (B-flat minor) as the flat sixth scale degree thereof. And E-flat might be borrowed from the minor dominant (C minor). I say "might," because in earlier works of classical music, these derivations usually become clear during the course of the works. As the late Patricia Carpenter has shown, the act of clarification becomes part of the narrative of the work.[6]

---

[5]See Schoenberg, *Structural Functions of Harmony* (New York: Norton, 1969), 20, 30.

[6]See, for example, Patricia Carpenter, "'Grundgestalt' as Tonal Function," *Music Theory Spectrum* 5 (1983):15-38; Carpenter, "Musical Form and Musical Idea: Reflections on a Theme of Schoenberg, Hanslick, and Kant," in *Music and Civilization: Essays in Honor of Paul Henry* (cont.)

In Example 3, I have sketched this expanded tonality as it might be represented on a table like that of Schoenberg's Chart of the Regions. The tonic region (represented by capital T) is expanded to encompass the source regions of the substitute pitches A-flat, G-flat, and E-flat.

In Example 4, I have arranged the regions of an F major tonality around the circle of fifths, a circle much like that in Schoenberg's *Harmonielehre*. For ease of reading, I have represented each region by its tonic's letter name instead of Schoenberg's region names. I have indicated in boxes the regions involved in these opening measures—F, c, f b♭. As Schoenberg held, however, pitch names express nothing of tonal relationship.[7] In Example 5, I have replaced pitch letter names with variables and formulae. As the legend to Example 5 notes, the letter

---

According to Schoenberg, regions other than tonic [T] are sources for chromatic substitutes. Thus:

A-flat might be borrowed from the tonic minor region [t] as scale degree flat-3 thereof.

G-flat might be borrowed from the subdominant minor region [sd] as scale degree flat-6.

E-flat might be borrowed from the minor-five region [v] as scale degree flat-3.

These regions as located on the Chart of the Regions:

	V
T	t
	sd

These regions as located on a Chart of the Regions in F, with letter names:

	c
F	f
	b♭

Example 3. Schoenberg: First Chamber Symphony, mm. 1-6, substitution.

Lang, ed. Edmond Strainchamps and Maria Rika Maniates (New York: Norton, 1985), 394-427; Carpenter, "A Problem of Organic Form: Schoenberg's Tonal Body," *Theory and Practice: The Journal of the Music Theory Society of New York State* 13 (1988): 31-64; Carpenter, "Aspects of Musical Space," in *Explorations in Music, the Arts, and Ideas: Essays in Honor of Leonard B. Meyer*, ed. Eugene Narmour and Ruth A. Solie (Stuyvesant, N.Y.: Pendragon Press, 1988), 341-74; Murray Dineen, "Problems of Tonality: Schoenberg and the Concept of Tonal Expression" (Ph.D. diss., Columbia University, 1988); Dineen, "From the Gerald Strang Bequest in (cont.)

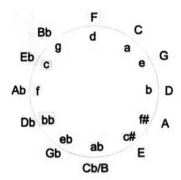

Example 4. Circle of fifths, with source regions for
substitutes indicated in boxes.

X indicates major regions, Y indicates minor regions, plus and minus signs indicate
steps to the right or left (respectively) around the circle. Again the regions in
question in these measures are indicated by boxes.

The notation of Example 5 implies that in lieu of the precise tonic pitch
centricity of Example 4, tonality can be seen to work by means of substitution
without regard to precise pitch identity. Tonal relation is created by moving
pitches from one region (a source region) to substitute for pitches in another (a
framing region). I will call this *formulaic tonality.*[8]

Let me take this now one step further. The First Chamber Symphony is
sometimes understood in the key of E major, since the key signature with
which it begins and ends contains four sharps, and the work concludes with an
E major chord. In most symphonies prior to Schoenberg's day, that would
generally suffice, at least superficially, to indicate a tonal centricity tied to a pitch
letter name. But this is not a superficial symphony, and it will not support a
superficial key attribution.

the Arnold Schoenberg Institute: Documents of a Learning," *Theory and Practice: The Journal of
the Music Theory Society of New York State* 18 (1993): 109-25; Dineen, "The Contrapuntal
Combination: Schoenberg's Old Hat," in *Music Theory and the Exploration of the Past,* ed. Christopher
Hatch and David W. Bernstein (Chicago: University of Chicago Press, 1993), 435-48; Dineen,
"Schoenberg on the Modes: The Antecedents of Extended Tonality," *College Music Symposium*
33-34 (1993-94):140-54; Dineen, "Schoenberg's Logic and Motor: Harmony and Motive in the
'Capriccio,' No. 1 of the *Fantasien,* Op. 116, by Johannes Brahms," *Gamut: The Journal of the
Georgia Association of Music Theorists* 10 (2001): 3-28; Dineen, "The Tonal Problem as a Method
of Analysis. In memoriam Patricia Carpenter," *Theory and Practice: The Journal of the Music Theory
Society of New York State* 30 (2005): 69–96; and Dineen, "Tonal Problem, Carpenter Narrative,
and Carpenter Motive in Schubert's Impromptu, op. 90, no. 3. In memoriam Patricia Carpenter,"
Theory and Practice: The Journal of the Music Theory Society of New York State 30 (2005): 97-120.
[7]See Schoenberg, *Theory of Harmony,* 32, and Schoenberg, *Models for Beginners in Composition,* ed.
Leonard Stein (Los Angeles: Belmont, 1972), 54.
[8]See Dineen, "Schoenberg's Modulatory Calculations," 98, 108-09.

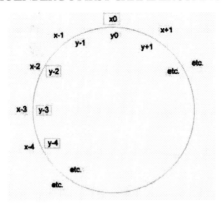

Example 5. Circle of fifths as variables,
with source regions indicated in boxes.

Notes: X indicates a region in major; Y indicates a region in minor. Integers
indicate steps on the circle of fifths. Plus (+) and minus (-) signs indicate
respective motion to the right or left on the circle.

In Example 6, I have re-situated the F major tonality of Example 4 in the
tonality of E major. In Example 7, I have re-situated the formulaic tonality of
Example 5 likewise in E major. Let me draw my conclusion: an actual tonal
center allied with a pitch is not important here. Schoenberg's tonality is formulaic.
All that matters is the expression of a coherent tonal relationship based on
interval. Where and with what pitches this takes place is irrelevant to the proof
of tonality. And therein Schoenberg sows seeds for the serial works to come.

The preceding description of the opening measures to the First Chamber
Symphony and its expanded tonality belong properly within that mode of art
criticism called *formalism*. That is to say, as a description it concentrates upon the
formal features of the work, as if these existed in their own right, "absolutely,"
to use an adverb drawn from common parlance, which means with only minimal
relation to a world outside the work's supposed boundaries. The theoretical
framework of this formalist mode allows for little evidence to be introduced
from outside the work proper. Appeal to a sort of biographical narrative is
admissible in some kinds of formalism; for example, a formalist might allow
the notion that Schoenberg conceived a vision of an expanded tonality which
he then applied to works such as the song *Lockung*, Op. 6, No. 7, and to the First
Chamber Symphony, Op. 9. For the strict, card-carrying formalist, the work of
art is hermetically sealed. My favorite formalist is Clive Bell, for he minces no
words when declaring his formalism:

The rapt philosopher, and he who contemplates a work of art, inhabit a
world with an intense and peculiar significance of its own; that significance is
unrelated to the significance of life. In this world the emotions of life find no
place. It is a world with emotions of its own. To appreciate a work of art we

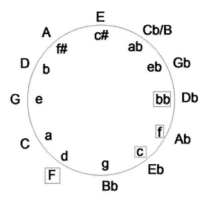

Example 6. Source regions and frame regions in an E-major tonality.

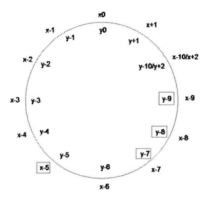

Example 7. Circle of fifths as variables, with source regions [y-7, y-8, y-9] and frame region [x-5].

need bring with us nothing but a sense of form and colour and a knowledge of three-dimensional space. [9]

And despite his avowed inabilities when it comes to criticizing music, he extends his formalism to negate the possibility that music might have any relationship to life, to the form or formal "significance" of life: "But at moments I do appreciate music as pure musical form, as sounds combined according to the laws of a mysterious necessity, as pure art with a tremendous significance of its own and no relation whatever to the significance of life. . . ."[10]

The late David Lewin spoke of approaching musical works by enlisting the aid of different colored lenses, meaning different theoretical frameworks.

[9]Clive Bell, *Art* (Oxford: Oxford University Press, 1987), 26-27.
[10]Ibid., 31.

So, for example, he might on one day look upon a work through the aid of Schenkerian spectacles, but then trade these for the perspectives of transformational theory, his own approach to analysis that has since become for music theorists a particularly profitable means of envisioning a work in formalist terms.[11]

In this essay, I shall switch from formalist lenses to a perspective informed by the writings of Theodor Adorno, formalism's very antipode. Adorno is dismissed regularly by formalists (in both classical and popular music studies) on account of his inability to appreciate music in their terms.[12] That is to say he cannot approach the musical artwork as an object of aesthetic value in and of itself (for example, along lines of the analysis above), value being thus an attribute of the work *sui generis*. Adorno can be read profitably, however, from the perspective of diagnostic value—that the value of a work lies in its ability to diagnose and thus illuminate the world outside itself. I shall read Adorno's appreciation of Schoenberg's Symphony and its relation to the twelve-tone technique in this manner—as a diagnosis—throughout the remainder of this essay, although I shall put myself from time to time in the guise of formalist so as to illuminate formalism's inherent differences with Adorno.

As a Marxist working in the world of Late Capitalism, or the Late Bourgeois as Adorno calls it, he makes a consistently unpleasant diagnosis of musical works in light of their world. And thus formalists, confusing Adorno's properly diagnostic approach with their own formalist aesthetic approach, dismiss him as unsympathetic, when in truth his very objectivity as a Marxist diagnostician demands that he be anti-sympathetic to such attributes as a work's formal aesthetic appearance. A particularly untoward development stems from this formalist misunderstanding of Adorno's project: the works which Adorno appears to dismiss in formalist aesthetic terms—for example, the repertoires of popular music and jazz—are in truth the repertoires most important to him as diagnostics. If he disparages a repertoire in aesthetic terms, as he does jazz and popular music, he does so on account of the world they diagnose, and not necessarily on account of the repertoire's formal aesthetic qualities. In truth it can be said that Adorno values a work of music in a directly converse proportion to its aesthetic disparagement at his hands: the more he rails against its aesthetic form, the more it rises in his esteem as a diagnostic.

It is for this reason that Adorno can value so highly Schoenberg's twelve-tone technique as a diagnostic while he disparages it so savagely in many of his

---

[11]See David Lewin, *Generalized Musical Intervals and Transformations* (New Haven: Yale University Press (1987), and Lewin, *Musical Form and Transformation: 4 Analytic Essays* (New Haven: Yale University Press, 1993).

[12]See, for example, Richard Middleton, *Studying Popular Music* (Milton Keynes: Open University Press, 1990), Chapter 2, and Theodore A. Gracyk, "Adorno, Jazz and the Aesthetics of Popular Music," *Musical Quarterly* 76/4 (Winter 1992): 526-42.

writings.[13] Mistaking Adorno's appreciation of the twelve-tone method as an aesthetic critique, formalists (in particular popular music scholars) denigrate Adorno as a twelve-tone elitist. By doing so, they ignore the fact that in Schoenberg's twelve-tone works, he diagnoses much the same symptoms of a malady displayed by jazz and even Stravinsky, as this essay's epigraph borrowed from Adorno suggests.[14] And since this diagnostic in the form of disparagement covers by extension the Chamber Symphony as well as Schoenberg's late works, the epigraph applies to the former as equally as to the latter.

In concluding this essay, I want to clarify the diagnostic aspect of Adorno's approach by examining remarks about Schoenberg's First Chamber Symphony made in *Philosophy of New Music*. The remarks are framed by Adorno's critique of the twelve-tone method, and should be seen in light of that critique. Let us begin by quoting Adorno on the first theme to Schoenberg's Symphony:

> If the young Schoenberg recognized that from the main theme of the First Chamber Symphony no "consequences" in the traditional sense could be drawn, the interdiction contained in that recognition remains in force for twelve-tone technique altogether. If one serial tone is as good as any other, how is it possible to "form a transition" without tearing the dynamic categories of form away from the compositional substance?[15]

Adorno says that in traditional music composition (with presumably middle-period Beethoven as its apogee) certain "consequences" were to be drawn from a theme, and that these consequences had a dynamic formal role—to form a transition, for example. The possibility of creating form by projecting consequences from a theme was inherent in the very "compositional substance," the material with which the composer worked. The compositional substance in Beethoven's music, for example, was diatonic tonality, where transitional passages would be in keys other than the tonic. The diatonic theme would be differentiated from chromatic transitions. As Adorno suggests, this differentiation lies within the compositional substance of the theme—its inherent diatonicism, compared with the work's transitions.

In essence, form rests upon a differentiation in pitch material, realized in the differentiation of a theme and its consequences (such as a transition). In a serial work, however, all tones are equal in kind—"as good as any other." All pitches are equal, and thus no distinction between diatonic and chromatic can be drawn inherently. And thus formal differentiation is impossible, unless one draws from the row (or forces upon it) categories of form to which it is inimical by its very nature.

---

[13]See, in particular, Theodor Adorno, *Philosophy of New Music*, trans. and ed. Robert Hullot-Kentor (Minneapolis: University of Minnesota Press, 2006).

[14]Ibid., 50.

[15]Ibid., 77-78.

When he speaks of the first theme of Schoenberg's Symphony, Adorno refers, I believe, to the cycle of fifths given to the French horn. He draws the conclusion, as I do, that there is a serial ethos to this theme—that none of the pitches is inherently different from any other pitch as a central point of tonal reference. Instead, in both twelve-tone works and Op. 9, identity resides in pre-determinate intervallic relationships—be it the complex of relationships inherent in the row or the simple fifth relationships of Op. 9.

Adorno's reading differs markedly from my formalist reading in its conclusions. In Adorno's case, Schoenberg stands on the verge of formal disintegration. In my case, fifth relation becomes merely another vehicle of form—a tonicizing musical idea (to be differentiated with other ideas such as the whole-tone relationships drawn at rehearsal number 2 in the cello solo, or at rehearsal number 11). Setting my formalist argument to one side, let us pursue Adorno's twelve-tone critique in the remainder of the essay. We begin with a lengthy quotation that stands at the heart of his critique:

> Every row is as much "the" row as the previous one was, no more, no less; it is even accidental which one counts as the "basic" row. What, then, does "development" mean? Each tone is thematically worked out in terms of its relation to the row and none is "free"; the various parts can produce a greater or fewer number of combinations, but none can bind itself more closely to the material than can the first statement of the row. The totality of the thematic labor in the preliminary forming of the material makes a tautology of the visible thematic labor in the composition itself. This is why "development," ultimately, in the sense of strict construction, becomes illusory . . . .[16]

In this quotation, Adorno places great value upon development, upon a free relationship of developmental tones to a theme, a relationship that allows for a distinction between developmental tones in terms of how closely they "bind" themselves to the theme. Secondly, he places great stock in a visible thematic labor—a working out—that relies upon this free relationship of tone to theme.

Neither free relationship nor authentic thematic labor is to be found in the twelve-tone technique, which Adorno thus disparages. In twelve-tone composition, all rows are fundamentally equal through the operation of transposition, inversion, and retrogression ("prime" being merely a term of convenience), for a twelve-tone work consists in principal entirely of row statements. There is no distinction, no differentiation, to be drawn between pitches thematic and developmental, for all pitches are part of the "row" and thus all pitches are thematic.

On Adorno's account, then, thematic development in twelve-tone music (achieved, for example, by exploiting the combinatorial properties of the row)

[16]Ibid., 78.

is illusory; serial composition is not a bona fide vehicle for creating developmental form. The only real process of forming takes place in the "preliminary forming of the material," as the composer plays freely with tones before locking them into the final form of the row. Every compositional act that takes place after the row is settled has thus been predetermined. Composition is merely the repetition of the row, albeit with considerable superficial variation, but at heart merely repetition. It follows that any subsequent shaping process that a composer tries to impose upon the form of a work is illusory. As Adorno points out in the passage quoted as this chapter's epigraph, any development of a theme that would take upon itself a historical character (as in the sonata form) is rendered inappropriate by the predetermined repetitive nature of the tone row: history is negated by the repetition of the row in twelve-tone composition. In this regard the twelve-tone works are the perfect diagnostic (alongside jazz and Stravinsky) of a world that "no longer knows history."[17]

We do not need to take the point of view of an orthodox or even "vulgar" Marxist to discern a faint whiff of commodity fetishism here. A discrepancy lies between what the work is thought to offer its listeners in terms of form and the truth—it offers little more than an illusion of form, a falsehood. This is the sort of discrepancy—between promise and reality—that lies at the heart of the bourgeois fetish for commodities. The discrepancy is merely complemented by Adorno's reference to the estrangement of two forms of labor: real (or useful) labor, which the composer brings to bear upon creating the row, and a phony labor (congealed labor-time linked to the commodifying of the work for the purposes of exchange) exerted so as to dress the work up, to give it a phony spontaneity.[18] This is at heart merely the timeless Marxist distinction between use and exchange value, and it arrives at the constant conclusion about fetishism and commodities—that commodity fetishism discerns a mystical sense of bona fide creation where in truth all valid creation has long since been replaced with emptiness, in this instance the empty repetition of the row.[19] Thus Adorno refers to twelve-tone works such as the Woodwind Quintet, Op. 26, with its sonata forms, as "constructed; its form has in a sense been petrified in twelve-tone technique in which the "dynamic components of the form stand like monuments to the past."[20] This is all too reminiscent of Lukács's *second nature*[21]

[17]On repetitive forms such as the fugue, see Patricia Carpenter, "Musical Form Regained," *Journal of Philosophy* 62/2 (January 21, 1965): 36-48; Carpenter, "The Janus-Aspect of Fugue: An Essay in the Phenomenology of Musical Form" (Ph.D. diss., Columbia University, 1971); and Dineen, "Fugue, Space, Noise, and Form," *International Studies in Philosophy* 36/1 (2004): 39-60.

[18]See Karl Marx, *Capital: A Critique of Political Economy*, vol. 1, trans. Ernst Mandel (London: Penguin, 1990), 130-31.

[19]See ibid., 163-65.

[20]Adorno, *Philosophy of New Music*, 78.

[21]See Georg Lukács, *The Theory of the Novel: A Historico-Philosophical Essay on the Forms of Great Epic Literature*, trans. Anna Bostock (Cambridge: M.I.T. Press, 1971), 63-64.

and Benjamin's archaicisms.[22] For Adorno, then, the twelve-tone technique kills the sense of time that integrates a theme with its developments.[23] As he writes:

> The continuum of subjective experiential time is no longer believed to have the power to integrate musical events and, as their unity, to give them meaning. Such discontinuity, however, kills the musical dynamic to which music owes its own existence. Once again [in twelve-tone composition] music masters time—but no longer by guaranteeing its fulfillment, but rather by negating time through the suspension of all music elements as a result of omnipresent construction.[24]

Having made the assertion that twelve-tone composition negates musical time by suspending the free relationship of tone to theme through the omnipresent preconstructed row, Adorno then makes the assertion, as noted above, that links Schoenberg to jazz and to Stravinsky: negation in these three instances is but a reflection of negation in the external world. The section following, entitled "The Idea of Twelve-Tone Technique," is nothing short of a wholesale damnation of Schoenberg's method.[25]

If all this appears as heresy to my formalist aesthetic ear attuned to the niceties of Schoenberg's row forms, I must remember that Adorno's task here is not to praise the composer but to diagnose—if not him directly, then his late capitalist world. As the vehicle of this diagnosis, Schoenberg's twelve-tone works are what Adorno calls in the following quotation a "canon of aesthetic objectification." By their rigidity, the row forms serve as a vehicle for an objective critique, one in which aesthetics, seen in its proper light as a diagnostic means, is put to a truly objective diagnostic status well beyond the limitations of formalism:

> The subject of new music, what its deposition transcribes, is the real, emancipated, isolated subject of the late bourgeois period. This real subjectivity, and the radical material that it has integrally structured, provides Schoenberg with a canon of aesthetic objectification. It is the measure of the depth of his work.[26]

In a lengthy and disturbing section entitled "Musical Domination of Nature," Adorno links Schoenberg with Oswald Spengler as diagnosticians of the bourgeois need for domination, for the repression of autonomy and freedom, this made manifest, as

---

[22]See Adorno, "A Portrait of Walter Benjamin," in *Prisms*, trans. Samuel and Shierry Weber (London: Spearman, 1967), 233.

[23]And in truth he discerns redeeming features in some of Schoenberg's early twelve-tone works, in the suites Opp. 25 and 29, for example, and in the rondo of the Third String Quartet, as well as what he calls "his most recent works," where the petrified sonata form is taken apart and reconstituted in a manner more sympathetic to the technique of the twelve-tone technique (*Philosophy of New Music*, 78).

[24]Adorno, *Philosophy of New Music*, 50.

[25]See ibid., 50-52.

[26]Ibid., 48.

Adorno puts it, in "a longing rising out of the primordial age of the bourgeoisie: to seize all that sounds in a regulatory grasp and [thus] dissolve the magic of music in human reason."[27] Domination "breaks through uncloaked," according to Spengler's appreciation, at the "end of the bourgeois era." Adorno says:

> Twelve-tone technique . . . is closer to that [bourgeois] ideal than Spengler, or indeed Schoenberg would have allowed himself to consider. . . . [T]welve-tone technique approaches the ideal of mastery as domination, whose boundlessness consists in the exclusion of whatever is heteronymous, of whatever is not integrated into the continuum of this technique.[28]

In other words, the twelve-tone technique is linked by the dominating rigidity of the row to a bourgeois society in which freedom too is subject to a domination equally rigid in both nature and application.

Again the formalist within me takes exception to these theses, since they do not accord the absolute aesthetics of a work's integrity. The formalist would ask: why introduce these unnecessary, extraneous elements—the row as predeterminate, the violation of time and history—into our appreciation of Schoenberg's works, which, being so carefully constructed, stand as absolute things in their own right, *l'art pour l'art*, as Schoenberg put it?[29]

The answer in properly formalist terms is that one is free to listen to Schoenberg as one will, and to change lenses in the way David Lewin did (although to my knowledge none of his lenses were tinged with a Marxist hue). But if one is to answer the question as Adorno might, to see Schoenberg through Adorno's lenses (were that possible, since our time is not his), one is constrained in this world of Late Capitalism to set aside the notion of a musical absolute, much as Schoenberg on Adorno's account was constrained to adopt the twelve-tone method by the nature of his bourgeois world. On the formalist account, Schoenberg's choice of the twelve-tone method was an act of free will. On Adorno's account, however, Schoenberg's development of the twelve-tone technique (by means of antecedents such as the First Chamber Symphony) had about it just as little freedom as did the relationship of the individual tone to the row form from which it springs.

[27]Ibid., 52-53.
[28]Ibid., 53.
[29]See Schoenberg, *Style and Idea*, 123

Precedents of Schoenberg's Compositional Practice in the Chamber Works of Joseph Haydn

Bryan Proksch

Arnold Schoenberg frequently resorted to citing works by canonic composers to elucidate similar traits in his own works. This mindset led him to argue that, among other things, Brahms was a "progressive" and Bach was a "twelve-tone" composer. Schoenberg never took a similar stance on Joseph Haydn's music in his essays, but as will be seen his analyses of Haydn's music frequently demonstrate the ways in which he appropriated central traits of Haydn's style in his own works. This paper will investigate the extent of Schoenberg's interest in Haydn, and the relevance of this interest to Schoenberg's compositional practice. There are a number of striking parallels between the two composers' practices, and these are especially evident in their respective chamber works. An examination of Schoenberg's analyses of Haydn's music and Schoenberg's approach to composition will demonstrate the ways in which Schoenberg adapted salient traits from Haydn's musical style in his own compositions, including the Second String Quartet in F-sharp minor, Op. 10.

Schoenberg had an extensive knowledge of Haydn's chamber music. He owned, analyzed, and even played many of Haydn's mature string quartets. While he appears to have been less familiar with most of Haydn's quartets prior to the Op. 20 set, there is ample evidence from in-score annotations and published analyses that he knew a large percentage of the quartets from Op. 20 all the way to the final Op. 77 set. Similarly, he knew many of Haydn's piano sonatas, though in this genre surviving evidence indicates that he had a detailed knowledge only of the works from Hob. XVI: 28-48. While Schoenberg owned the scores of a large number of Haydn's piano trios, the only work in this genre he ever analyzed was Hob. XV: 29.[1]

Haydn's music stands out in Schoenberg's library for the large number of scores that contain handwritten analyses. A similar number of analyses appear in

---

[1] A detailed discussion of Schoenberg's knowledge of Haydn is available in Bryan Proksch, "Haydn's 'London' Symphony and Schoenberg's Analytic Methods," in *Eisenstadt Haydn-Berichte* 3, ed. Georg Feder and Walter Reicher (Tutzing: Hans Schneider, 2004) 11-29.

Bryan Proksch is an Assistant Professor of musicology and music theory at McNeese State University in Lake Charles, Louisiana. He has published articles on cyclic integration in the music of the Classical era, Schoenberg's reception of Haydn, Kent Kennan's use of quartal harmony, and the trumpet in Baroque England. Dr. Proksch earned his Ph.D. in 2006 from the University of North Carolina at Chapel Hill.

his scores of Bach, Beethoven, Brahms, Mahler, and Mozart. This indicates the esteem in which he held Haydn's music. More importantly it means that although Schoenberg would never write an extended essay on Haydn, we can nevertheless create a clear picture of Schoenberg's views on Haydn's music through these scores as well as his occasional references to Haydn in his essays and textbooks.

In general, Schoenberg stands apart from his late nineteenth- and early twentieth-century counterparts in that he—unlike Robert Schumann, Adolph Bernhard Marx, and others—did not let his interest in Beethoven's music dissuade him from making a serious inquiry into Haydn's practice. On occasion Schoenberg even defended Haydn's practice in the face of criticism by others. For instance, Richard Wagner attacked Haydn's approach to harmony, specifically the way in which he resorted to multiple cadences to define a new key area, as part of what was "grandfatherly" about "Papa" Haydn's music. Schoenberg argued that Wagner was in error on two points.[2] First, he noted that a single cadence alone is insufficient to defining a new key, therefore Haydn's cadences were nothing more than a necessity for solidifying a modulation. Second, he argued that any "grandfatherly" tendencies in Haydn's music were a result of a compromise on Haydn's part to assist the audience in understanding his harmonic goals. In this sense Haydn was aiding his audience without compromising on issues such as distant key relationships and striking harmonic motion.

In applying his own unique brand of music analysis to Haydn's music— by analyzing this repertoire for *Grundgestalten*, developing variation, and formal patterns—Schoenberg tacitly recognized Haydn's innovations and compositional accomplishments while at the same time affirming Haydn's continuing relevance to music theory and to Schoenberg's own compositional practice. Relative to other early twentieth-century theorists and musicologists, Schoenberg was essentially half a century ahead of his time in his understanding of Haydn. This interest in Haydn's music was also inherited by some of his most influential disciples, including for instance Rudolph Réti and Hans Keller. Yet in the end Schoenberg's interest in Haydn was driven at least in part by his desire to link the practice of the Second Viennese School to its heritage in the traditions of the First Viennese School, giving Schoenberg's inquiry a distinctly personal flavor.

Schoenberg's Analyses of Haydn's Music

Schoenberg's published and unpublished analyses demonstrate his interest in several areas of Haydn's style, including form, phrase structure, harmony, and developing variation. He uncovered instances of developing variation in Haydn's music on a par with that of most other composers. Schoenberg also took a particular interest in the ways in which Haydn maintained a sense of

[2]Arnold Schoenberg, "Problems of Harmony," in *Style and Idea: Selected Writings of Arnold Schoenberg*, trans. Leo Black (Berkeley: University of California Press, 1975), 274.

coherence and intelligibility while simultaneously including irregularities and idiosyncrasies of style. Many of Schoenberg's analyses note things such as odd-measured phrases and unexpected twists that were peculiar to Haydn's music and in some way at odds with more conventional Classical-era works. The question for Schoenberg was how Haydn managed to integrate these oddities into compositions that somehow maintained a logical and understandable framework.

Of all the diverse ways in which Schoenberg analyzed Haydn's music, his most sustained interest was in Haydn's use of odd or unconventional phrase structures. Schoenberg's interest in Haydn's phrase structures was, in a sense, a study of the ways in which one could foster a sense of intelligibility and regularity without the aid of conventional gestures. Schoenberg tells us in his 1947 essay "Brahms the Progressive" that asymmetric phrase structures eliminate one of the "most efficient aids to comprehension."[3] The creation of comprehension in the absence of a tonal framework was, naturally, a problem that Schoenberg had to address in his own works. He latched onto Haydn in his examination of irregular phrase structure because "irregularity is more frequently present" in his works than in Beethoven's.[4] His consistent reference to Haydn's minuets is particularly insightful, considering that regular phrase patterns were the expected norm in this stylized dance form. Schoenberg points out that Haydn's departures from conventional phrase structure were a result of his emotional approach to composition, as if Haydn worked in the "realm of song," and indicate a dismissal of abstract "dance music." He goes on to argue that Haydn's phrase structures were similar in conception and emotional content to the music of Brahms.

Schoenberg approaches Haydn's irregular phrase structures from two different angles. In some cases, such as in the minuet of Op. 76/2 ("Quinten"), he sees a connection back to the contrapuntal unfolding and spinning out of phrases used by J.S. Bach (Example 1). Schoenberg notes that the use of canon in this minuet creates an ambiguity of phrase length atypical of a dance movement. The phrase can be divided in sections of either 5+6 measures (divided at m. 6) or 4+4+3 (divided at mm. 4 and 8), depending upon which voice takes precedence.[5] Schoenberg saw this movement as Baroque in conception and structure, an example of Baroque influence lingering in the background of Haydn's art.

Schoenberg also saw an emphasis on small-scale rhythmic/motivic development as the driving force behind Haydn's odd-measured phrase structures. He examines another minuet, that of Haydn's String Quartet in G

---

[3]Schoenberg, "Brahms the Progressive," in *Style and Idea*, 411.

[4]Ibid., 410.

[5]Arnold Schoenberg, *Fundamentals of Musical Composition*, ed. Gerald Strang and Leonard Stein (New York, 1967), 142 and 146. There are of course additional possibilities for breaking up this phrase that Schoenberg does not mention (5+6 seems equally valid, for example).

Example 1. Schoenberg's analysis of Haydn's String Quartet in D minor ("Quinten"), Op. 76/2/iii.[6]

Example 2. Schoenberg's Analysis of Haydn's String Quartet in G Major, Op. 54/1/iii (bold/large print denotes Schoenberg's analysis, *italics* denote my additional remarks, ossia is Schoenberg's).[7]

[6]In creating these examples I have used the editions owned by Schoenberg, even in cases where a newer critical edition is available.

[7]Arnold Schoenberg, *Fundamentals of Musical Composition*, 26 and 141-42, with examples taken from 34 and 145-46.

major Op. 54/1, in exactly this manner in two separate sections of *Fundamentals of Musical Composition* (harmonic caesura and minuet form). Example 2 is a composite of these analyses created by combining Schoenberg's prose comments with his musical examples.

Haydn's approach to irregular phrases evolves over the course of the movement, and this was of great import for Schoenberg. He begins by pointing out the ten-measure phrases of Op. 54/1/iii and the manner in which Haydn created an irregular-length phrase (5+5) by stretching and distorting a standard eight-measure (4+4) period structure. The ossia above the top system of Example 2 shows Schoenberg's reconstruction of the "original" undistorted eight-measure period. The A and A[1] sections of this work both maintain a rigid adherence to five-measure sub-phrases. The deceptive cadence at measure 34, as shown in the second system of the example, forces the movement into an additional coda phrase. In this coda, Haydn changes his approach to the ten-measure phrase by building it using a sentence structure commencing with a rest (1+9). Schoenberg argues that this change in phrase structure gives the movement a sense of closure that would not have been possible by simply ending the movement with another 5+5-measure period. In essence, the regularity Haydn set up using an irregular 5+5-measure phrase needed to change before the movement could reach a point of closure.

Rhythmic and motivic development lie at the heart of this movement's irregular phrase structures. The motives marked "a" and "a′″" by Schoenberg receive constant developmental attention throughout the movement. In the opening phrase Haydn repeats both "a" and "a′." A further-developed form of "a′″" appears at measure 7. The descending eighth-note run in the first violin (which I have labeled as motive "b" in the example) is related to similar gestures in the viola in measure 4 and cello in measure 5. Haydn unexpectedly inserts motive "b" at measure 8 to help round out the phrase by developing a secondary motive, and this insertion creates the altered ten-measure period.

In contrast to the extractable insertions of the movement's opening phrase, the closing phrase is an excellent example of the use of organic growth through motivic liquidation. None of the measures in this final phrase could be extracted without destroying its integrity; each measure is essential. In measures 39-42, Haydn liquidates the "a" motive through constant repetition. This integral "phrase extension," as Schoenberg thought of it, is a much different approach to the distortion of phrase structure than seen in the movement's other phrases.[8] It is markedly closer in practice to the continual growth of developing variation than it is to a normal period construction.

---

[8]In his score of the finale of Haydn's String Quartet in C major, Op. 76/3, Schoenberg labels a similar passage with the word "extension."

In fact, developing variation is at the heart of what is happening in this quartet movement. Schoenberg also latches onto Haydn's rhythmic variations in this movement in much the same way that he does with the development of melodic motives. The dotted anacrusis gesture of "a" becomes an even eighth-note anacrusis already in the second measure, by which time it has been metrically displaced to the downbeat. When the final phrase of the example arrives (mm. 39ff.), the anacrusis in both forms (dotted and even) becomes a center of motivic development. This rhythmic development provides a sense of closure to the movement in much the same way as the changing phrase structure, as Haydn finally exhausts the various possibilities for this rhythmic gesture.

How did this type of phrase and motivic analysis translate into Schoenberg's compositional practice? The opening phrase of his Second String Quartet in F-sharp minor, Op. 10 (Example 3), actually commences with a five-measure antecedent phrase. A brief moment of stasis follows in measure 6, before Schoenberg concludes the phrase with a "normal" four-measure consequent. The heart of this opening, like Haydn's, is a sentence structure reliant on the development of a short rhythmic motive. Despite the oddity of opening with a five-measure phrase, Schoenberg maintains a sense of intelligibility through consistency of motive and an underlying conventional phrase structure. When one takes the measures of stasis into account, the actual amount of time passing in the opening is a regular eight measures, yet the stasis hides this regularity. This is Schoenberg's solution to creating a normal-sounding phrase that is simultaneously conventional and unconventional. It is, above all, intelligible as a parallel period despite its departures from a four-measure norm.

Developing variation, naturally, is at the center of this opening phrase. The "a" and "a‴" motives marked in the example show how Schoenberg's treatment parallels Haydn's in its use of sentence structure and motivic development. At measure 10, the motive receives further development as an "a′‴" motive. The rhythm constantly shifts from dotted eighth-notes to straight eighth-notes, and the placement of each within the meter changes from measure to measure. Severine Neff has shown that this opening phrase is the *Grundgestalt* or basic complex of ideas that Schoenberg develops over the course of the entire Quartet, in much the same way as Haydn consistently developed a small handful of motives to create an intelligible structure in Op. 54/1/iii.[9] Schoenberg's Op. 10 includes all the salient traits of Haydn's developmental technique writ large.

---

[9]Arnold Schoenberg, *The Second String Quartet in F-sharp minor, opus 10*, ed. Severine Neff (New York: W.W. Norton, 2006), 129ff.

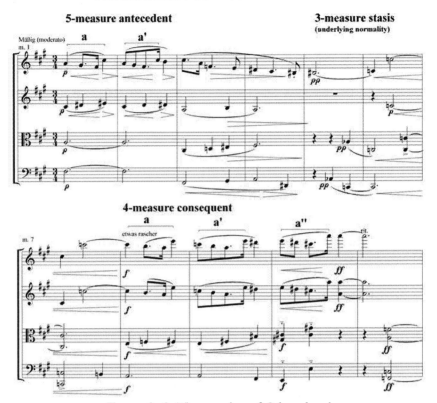

Example 3. The opening of Schoenberg's
Second String Quartet in F-sharp minor, Op. 10.

Schoenberg's Interest in Haydn's Harmonic Language

Outside of phrase analysis and motivic development, Schoenberg's other analytic interest in Haydn revolves around harmonic language. He concentrates in particular on Haydn's use of harmonic alteration as an element of developing variation. In fact, he cites harmonic development as one of Haydn's primary innovations as a composer. He felt that Haydn did more with less material than most other composers. In *Structural Functions of Harmony*, Schoenberg hints at a preference for Haydn's harmonic economy and ingenuity:

> Long segments of a Haydn theme may be based on one or two harmonies only, while the first theme of Schumann's Piano Quintet requires a rich succession of harmonies. Nevertheless, [as my analyses show], the distance of [harmonic] regions reached in Haydn's "Surprise" symphony is greater than that of those in Schumann's example.[10]

[10]Schoenberg, *Structural Functions of Harmony* (New York: W.W. Norton, 1969), 164.

Figure 1: Schoenberg's analysis of Haydn's String Quartet in C major ("Emperor"), Op. 76/3/ii (*top:* the theme; *bottom:* variation IV).[11]

Schoenberg similarly derides the theme and variation movements of Handel and the Baroque in a similar fashion, calling them "annoying" because of their focus on pianistic figuration at the expense of substantive development. He then cites the slow movement of Haydn's String Quartet in C major, Op. 76/3 ("Emperor") as an instance of the enrichment of harmony propelling a set of variations and maintaining the listeners' interest (Figure 1).[12] In this slow

[11] *Structural Functions of Harmony*, 90-91

[12] Arnold Schoenberg, *Fundamentals of Musical Composition*, ed. Leonard Stein, (New York: W.W. Norton, 1969), 164.

movement, unity appears in the recurring theme while harmonic changes provide the much-needed variety that sustains the listeners' interest throughout.

Schoenberg specifically cites the fourth variation of Haydn's movement for its use of harmonic development. Haydn opens the variation off-tonic on a submediant chord (vi) which at first glance seems to be nothing more than the cliché gesture introducing a conventional *minore* variation. This turns out not to be the case, as the variation remains in the tonic major despite the opening chord. Haydn moves to major by including a number of secondary chords that help him modulate to the dominant at the end of the A phrase. The variation then continues in major and concludes with a strong tonic major cadence. Schoenberg interprets the appearance of the submediant chord at the outset of this variation as a development of the tonic chord, a substitute of sorts that is as much a harmonic element of developing variation as the inserted secondary dominant chords.

Haydn's harmonic elaboration also appears in the B and A¹ phrases of the fourth variation. The B phrase of this variation is a four-measure dominant pedal, as in the first appearance of the theme. However, this time Haydn does not terminate his pedal to prepare for the A¹ phrase; the pedal instead continues to sound throughout the entirety of the B phrase. The A¹ phrase is the most heavily altered phrase of the variation. Haydn vastly increases his harmonic rhythm now, to the point where secondary chords appear on practically every eighth note. Harmonic variation and development appear pervasively in this movement. For Schoenberg, Haydn's variation procedures here (and throughout the set) are premised on harmony rather than melody, a fact underscored by Haydn's unwillingness to alter the melody in any way over the course of the fourth variation.

The theme of Op. 76/3/ii, Haydn's "Kaiser-Hymn," attracted Schoenberg's compositional interest in 1925, when he wrote a chamber-ensemble arrangement of Johann Strauss Jr.'s "Emperor Waltz." Schoenberg discovered that the opening of Haydn's melody fit contrapuntally with Strauss's waltz and decided to include fragments of the hymn throughout his arrangement as a countermelody. While this combination of Kaiser-related compositions was probably more due to the status of the hymn as a national anthem at a time of political strife than it was a response to Haydn's quartet movement, it nevertheless stands as another example of Schoenberg showing an affinity for Haydn in his chamber music.[13]

---

[12]Facsimile of Leonard Stein's manuscript proofs courtesy of the Arnold Schoenberg Center, the Leonard Stein Satellite Collection.

[13]Zoë Lang proposed that Schoenberg's inclusion was meant as a political statement opposed to radicalism in the Austrian government at the time. Zoë Lang, "Johann Strauss Jr.'s Emperor Waltz (1889) as Cultural Symbol," Conference of the Southern Chapter of the American Musicological Society (29 February 2008).

In the theme and variations movement of Schoenberg's Second String Quartet, harmony is not varied in the same way as in Haydn's quartet. In fact, each of the five variations in the slow movement of Op. 10 appears on pitch and with the same basic harmonic motion. Perhaps Schoenberg opted to retain his harmonic motion in each variation because this is one of the few elements that readily delineate the movement's form. After stating his opening motive, Schoenberg's variations head off in many different directions. Haydn's harmonic changes reflect a desire to keep things interesting within a highly predictable structure. Schoenberg's lack of changes indicates a desire to maintain formal coherence throughout a set of very unpredictable variations. It is unfortunate that Op. 76/6 was the only one of Haydn's Op. 76 quartets that Schoenberg neither owned nor, apparently, analyzed. The slow, fantasia, movement of that work is arguably Haydn's most harmonically ingenious. It opens in B major but modulates to G major ($\flat$VI), B$\flat$ major ($\flat$I), and A flat major ($\flat\flat$VII) over the course of its first sixty measures, $\flat$I is rarely seen, of course, because it is so istant from the tonic, and Schoenberg thought of this region as a transformative tonic, a key area that threatens to break the very system of tonality.[14] Yet Schoenberg's Second String Quartet modulates to $\flat$I already at measure 11 (the last measure of Example 1) and $\flat$I is a crucial harmonic region for the entire Quartet. Perhaps Schoenberg knew Op. 76/6, or, what is more likely, perhaps his harmonic language was so rooted in the classical tradition that he, like Haydn, could not help but explore even the furthest regions of tonality.

Schoenberg's Reception of Haydn's Music

Having examined a number of Schoenberg's analyses, the question remains as to what he actually thought of Haydn's music, and its place in music history. To be sure, he saw Haydn as the composer who linked J.S. Bach's contrapuntal mode of composition with Beethoven's motivic mode of composition. This is also how he viewed Mozart in many ways, but Haydn and Mozart had somewhat different influences on the course of Schoenberg's version of music history. Haydn's innovations lay in his quirky phrase structures, and his insistence on the continuous development of motives and harmonies, while Mozart later took these innovations and furthered them.[15] Beethoven, using Haydn and Mozart's practice as guides, then found a way to instill dramatic function into his music.[16] In viewing Beethoven in this light, Schoenberg participated in a long tradition of German-language music criticism from the nineteenth century, and his views

---

[14]For a discussion of $\flat$I in the Quartet and Schoenberg's analytic writings see Neff, ed., *Second String Quartet*, 128ff.

[15]Schoenberg, *Structural Functions*, 149 and 167-68.

[16]E.g. Ibid., 153 and 167-68. Schoenberg notes the harmonic function of Haydn's and Mozart's slow introductions in comparison to the dramatic function of Beethoven's.

are remarkably similar to those of, for example, Richard Wagner, A.B. Marx, and E.T.A. Hoffmann. But unlike these earlier commentators, Schoenberg granted more than simple *precedence* to Haydn. In essence, he viewed Haydn as an equal to Mozart, as a palpable influence on Beethoven's practice, and did not participate in the typical dismissals of Haydn's music as old-fashioned or worn-out. Schoenberg was thus among the first theorists to reverse the nineteenth-century tendency to see Haydn as a subordinate and merely conventional or convention-defining composer.

Assessing Haydn's relative position in Schoenberg's grand scheme of music history is somewhat more difficult. For example, in his unfinished orchestration textbook, Schoenberg plotted out the ratio of examples to be included by each composer before beginning writing. He predetermined to have twenty percent of his examples taken from Beethoven and eighteen percent from Mozart. Haydn was his third-ranked composer at twelve percent.[17] In a revised version of this hypothetical table of contents, Haydn received a lesser percentage but was still ranked third in number of examples. A few of the examples for this text were actually written up for publication, including excerpts from the slow movements of Haydn's Symphonies Nos. 92 ("Oxford") and 100 ("Military"). Schoenberg's proposed reliance on Haydn in an orchestration text is all the more interesting considering the greater orchestral palates at the disposal of nineteenth-century composers. The simple fact that Schoenberg would include more examples from Haydn than from a number of later composers such as Berlioz, Strauss, and Mahler, indicates his regard for Haydn's sensitivity in matters of texture and timbre. The occasional comment in Schoenberg's published analyses supports this view of his esteem for Haydn's practice.

Just as Schoenberg preferred Haydn's orchestration, he favored Haydn's approach to theme and variation movements over those of Handel in particular, and the Baroque in general. In a letter to Pau Casals on his adaptation of a harpsichord concerto by G.M. Monn, Schoenberg remarked how he had "removed the defects of the Handelian style (prevailing in the original work)" by discarding empty sequences and replacing them with "real *substance*."[18] He did this in an effort to avoid making the theme seem more trivial with each appearance. In the end Schoenberg thought that he had "succeeded in making the whole thing approximate, say, to Haydn's style." By this he presumably meant that he had added elements of developing variation and had found a way to incorporate irregularity without disrupting the intelligibility of the music.

Schoenberg found a way to include other Haydnesque gestures in his music on a number of occasions. The similar approaches to developing variation in Haydn's Op. 76 quartets and Schoenberg's Op. 10, the "Haydnizing" of

---

[17]Schoenberg Center catalog #T-68-12-13 (with thanks to Eike Fess).

[18]Arnold Schoenberg, *Arnold Schoenberg Letters*, ed. Erwin Stein, trans. Eithne Wilkins and Ernst Kaiser (New York: St. Martins's Press, 1965), 171. Emphasis in original.

Monn's concerto, and the inclusion of Haydn's "Kaiser-Hymn" in Schoenberg's arrangement of Strauss Jr.'s "Kaiser-Waltz" are only the tip of the proverbial iceberg of parallels, both general and specific, between the two. It is difficult, for instance, not to hear the bright C major "Let there be light" moment of Haydn's oratorio *The Creation* when the sun rises in C major at the end of Schoenberg's oratorio *Gurrelieder*, for example. Schoenberg owned a copy of *The Creation* and, as evidenced by performance annotations in his score, he participated in at least one performance of this, one of Haydn's most popular works. There are also connections between the two composers' works of a more general nature. Schoenberg's placement of the Scherzo movements of the Op. 9 Chamber Symphony and of Op. 10 in the second position, ahead of the slow movement, harkens back to Haydn's practice in the Op. 33 quartets. In Op. 33 Haydn consistently placed his scherzi as second movements. Schoenberg owned copies of Op. 33/2-4, so would have been well aware of the precedent he was following when writing Op. 9.[19]

For Schoenberg, Haydn stands among the greatest historical composers in importance, lasting impact, compositional technique, and economy of means. He recognized Haydn's numerous innovations, the composer's transitional role on music written after Bach, and Haydn's influences on Beethoven and the music of the nineteenth century. Schoenberg's interest in Haydn's phrase structure, harmonic motion, and developing variation was intense, and he frequently used examples from Haydn's output to demonstrate the continuity of tradition from Bach's music up to his own time. And, as I have argued, there are distinct similarities between Haydn' chamber music and that of Schoenberg. Clearly Schoenberg's deep interest in Haydn's music influenced his musical practice, style, and approach to composition.

---

[19]It would seem that Schoenberg believed that Haydn's label of "Scherzo," typically referred to as part of the new style of Op. 33, was little more than a relabeling of a minuet: in the Scherzo chapter of *Fundamentals of Musical Composition* he makes no reference to Haydn's Op. 33 quartets.

OTTAWA SYMPOSIUM AND
CHAMBER MUSIC FESTIVAL

Opening of Multi-Media Exhibition ("Arnold Schoenberg: 1874-1951"),
Christ Church Cathedral, Ottawa, 25-31 July 2007.
(photo by Mike Heffernan)

Nuria Schoenberg-Nono opens the Exhibition.

(photo by Mike Heffernan)

Christian Meyer.
(photo by Mike Heffernan)

I Feel the Air of Another Planet (1990), Dennis Spiteri,
Acrylic on Canvas, 221 cm x 358 cm.
(reproduced by permission of the artist)

Nuria Schoenberg-Nono with James Wright.

The Carleton University student team (left to right): Erica Vincent, Kate Morrison, Brady Leafloor, Nate Meneer, Sarah Stephens, Curtis Perry, Dan Salinas.

Canadian composer Eldon Rathburn (1916-2008), attending
the opening of the Schoenberg Exhibition.
(photo by Mike Heffernan)

Ronald, Nuria, and Lawrence Schoenberg preparing their
conference presentation.
(photo by Barbara Schoenberg)

Severine Neff, Anne Schoenberg, and Ronald Schoenberg, under a giant bronze sculpture ("Maman" by Louise Bourgeois) outside the National Gallery of Canada, Ottawa.

Keynote speaker Allen Forte, with Madeleine Forte, outside the National Gallery of Canada, Ottawa.

Soprano Martha Guth and the Moscow String Quartet (Eugenia Alikhanova, Galina Kokhanovskaya, Tatiana Kokhanovskaya, Olga Ogranovitch), perform Schoenberg's String Quartet No. 2 in F-sharp minor, Op. 10, at the Ottawa International Chamber Music Festival, 26 July 2007.
(photo by Mike Heffernan)

The Vienna Trio (Wolfgang Redik, Stephan Mendl, Matthias Gredler) perform Eduard Steuermann's trio arrangement of Schoenberg's *Transfigured Night* at the Ottawa International Chamber Music Festival, 29 July 2007.
(photo by Mike Heffernan)

Lawrence and Ronald Schoenberg with Canadian composer Eldon Rathburn,
holding a photo taken of the young Schoenberg children
by Rathburn when he visited the family home in 1946.
(photo by Barbara Schoenberg)

Back (left to right): Christian Meyer, Ronald Schoenberg, Nuria Schoenberg-Nono, Lawrence Schoenberg, James Wright, Alan Gillmor, Susan Gillmor.

Front (left to right): John Frecker, Anne Schoenberg, Barbara Zeisl Schoenberg, Dennis Spiteri, Dianne Parsonage. Ottawa International Chamber Music Festival, 26-29 July 2007.

PERFORMANCE, RECEPTION, AND
INTERNATIONAL INFLUENCE

Echoes of *Pierrot Lunaire* in American Music

Sabine Feisst*

Few twentieth-century compositions have affected as many American composers as Schoenberg's melodrama cycle *Thrice Seven Poems from Albert Giraud's Pierrot Lunaire*, Op. 21, for *Sprechstimme* and mixed ensemble (1912). But since it is primarily seen as a potent model for European composers, we may not recognize how thoroughly the work has infiltrated American musical consciousness.[1] Its absence from accounts of American music can be attributed to historiographical efforts to minimize the impact of Europeans on American music, to "anxiety of influence" on the part of certain composers and to the fact that its once-new features are now customarily utilized. In any case there have been countless American compositions echoing *Pierrot*'s unique instrumentation, theatricality, musical language, cyclic structure, vocal treatment, and notation. American composers have paid tribute to *Pierrot* through imitation, quotation, "misreading," and parody in a variety of genres including chamber works, operas, and radio song-plays. What follows will elucidate the manifold influences of *Pierrot* on the music of several generations of American composers.

*Many thanks to Susan Youens, Don Gillespie, Therese Muxeneder (Arnold Schoenberg Center, Vienna), and Joseph Auner for their comments on previous drafts of this essay. I would also like to acknowledge the generous grant from the Deutsche Forschungsgemeinschaft which enabled me to do extensive research on this topic.

[1]See, for instance, Andreas Meyer, *Ensemblelieder in der frühen Nachfolge (1912-17) von Arnold Schönbergs "Pierrot lunaire": Eine Studie über Einfluß und "Misreading"* (Munich: Fink-Verlag, 2000).

Sabine Feisst is an Associate Professor of Music History and Literature at Arizona State University. Her research interests focus on the music of the twentieth and twenty-first centuries, including the music of Arnold Schoenberg, improvisation, experimental music, film music, and eco-criticism with respect to music. Her publications include the book *Der Begriff "Improvisation" in der neuen Musik* (The Idea of Improvisation in New Music, 1997) and chapters in *Schoenberg and His World* (1999), *Edgard Varèse. Composer, Sound Sculptor, Visionary (1883-1965)* (2006) and *Geschichte der Musik im 20. Jahrhundert, 1925-1945* (2006). She also contributed articles to *Archiv für Musikwissenschaft*, *The Musical Quarterly*, *Journal of the Arnold Schönberg Center*, *MusikTexte*, *Chamber Music America*, *The Cue Sheet*, and *21st-Century Music*.

Early Reactions

Early European *Pierrot* performances in the 1910s sparked heated debates in the American press. Many critics predictably dismissed it. Yet the work, available as a pocket score since 1914, soon aroused the interest of American composers. In 1915 experimental composer Henry Cowell, who later befriended Schoenberg, conceived the dramatic work *Red Silence* for speaker, flute, violin, cello, and piano. Charles Griffes, as interested in new musical currents as Cowell, also followed Schoenberg's developments with interest; and the unusual chamber instrumentation and theatrical implications of his *Sho-jo*, a pantomime, and *The Kairn of Koridwen*, a dance-drama (both 1917), show an obvious affinity with *Pierrot*. In 1917 Griffes himself informed a representative of the *New York American* about the *The Kairn*'s kinship with *Pierrot*.[2] Charles Ives also used *Sprechstimme* techniques and explored the mixed chamber ensemble with and without voice independently from Schoenberg, even before 1912. Yet Ives's music only gradually became known from the 1920s onward.[3]

The American *Pierrot* Premiere and Its Aftermath

After World War I, which had halted the American reception of *Pierrot*, Varèse and his newly founded International Composers' Guild organized the work's first performance in America. Louis Gruenberg, a Russian-American Busoni student, had witnessed a *Pierrot* performance in Berlin and directed the American première in February 1923 in New York City, with soprano Greta Torpadie.[4] The event was felt as the advent of something quite new.

A number of prominent composers were in the audience for this sold-out and much-discussed performance, including Marion Bauer, Carl Engel, George Gershwin, Frederick Jacobi, Carl Ruggles, Carlos Salzedo, Lazare

---

[2]*Sho-jo* was written for flute, clarinet, oboe, strings, harp, and percussion, and *The Kairn of Koridwen* for flute, two clarinets, two horns, harp, celesta, and piano (Philadelphia: Kallisti Music Press, 1993). See Edward Maisel, "Liner Notes," for *The Kairn of Koridwen* (Koch International Classics 3-7216-2, 1994).

[3]Ives used *Sprechstimme* in such songs as "Vote for Names!" (1912), "Soliloquy" (ca. 1913, rev. 1933), and "Nov. 2, 1920" (1920-21). Both Ives and Schoenberg were early in their careers musically active in theatres and cabarets, which may have been the inspiration for their utilization of small mixed ensembles. Some of the performers of the *Pierrot* world premiere were recruited from the salon orchestra of the Berlin "Nachtcafé Kutschera." See Gabriele Beinhorn, *Das Groteske in der Musik: Arnold Schönbergs 'Pierrot lunaire'* (Pfaffenweiler: Centaurus, 1989), 211-12; see also Bryan R. Simms, "Twentieth-Century Composers Return to the Small Ensemble," in *The Orchestra: Origins and Transformations*, ed. Joan Peyser (New York: Schirmer, 1986), 460-74.

[4]For more details see Claire Reis, *Composers, Conductors and Critics* (New York: Oxford University Press, 1955), 10-14. The event interfered with Schoenberg's plans for an American tour with *Pierrot* and *Gurrelieder*. "Schoenberg Doesn't Want His *Pierrot lunaire* Played" (*New York Herald*, 14 January 1923).

Saminsky, Varèse, and Emerson Whithorne. Many of them were undoubtedly inspired by *Pierrot* to pursue the composition of vocal chamber works.[5] Carl Ruggles was one of those who attended and remembered that everybody talked about the event and rushed to obtain scores. Ruggles himself reacted by quickly embarking on *Vox Clamans in Deserto* (1923-24), a projected cycle of seven songs for mezzo-soprano and chamber ensemble.[6] The cycle reflects Ruggles's typically generous use of dissonance and controlled repetition, but it is more contrapuntal and rhythmically more complex than such earlier works as *Angels* (1921). The vocal part (not conceived in *Sprechstimme*) comprises almost two octaves and a multitude of dissonant intervals and is rarely supported by the instruments. Moreover Ruggles also used *Pierrot* for teaching purposes, arranging "Der kranke Mond" (originally for flute and voice) for clarinet and horn and giving it the new title *Composition in Two Part Dissonant Counterpoint.*[7]

It may not have been pure coincidence that Otto Luening's *Soundless Song* for soprano, flute, clarinet, string quartet, piano, dancers, and light (1923-24) and Gruenberg's *Daniel Jazz* (1923), his first work for solo voice and chamber ensemble, were written right after *Pierrot* received its American premiere. Luening's seven-movement work comprises an unaccompanied spoken prologue, string quartet movements, woodwind duets, sections for voice and piano, and a tutti finale. It even features "a primitive kind of twelve-tone manipulation in the accompaniment around a diatonic melody set to [Luening's] own esoteric words."

[5]Responses to this event are documented in *Dossier de Presse de Pierrot lunaire d'Arnold Schönberg*, ed. François Lesure (Geneva: Minkoff, 1985), and David Metzer, "The Ascendancy of Musical Modernism in New York City, 1915-29" (Ph.D. diss., Yale University, 1993), 313-41, and "The New York Reception of 'Pierrot lunaire': The 1923 Premiere and Its Aftermath," *Musical Quarterly* 78/4 (Winter 1994): 669-99. However, several vocal chamber works influenced by *Pierrot* received American premieres in New York before *Pierrot*: Stravinsky's *Three Japanese Lyrics* in 1917, *Pribaoutki* in 1918 and *Berceuses du chat* in 1919; two of Maurice Delage's *Quatre poèmes hindous* in 1920, and Varèse's *Offrandes* in 1922. In 1920 Eva Gauthier gave a whole recital of vocal chamber music including Ravel's "Soupir" (from *Trois Poèmes de Mallarmé*) and works by Bainbridge Crist, Samuel Gardner, and Wintter Watts. Those performances, which received much less critical attention than *Pierrot*, together with the American premieres of Stravinsky's *Renard* (1915-16) in 1923, *Histoire du soldat* (1918) in 1924, and Webern's *Fünf geistliche Lieder* (1917-22) in 1926, all vocal chamber works, confirmed and increased the topicality of this medium, partly induced by jazz bands and theatre music groups.

[6]Marilyn Ziffrin, *Carl Ruggles: Composer, Painter, and Storyteller* (Urbana: University of Illinois Press, 1994), 84. The scoring is for flute, oboe, clarinet, bassoon, horn, two trumpets, a string sextet, and piano. He chose poems by Browning, Keats, Charles H. Meltzer, Shelley, and Whitman as well as a text of his own, but completed only three (Browning's "Parting at Morning," Meltzer's "Son of Mine," and Whitman's "A Clear Midnight"). The completed settings of *Vox Clamans in Deserto* were premiered at a concert of the International Composers' Guild in 1924. Torpadie was the vocalist and Salzedo the conductor. Unhappy with its premiere, Ruggles withdrew the work.

[7]On a separate note Ruggles reveals the purpose of this arrangement: "I think that's from *Pierrot lunaire* that was down in Florida, it may be called 'The Washerwoman' [sic]. I copied it for some of the students." Ruggles Papers, Yale University.

The second movement entitled "Moonlight" includes the *Pierrot*-like passage "I am wand'ring thru the pale moonlight of ages inhaling the perfume of unborn fruit."[8] Gruenberg's work, on the other hand, is based on a text by Vachel Lindsay and reveals (partly due to the replacement of the flute with a trumpet) the influence of American jazz bands and Stravinsky's *Histoire du soldat*. Soon to emerge as well were works for similar forces by Samuel Barlow, Frederick Jacobi, Richard Hammond, Lazare Saminsky, William Grant Still, and Emerson Whithorne.

Further American Performances and Reactions until World War II

Cowell, who after the American *Pierrot* premiere had composed *Four Combinations for Three Instruments* (1924) featuring *Pierrot*–like instrumental combinations changing in each of its four movements, reviewed the second New York *Pierrot* performance in 1925.[9] Declaring the work as a "classic of modern music" and as a "precursor of many recent chamber works by others," he also remarked on its unprecedented "stripped to the bone" economy, form, and strange vocal treatment.[10] In 1930 Cowell gave *Pierrot*'s West Coast premiere in San Francisco and introduced it to composers like John Becker, John Cage, Lou Harrison, and Harry Partch. Considering *Pierrot* a unique adventure, Partch began to explore the musical "simulation of speech" with his *Lyrics by Li Po* (1930-33) for intoning voice and adapted viola and credited Schoenberg for his *Sprechstimme* experiments. It is perhaps no coincidence that Partch recruited Rudolphine Radil, the vocalist of the West Coast *Pierrot* premiere, to perform his *Lyrics by Li Po*.[11]

---

[8]Otto Luening, *The Odyssey of an American Composer* (New York: Charles Scribner, 1980), 241, 484. It is, however, not certain whether Luening, who lived in Chicago at that time, attended the American *Pierrot* premiere. Yet, he would have read and heard much about this event. During his European sojourn (1912-20), he had the opportunity to discover the work. The *Soundless Song* is not published, but is recorded on Parnassus (PACD96-025, 1998).

[9]This performance, featuring again Torpadie as vocalist, was organized by the League of Composers, founded after an intense dispute over a proposed repeat performance of *Pierrot*. The premise of the International Composers' Guild was that works were not to be repeated.

[10]Henry Cowell, "America Takes Front Rank in Year's Modernist Output," *Musical America* 41/23 (28 March, 1925): 5, 35.

[11]Bob Gilmore, *Harry Partch. A Biography* (New Haven: Yale University Press, 1998), 74-85; and "Spoken Word Basis for New Musical Notation" [May 1932], in *Enclosure 3: Harry Partch*, ed. Philip Blackburn (Saint Paul: American Composers Forum, 1997), 16. In 1949 Partch again positively commented on the use of *Sprechstimme* in *Pierrot*: "The execution of *Pierrot lunaire*, under Schönberg's direction, shows these glides to be vastly but effectively exaggerated, and to do no harm to the drama, or melodrama, of the piece, but rather to enhance it. Further, the words are heard as spoken words." Harry Partch, "The Schönberg Adventure," in *Genesis of a Music*, 2nd ed. (New York: Da Capo, 1974), 40-41.

By the late 1920s and early 1930s *Pierrot* was being presented in major American cities (Chicago 1926; New York and Boston 1928; Philadelphia 1929, New York 1933), involving such prominent figures as Aaron Copland and Marc Blitzstein. The latter, a rebellious Schoenberg student, played the piano part of *Pierrot* at its Philadelphia premiere and lectured on this work. Although Blitzstein regarded *Pierrot* favorably, he disliked many other works by Schoenberg and disagreed with his aesthetics.[12]

With the onset of the Great Depression, populist political influences together with musical conservatism began to thrust uncompromising works like Schoenberg's into the background. Blitzstein, Copland, Ruth Crawford, and Elie Siegmeister, along with émigré composers Hanns Eisler and Kurt Weill, questioned the elitist tendencies of such music and included political and social content—to ensure comprehensibility often in the form of narrated text—into their own works. In 1937, Blitzstein parodied not only the principle of "art for art's sake" and American art patronage, but *Pierrot* itself in his autobiographical radio song-play *I've Got the Tune*.[13] In it, an arts patroness named Madame Arbutus recites in *Sprechstimme*: "The moon is a happy cheese tonight, I swoon!... It is so grand to be so bored! You can afford the kind of music you cannot stand." Parody notwithstanding, Schoenberg himself seemed to have followed the trend of politically inspired works in the 1940s. His *Ode to Napoleon* (1942) for speaker, string quartet, and piano and *A Survivor from Warsaw* (1947) for speaker, male choir, and orchestra are vivid musical indictments of Hitler and the Holocaust and feature a simpler type of *Sprechstimme* in the interest of realism of word setting.

During his American period Schoenberg conducted performances of *Pierrot* in San Francisco and New York. In 1940 he directed its premiere recording. Erika Stiedry-Wagner was the vocalist and Nicolas Slonimsky wrote the liner notes and summaries of each poem. Issued by Columbia Records, this recording marked a milestone with regard to the work's availability to American audiences, as *Pierrot* performances had become rare during the war years.[14] Lou Harrison, who studied with Schoenberg in 1943, remembered listening to that recording

---

[12]Marc Blitzstein, "Toward a New Form," *Musical Quarterly* 20/2 (1934): 216.

[13]Eric A. Gordon, *Mark the Music: The Life and Work of Marc Blitzstein* (New York: St. Martin's Press, 1989), 153-54. Blitzstein's *Pierrot* parody alludes to his complicated relationship with Schoenberg. A similar parody of American art patronesses also occurs in Blitzstein's *The Cradle Will Rock*. His ridiculing of art patrons was not uncommon. See Carol Oja, "Women Patrons and Crusaders for Modernist Music," in *Cultivating Music in America: Women Patrons and Activists since 1860*, ed. Ralph P. Locke and Cyrilla Barr (Berkeley: University of California Press, 1996), 250-54.

[14]Columbia M 461 (71157-D/160-D), released in 1941. For details on the recording history see Dika Newlin, *Schoenberg Remembered: Diaries and Recollections 1938-1976* (New York: Pendragon Press, 1980), 240-59. The League of Composers sponsored this recording project. Schoenberg, however, did not like the recording as much as the following New York performance in November 1940, which was also broadcast. Letter from Leonard Stein to the author (14 October 2000).

[15]Telephone conversation with Lou Harrison (9 September 2000).

daily after it was released.[15] Similarly Gunther Schuller recalled that hearing that record was a "mind- and ear-expanding experience."[16] Before the end of World War II, in 1944, émigré composer Ingolf Dahl conducted the first performance of an English-language version of *Pierrot* (endorsed by Schoenberg) at the "Evenings on the Roof" concert series in Los Angeles.[17]

Pierrot Lunaire Reception after World War II

After World War II *Pierrot* performances were on the rise and the work continued to bear offspring in American music. Along with Stravinsky's *L'histoire du soldat*, *Pierrot* became widely acknowledged as a significant source of inspiration for new American chamber music. Lukas Foss proclaimed in a 1975 interview: "Our new music roughly begins with *Pierrot lunaire*."[18] Composers from Milton Babbitt to Pauline Oliveros made no secret of their debt to Schoenberg's groundbreaking melodrama cycle, a debt that is evidenced as homage, parody, quotations, and allusions to the work's instrumentation, vocal treatment, structure, and theatricality. At the approach of the work's seventy-fifth anniversary in 1987, Leonard Stein, then director of the Arnold Schoenberg Institute, decided to highlight the fact that American composers never stopped creating works that followed in *Pierrot*'s footsteps by initiating the so-called "*Pierrot* Project." He invited sixteen prominent composers—among them Babbitt, Miriam Gideon, Stephen "Lucky" Mosko, and Schoenberg students Richard Hoffmann and Leonard Rosenman—to pay homage to the work by employing the original instrumentation for pieces based on the twenty-nine Giraud-Hartleben poems not included in Schoenberg's cycle.[19] The use of a vocalist was elective. The project yielded numerous novel pieces—single songs and song cycles—displaying various techniques and quotations from *Pierrot* as well as several other Schoenbergian features, adding to the growing literature related to this work.[20]

---

[16]Gunther Schuller, "Producer's Note," *Schoenberg, "Pierrot lunaire"* with the New York New Music Ensemble, Robert Black, conductor, Phyllis Bryn-Julson, voice (GM Recordings GM2030CD, 1992).

[17]Dahl allegedly translated the Giraud/Hartleben texts together with Carl Beier. See Dorothy Crawford, *Evenings On and Off the Roof: Pioneering Concerts in Los Angeles, 1939-1971* (Berkeley: University of California Press, 1995), 66-67. Yet toward the end of his life, Schoenberg found out that they had plagiarized a translation by the physician Hans Wachtel. See letter from Arnold Schoenberg to Fritz Stiedry (21 July 1949), Arnold Schoenberg Center, Vienna.

[18]Cole Gagne and Tracy Caras, *Soundpieces. Interviews with American Composers* (Metuchen, N.J.: Scarecrow Press, 1982), 205.

[19]Other composers in this project included: Leslie Bassett, Susan Blaustein, Paul Cooper, John Harbison, Donald Harris, Karl Kohn, William Kraft, Ursula Mamlok, Mark Neikrug, Mel Powell, and Roger Reynolds. Stein himself also set one of the poems. For more details see the Appendix.

[20]The premieres of the *Pierrot* Project settings were programmed with Schoenberg's *Pierrot* in four concerts with the San Francisco Contemporary Music Players, Jean-Louis LeRoux, conductor, and Miriam Abramowitsch, voice (1988, Los Angeles); the New York New (cont.)

The *Pierrot* Ensemble

One of the most striking aspects of *Pierrot*'s reception history is the widespread adoption of its instrumentation and the proliferation of works for small mixed ensembles.[21] John Harbison, who modeled several works on *Pierrot*'s scoring, went so far as to say that "the *Pierrot* ensemble has replaced the string quartet as the standard denomination for chamber music in our time."[22] Although a challenging type of soloistic instrumentation, the scoring for a small heterogeneous ensemble of flute (interchangeable with piccolo), clarinet (interchangeable with bass clarinet), violin (interchangeable with viola), cello, and piano allows for maximum differentiation in instrumental color. Joan Tower, who repeatedly composed for *Pierrot*–like ensembles, suggested that it was like a little symphony orchestra.[23] The "broken consort" of five players using eight instruments and voice, not only tempted many composers to explore further its timbral and structural possibilities but lent itself to limited budgets for new music and made touring easier than with larger groups. *Pierrot*'s scoring has therefore shaped the configuration of numerous American ensembles (Aeolian Chamber Players, California E.A.R. Unit, Da Capo Chamber Players, New York New Music Ensemble, and eighth blackbird, among many).[24] *Pierrot* was often at the center of these groups' repertory. Most of them commissioned compositions from a wide variety of American composers, leading to hundreds of new stylistically very different works for this scoring, including atonal, serialist, neo-classical, neo-romantic, and experimental compositions.

Due to the inherent variability of the *Pierrot* group, composers often toyed with the original instrumentation by replacing, omitting, or adding an instrument

---

Music Ensemble directed by Robert Black, featuring vocalist Christine Schadeberg (1988, Los Angeles); the Da Capo Chamber Players and Lucy Shelton, voice (1989, Los Angeles); and Sonor under John Fonville and Keith Humble, with Carol Plantamura, voice (1990, San Diego).

[21]The *Pierrot* ensemble was also frequently employed by European composers, if never on this scale.

[22]John Harbison, "Schoenberg and After: The Song Cycle Transformed," *From Pierrot to Marteau*, ed. Leonard Stein (Los Angeles: Arnold Schoenberg Institute, 1987), 5. Harbison's works for the *Pierrot* ensemble include "Rot und Weiss" and "Im Spiegel" (both written for the *Pierrot* Project in 1988).

[23]Conversation with Joan Tower (23 May 2000). During the existence of the Society for Private Musical Performances (1918-21) many orchestral works were scored for ensembles related to *Pierrot*.

[24]Many more such American ensembles can be found in *Contemporary Music Ensembles: A Directory* (New York: American Music Center, 1998). Some of them, the New York New Music Ensemble (also referred to as "Pierrot Plus Percussion") and the Da Capo Chamber Players, recorded *Pierrot*. Though not as numerous as in America, several European groups are also modeled after the *Pierrot* ensemble, for instance, the British "Pierrot Players" (founded in 1967, renamed in 1971 as "The Fires of London") and the (Cambridge) "New Music Players" (since 1991), the German "ensemble recherche" (since 1984) and the "*Pierrot lunaire* Ensemble Wien" (since 1996).

or two. For example, Babbitt dispensed with the voice in *Arie Da Capo* (1973-74), written for the Da Capo Chamber Players; he omitted both voice and piano in Composition for Four Instruments (1948) and excluded the piano in *The Head of the Bed* (1982).

Most common, however, was the use of the so-called "*Pierrot* quintet" without voice. Among the composers who wrote for the *Pierrot* quintet are Charles Wuorinen, Tower, George Crumb, and Oliveros. In her short and tonal one-movement piece *Petroushskates* (1980), written for the Da Capo Chamber Players of which she was the co-founder and pianist, Tower brilliantly utilized the *Pierrot* quintet's instruments. Inspired by Stravinsky's *Petrushka* and Olympic figure skating, Tower consequently used the piano as a virtuoso solo instrument and often divided the whole group into synchronously gliding pairs of instruments evocative of skaters to create "seamless action" and "a sort of musical carnival on ice."[25]

Many American composers also used a *Pierrot* ensemble, in which percussion instruments are substituted for the vocal part.[26] Commonly called "*Pierrot* Plus Percussion," this type of scoring not only enlarges the timbral palette, but it also provides greater sonic balance since percussion instruments allow the piano's sonorities to blend better with the rest of the ensemble. *Pierrot* plus percussion was taken up by Earle Brown, John Cage, Morton Feldman, Elliott Carter, and George Perle, to name a few. In *Tracking Pierrot* (1992), which Brown wrote in admiration of the *Pierrot* instrumentation, the *Pierrot* ensemble is enriched with vibraphone and marimba. He explored—without trying to invoke the "angst and moon-madness"—the possibilities of instrumental interaction and sonic variability in company with his trademark open-form approach, allowing the conductor to shape the written-out materials on the spur of the moment.[27] Feldman, on the other hand, requires two performers to handle the arsenal of percussion instruments added to the *Pierrot* quintet in his delicate work *For Frank O'Hara* (1973).

Besides purely instrumental works, numerous other compositions add voice to the *Pierrot* quintet. The inclusion of voice, however, renders this instrumentation more complex and problematical due to the disintegrating sonorities and tricky sonic balance. For the singer it is often difficult to compete with soloistic instruments, particularly in complex textures. Not surprisingly this approach has been favored by composers whose music is characterized by complex textures (Vivian Fine, Ursula Mamlok, Seymour Shifrin,

---

[25]Ellen K. Grolman, *Joan Tower: The Comprehensive Bio-Bibliography* (Lanham, Maryland: Scarecrow Press, 2007), 89.

[26]The soloistic use of percussion points to *L'histoire du soldat*, one of the first chamber works to give musical significance to a percussion set.

[27]Earle Brown, "Program Notes," S.E.M. Ensemble concert, Alice Tully Hall, New York City, 22 May 2000.

Example 1. Milton Babbitt: "Souper," mm. 1-6.

(Copyright © C. F. Peters Corporation 1987. Quoted by permission)

Louise Talma, and Hugo Weisgall, among others). Moreover participants in the *Pierrot* Project including Babbitt, Leslie Bassett, Susan Blaustein, Gideon, and Mamlok chose this scoring which reflects the instrumentation of Schoenberg's "Heimfahrt" (flute, clarinet, violin, cello, piano). Babbitt's *Pierrot* Project setting "Souper" (1987) which features a lyrical moonlit gondola scene similar to that of "Heimfahrt," accounts for his choice of the "Heimfahrt" instrumentation.

The full ensemble is used throughout the piece, and Babbitt's setting, based on a trichordal super-array, contains various motives from Schoenberg's *Pierrot* setting. The opening of "Souper" displays quotations from "Der kranke Mond" (flute), "Valse de Chopin" (clarinet), "Columbine" (violin), "Serenade" (cello), and "Mondestrunken" (piano). All of these motives are developed by each of the instruments.[28] This is why Babbitt subtitled "Souper" "A Quodlibet." The syllabic vocal part, which is conceived as *Sprechgesang* and follows the German diction closely, is woven into a complex polyphonic texture (see Example 1).

Vocal Technique

After 1945—and certainly thanks to such inspiring vocalists as Stiedry-Wagner, Alice Howland, Bethany Beardslee, Cathy Berberian, and Jan DeGaetani—*Pierrot* also became a guiding star when composers started exploring new vocal resources.[29] Schoenberg often (yet unjustly) received credit for the invention of *Sprechstimme* and its notation. But he provided a new, stylized and structurally more integrated form of the traditional, mostly narrative melodrama. It is perhaps thanks to *Pierrot* that the concept of melodrama, once considered problematical and of minor aesthetic value, became a respected and challenging "genre" because of the new aesthetic premises. Moreover the novel use of *Sprechstimme* in *Pierrot* became the point of departure for various experimental tendencies exemplified in works for speaking voices by such composers as Kenneth Gaburo, Charles Amirkhanian, Robert Ashley, and Laurie Anderson.

While most of these composers explored the domain between singing and speaking further without referring to the Schoenbergian precedent, others related their efforts directly to Schoenberg's seminal work. Such is the case with the composers of the *Pierrot* Project Babbitt, Harbison, Hoffmann, and Mosko. Hoffmann employed *Sprechstimme* in his setting of Giraud/Hartleben's "Das Alphabet," (1986). This poem, in which lieutenant Harlequin heads the shimmering army of all letters of the alphabet, inspired Hoffmann to use the "musical alphabet," that is the complete chromatic pitch material. The poem's verses are musically spelled out by pitches corresponding to letters and syllables of words. Not only the vocalist, but also the members of the *Pierrot* quintet spell out single letters verbally and recite words whereby pitch is indeterminate and rhythm determined.

Other provocative reinterpretations of *Pierrot*'s vocal part are found in the experimental *Variations … Beyond Pierrot* (1993-94) by Larry Austin—not a participant in the *Pierrot* Project. In this tripartite "sound-play" for soprano (or tenor), *Pierrot* quintet, hypermedia system, and computer music recitation on

[28]Letter from Milton Babbitt to the author (21 April 2000).

[29]Judith Bettina, Phyllis Bryn-Julson, Lucy Shelton, and Susan Narucki among others have continued the legacy of *Pierrot* performances.

5. VOICE: *Valse de Chopin. Wie ein blasser Tropfen Bluts! Färbt die Lippen einer Kranken. Wilder Lust Accorde stören,*

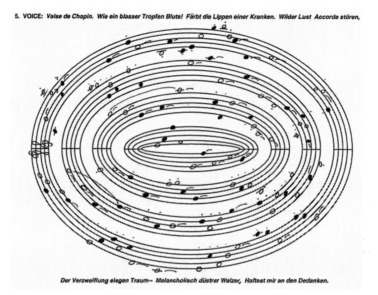

Der Verzweiflung eisgen Traum— Melancholisch düstrer Walzer, Haftest mir an den Gedanken.

Example 2a: Larry Austin, *Variations... beyond Pierrot.*
Excerpt from "Valse de Chopin."

(Copyright © Larry Austin Music 1995. Quoted by permission)

tape, Austin made extensive use of *Sprechstimme*.[30] For the computer music recitation, Austin employed the first two and other selected lines from twenty of the twenty-one poems used by Schoenberg, which are read in English, French, German, and Japanese, recorded and computer-processed.[31] In addition, the live vocalist speaks, speak-sings, and sings in four languages and freely interprets with the instrumentalists the computer music recitations (aural cues) and the *moon-scores* (visual cues), which show concentric oval-shaped staves covered with so-called "moon-pitches" (see Example 2). Furthermore, the live musicians, whose sounds are processed in real-time using a multi-effect digital signal and a digital delay processor, evoke, together with the tape and theatrical actions, a non-narrative *commedia dell'arte*.

For some, an aversion to novel twentieth-century compositional techniques such as *Sprechstimme* became a creative impetus. Betsy Jolas, for instance, had an aversion to *Pierrot*'s *Sprechstimme* part. Considering the work a disguised *Lieder* cycle with "virtual" melodies obscured by spoken voice, she composed *Episode Second: Ohne Worte* for flute solo (1977) to excavate and recompose the hidden melos in *Pierrot*'s vocal part. While the material of *Episode Second*, a virtuoso

[30]*Variations* was commissioned in 1993 by the Canadian group Thira whose core members form a *Pierrot* ensemble.
[31]Given his Catholicism, Austin skipped the blasphemous "Rote Messe" of Schoenberg's cycle.

Example 2b: Photograph by Gerry Kopelow. Members of the Canadian group Thira performing Larry Austin, *Variations... beyond Pierrot.*

(Copyright © Larry Austin Music 1995. Used by permission)

"free concerting paraphrase," is entirely drawn from Schoenberg, the subtitle of the piece, *Ohne Worte*, implies that the source of inspiration was a vocal work and that the re-composition dispenses with words (and *Sprechstimme*).[32]

Like Jolas, John Adams also expressed reservations against certain aspects of Schoenberg's music. Thus he included a parody of *Pierrot* in one scene of his second opera, *The Death of Klinghoffer* (1990-91). Among the various characters who witness and describe the hijacking of the cruise ship *Achille Lauro* is an arrogant Austrian woman recounting the event in *Sprechstimme* to the accompaniment of a *Pierrot*-ensemble. By identifying an Austrian snob with the music of an Austrian-born Jewish émigré composer in the context of an Arab-Israeli conflict Adams undoubtedly added to the opera's semantic complexity and reinforced its controversial anti-Semitic overtones.

Theatricality

If Schoenberg's melodramas are "songs" without singing ("music to spoken words," "spoken songs"), they could also be viewed as a kind of non-narrative "theatre" without staging. The score of *Pierrot* contains no stage directions, yet like most other melodramas, it implies theatrical aspects due to the text's evocation of often grotesque *commedia dell'arte*-like scenes, the work's designation for a *diseuse* (a female professional reciter) and actress and the exaggerated *Sprechstimme*-technique, which prompts expressive miming and gestures. The world premiere and further *Pierrot* performances were semi-staged according to staging customs at cabarets. Since 1926 *Pierrot* has continuously received staged and choreographed performances in America, including Glen Tetley's remarkable 1962 choreography with set and costumes designed by Rouben Ter-Arutunian, which was presented by Rudolf Nureyev in 1977. Such visualizations may have led Lukas Foss and others to consider *Pierrot* a "mixed-media" piece.[33] Blurring the strict division between music theatre and concert works, *Pierrot* was indubitably a forerunner of chamber works that strive for theatricality.[34] Visual and dramatic elements enriched American concert works before 1945 occasionally, and afterwards extensively, when multimedia works became the focus of the avant-garde.

[32]Betsy Jolas, *"Pierrot lunaire—Episode Second,"* in *Molto Espressivo*, ed. Alban Ramaut (Paris: L'Harmattan, 1999), 155-62; and "Program Note" for a New York New Music Ensemble concert on 21 November 1988 in New York City.

[33]See Gagne and Caras, *Soundpieces*, 205.

[34]In the late nineteenth and early twentieth century, the American melodrama, popular in theatres since the eighteenth century, was gradually replaced by non-theatrical melodramas for voice and piano presented on the concert stage. Anne Dhu Shapiro, "Action Music in American Pantomime and Melodrama, 1730-1913," *American Music* 2/4 (Winter 1984): 49-72.

Example 3. Leonard Rosenman: "Absinth" from
Looking Back at Faded Chandeliers, mm. 48-55.

(Copyright © Peermusic Classical 1990. Quoted by permission)

Several composers participating in the *Pierrot* Project used straightforward theatrical elements in their Giraud/Hartleben settings. Rosenman, who due to his background in film composition frequently enriched his works for the concert stage with theatrical components, included scenic actions in the final song ("Absinth") of his *Pierrot* triptych *Looking Back at Faded Chandeliers* (1990): "Die Estrade," "Moquerie," and "Absinth."[35] The last poem's image of sticky polyps sinking the poet's boat in a surging ocean of absinth, prompted Rosenman to demand that the singer sip from a glass with absinthe and gradually shift into a state of inebriation. The musical flow becomes more and more corrupted by superimposed bits of heterogeneous musical pieces—all of which suggests a drunk losing her balance as the world around her spins out of control (see Example 3). Mosko also resorted to subtle theatrical gestures in his 1988 *Pierrot* Project setting of "Schweres Loos," a fanciful poem featuring gluttonous bon-vivants derided by comic characters and black-blue insects. Emphasizing the grotesque mood, Mosko not only uses manifold vocal expressions ("muttering somewhat inaudibly," "(sing) like Marlene Dietrich," "almost screaming out of control"), but also asks the vocalist to act "amused with a hint of a smile" and "a bit bewildered" and to "stare somewhat sardonically at clarinetist during fermata."[36]

On the other end of the spectrum are such pieces as Pauline Oliveros's *Aeolian Partitions* (1969), commissioned by the Aeolian Chamber Players. The work's scoring for *Pierrot* quintet and its theatrical elements (use of proscenium stage, lighting, props, and costuming) relate to Schoenberg's melodrama cycle and its performance tradition. However, the musicians' reliance on mostly verbal performance instructions, the fact that the performers have to act as well as play and improvise on their instruments, and use meditation, telepathy, and interact with the audience, point to a myriad of other influences.

The Cyclic Aspect

In 1944 composer-critic Virgil Thomson noted in a *New York Herald Tribune* article that *"Pierrot's* little feelings, though they seem enormous and are unquestionably fascinating when studied through the Schoenberg microscope for forty-five minutes of concert time, often appear in retrospect as less interesting than the mechanism through which they have been viewed."[37] Though critical

---

[35] Initially Rosenman set only one Giraud/Hartleben poem for the *Pierrot* Project: "Die Estrade," But thereafter he added two more settings, "Moquerie" and "Absinth," titling the group *Looking Back at Faded Chandeliers* (New York: Peermusic, 1990).

[36] The alto vocal part is accompanied by an unusual instrumental combination not used in *Pierrot*: two widely spaced winds, piccolo, flute, and bass clarinet, and violin. Furthermore Mosko referred to Schoenberg with a seven-note chord containing letters of his name (used in the instrumental parts) and a complementary five-tone set (displayed in the vocal part), which form a twelve-tone series.

[37] Virgil Thomson, "Schoenberg's Music," *New York Herald Tribune*, 10 September 1944.

of the *Pierrot* poems, Thomson acknowledged Schoenberg's skillful treatment of the texts and hinted at the cycle's sophisticated layout shaped through extra-musical ideas, timbre, and texture rather than through an overarching concept of tonality. Indeed *Pierrot* "enlarged the conception of what a song cycle might be" and set an example for a wide range of novel multipartite vocal chamber music works.[38] Just as Boulez did with *Le Marteau sans maître* (1953-55), American composers created numerous exceptional cycles following *Pierrot*'s footsteps.

The *Pierrot* Project led six composers (Leslie Bassett, Paul Cooper, Donald Harris, William Kraft, Roger Reynolds, and Leonard Rosenman) to create cycles of mostly three structurally related settings for soprano and *Pierrot* quintet. Kraft's *Settings from Pierrot lunaire* (1987-90) for soprano and "*Pierrot* plus percussion" is the most elaborate cycle of the *Pierrot* Project and reflects his background as a percussionist. The settings "Feerie," "Mein Bruder," "Harlequinade," and "Selbstmord" are introduced by a prelude and joined by three instrumental interludes enriched by colorful percussion sounds.[39] The songs progress with increasing tension toward the final setting, Pierrot's suicide, which is interpreted as a grotesque and wild dream introduced by the energetic, improvisatory third interlude, "Fantasmagoria." Kraft based his cycle on a seven-tone and five-tone set to form a twelve-tone row, another reverence to Schoenberg. Reynolds, like Kraft, linked the three settings of his cycle *Not Only Night* (1988) by transitional instrumental interludes. Yet he added to the *Pierrot* ensemble an electronic tape. The most unusual aspect of Reynolds's work, however, is his quotation of Schoenberg's entire setting of "Nacht" as his cycle's centerpiece. Reynolds surrounded it with two of his own *Pierrot* settings, "Abend" for soprano, flute, and piano and "Morgen" for soprano, piccolo, and clarinet, which are tied to "Nacht" through the incorporation of melodic snippets from the instrumental part of "Nacht" and the use of twelve-tone rows derived from pitch material of "Nacht." Reynolds's arrangement of a sunset poem, followed by "Nacht" and finally a daylight poem, reflects in microcosm the conception of Schoenberg's cycle, which begins at darkness, drifts into darker spheres, and finally reaches dawn and daylight in the last two poems.

Other prominent examples of song cycles outside the *Pierrot* Project include Shifrin's three Thomas Hardy settings, *Satires of Circumstance* (1964), Weisgall's ten-part setting of Robert Herrick's *The Hesperides, Fancies and Inventions* (1970), Gideon's *Voices from Elysium* (1979), and Talma's *Diadem* (1980), the latter two based on ancient poetry. All of these works feature voice and *Pierrot* quintet. Yet while Shifrin and Talma used the full ensemble throughout their cycles with delicate refinement, Weisgall and Gideon chose, like Schoenberg, timbral rotation in each song.

---

[38]John Harbison, "Schoenberg and After: The Song Cycle Transformed," in Stein, ed., *From Pierrot to Marteau*, 5.

[39]For the *Pierrot* Project Kraft initially set three poems and later added a setting of "Selbstmord" and instrumental interludes. The work is recorded with Kraft on percussion and the Boston Musica Viva under Richard Pittman (Albany Records, Troy 218).

Number Symbolism

American composers were also interested in such structural aspects as the control of atonality, pitch organization, counterpoint, individualization of instruments and melodic lines, and interplay between voice and ensemble. Perle described *Pierrot* as a "sort of compendium of all the styles and techniques that Schoenberg had evolved in his earliest 'free' atonal works less than four years earlier, and it introduces some new elements as well."[40] Schoenberg's number symbolism in the title and, to a certain degree, in the musical texture became a much-disputed issue in the 1980s and 1990s. Perle suggested that Schoenberg might have chosen the "lucky numbers," three and seven, because each of the Giraud/Hartleben poems comprises thirteen lines, a numerologically unlucky number. Perle did not see any intrinsic musical meaning in the use of magic numbers,[41] but Colin Sterne, who analyzed *Pierrot* according to numerological principles, emphasized the impact of certain numbers such as three, seven, one, eleven, and twenty-two on the overall structure of the work (instrumentation, pitch values, time span values, intervallic values, and quantitative pitch values).[42] Claudio Spies's *Dreimal sieben... and BIS* (1991-96) for oboe and piano, although devoid of any numerological meaning, reflects *Pierrot* in its title and in its compositional structure.[43] The numbers three and seven and also their product twenty-one govern tempo indications, the length of phrases, beat patterns, and produce the pitches for the piece's peculiar twelve-tone set, which can be divided into three similar three-tone groups and seven different three-tone groups. In contrast, Crumb's *Black Angels (Thirteen Images from the Dark Land)* (1970) for electric string quartet incorporating text fragments spoken by the quartet players, is tangentially related to *Pierrot* in its use of numbers (three, seven, thirteen) and number symbolism. Crumb expressed these "'magical' relationships . . . in terms of phrase-length, groupings of single tones, durations, patterns of repetition, etc." In its portrayal of a three-stage "voyage of the soul," *Black Angels*, however, also shows a kinship to *Pierrot*'s journey reflecting "Departure," "Absence," and "Return."[44]

[40]George Perle, "Liner Notes" for *Pierrot lunaire*, Columbia Chamber Ensemble, Robert Craft, conductor, Bethany Beardslee, voice (Columbia M2L 279, 1963).

[41]George Perle, "*Pierrot lunaire*," in *The Commonwealth of Music: In Honor of Curt Sachs*, ed. Gustave Reese and Rose Brandel (New York: Free Press, 1965), 308.

[42]Colin Sterne, "Pythagoras and *Pierrot*: An Approach to Schoenberg's Use of Numerology in the Construction of *Pierrot lunaire*," *Perspectives of New Music* 21/1-2 (Fall-Winter 1982/Spring-Summer 1983): 506-34, and *Arnold Schoenberg: The Composer as Numerologist* (Lewiston, N.Y.: Edwin Mellen, 1993), 59-119.

[43]Claudio Spies, "Einführung in *Dreimal sieben...*," in *Stil oder Gedanke? Zur Schönberg-Rezeption in Amerika und Europa*, ed. Stefan Litwin and Klaus Velten (Saarbrücken: Pfau, 1995), 246-47.

[44]*George Crumb: Profile of a Composer*, ed. Don Gillespie (New York: C.F. Peters, 1986), 24, 107. Conversation with Crumb (New York City, 24 April 2000).

Epilogue

Schoenberg's *Pierrot*, a touchstone piece for composers world-wide, has provoked a particularly strong response in America. Yet despite the many echoes of *Pierrot* in American music, its text and vocal part were for a long time a source of misconception. *Pierrot* was viewed as a work revealing angst, neurosis, hysteria, and severity, rather than irony, satire, and lightness.[45] Leonard Bernstein remarked that *Pierrot* "always leaves me feeling a little bit sick. . . . Somewhere in the middle of this piece you have the great desire to run and open the window, breathe a lungful of healthy, clean air."[46] Thus elements of irony, intrinsic criticism of contemporary issues, and self-criticism were perhaps not perceived.[47] David Hamilton aptly observed that *Pierrot*'s "effect, especially to American listeners unfamiliar with the stylistic context, was not in the least ironic or parodistic but intensely emotional, often hysterical."[48] In 1940, during the preparations for the premiere recording of *Pierrot*, Schoenberg called for a cooler approach and greater comprehensibility of the words. He strove for "that light ironic-satirical tone in which the piece was actually conceived" (perhaps taking into account the changing attitudes of a later time), and decided to speed up the performance time by almost fifteen minutes. He also pleaded for performances in English.[49] Decades later, Aaron Copland noticed those changes of tempo and tone and assumed that Schoenberg was "downplaying the 'latent hysteria' of *Pierrot lunaire*."[50] He was not aware of earlier documents from 1912 and 1928, revealing Schoenberg's detached attitude toward the text and his idea of a "light" and dispassionate performance style.[51] However, new English translations, especially Andrew Porter's from 1984, and a number of ambitious performances and recordings, have helped to establish a lighter performance style.[52]

[45]Lazare Saminsky, *Music of Our Day: Essentials and Prophecies* (New York: T.Y. Crowell, 1932), 144; Aaron Copland, *The New Music, 1900-1960* (New York: Norton, 1968), 44.

[46]Leonard Bernstein, *The Joy of Music* (New York: Simon & Schuster, 1959), 203.

[47]Beinhorn, *Das Groteske in der Musik*, 181, 211-24.

[48]David Hamilton, "Moonlighting," in Stein, ed., *From Pierrot to Marteau*, 46.

[49]Letter from Arnold Schoenberg to Erika Stiedry-Wagner (31 August 1940), *Arnold Schönberg: Sämtliche Werke*, Series B, Vol. 24, 1, ed. Reinhold Brinkmann (Mainz: Schott Musik International and Vienna: Universal Edition, 1995), 302.

[50]Aaron Copland, "When Private Worlds and Public Worlds Meet," *New York Times*, 9 June 1968, II, 17; see also Howard Pollack, *Aaron Copland: The Life and Work of an Uncommon Man* (New York: Henry Holt, 1999), 536.

[51]"With regard to subject, content, it [Giraud's *Pierrot lunaire*] is perhaps not a matter dear to my heart. But with regard to form definitely" (letter from Schoenberg to Wassily Kandinsky, 19 August 1912, trans. by the author). "And I always emphasized that these pieces should be performed in a light and not in an emotive manner," Arnold Schoenberg, "Pathos," 7 April 1928, *Arnold Schönberg, Sämtliche Werke*, 301 (trans. by the author).

[52]Andrew Porter, "*Pierrot lunaire* – English Translation," in Stein, ed., *From Pierrot to Marteau*, 28-29; and see *Arnold Schoenberg, "Pierrot lunaire" (German and Porter's English versions – Performed without Conductor)*, Lucy Shelton with the Da Capo Chamber Players, Bridge (BCD 9032, 1992).

Although Schoenberg's influence on American composers of the twentieth century is regularly being questioned, the impact of such pivotal works as *Pierrot* certainly remains undoubted.[53] During the last century, *Pierrot* has echoed through innumerable compositions in many different styles. *Pierrot Lunaire*, which Stravinsky once called the "solar plexus of early twentieth-century music," subtly continues to resonate through American works of the new century.[54]

Appendix
The "*Pierrot* Project" (1987)

Milton Babbitt	"Souper" for *Sprechstimme*, fl., cl., vln., vc., pf. (1988, C. F. Peters)
Leslie Bassett	*Pierrot Songs* ("Die Wolken," "Eine Bühne," "Herbst,") for soprano, fl., cl., vln., vc., pf. (1988, C. F. Peters)
Susan Blaustein	*Harlequinade!* ("Köpfe, Köpfe!," "Harlequin") for soprano, fl., cl., vln., vc., pf. (1989, unpublished)
Paul Cooper	Rondels Bergamasques ("Landschaft," "Die Wolken," "Sonnen-Ende") for Soprano, fl., bcl., via., vc., pf. (1988, Edition Wilhelm Hansen)
Miriam Gideon	"Böhmischer Kristall" for soprano, fl., cl., vln., vc., pf. (1988, American Composers Alliance)
John Harbison	"Rot und Weiss," for *Sprechstimme*, fl., vln., vc.; "Im Spiegel" for *Sprechstimme*, vln., pf. (1988, Associated Music Publishers)
Donald Harris	*Pierrot Lieder* ("Der Koch," "Nordpohlfahrt," "Selbstmord") for soprano, fl., alto fl., cl., bcl., vln., vla., vc., pf. (1988, Gunmar)
Richard Hoffmann	"Das Alphabet," for *Sprechstimme*, fl., bcl., vln., vc., pf.; "Das heilige Weiss" for soprano, picc., vln., pf. (1986, unpublished)
Karl Kohn	"Pantomime," "Die Kirche" for soprano, fl., cl., vln., vc., pf. (1986-87, unpublished)
William Kraft	"Mein Bruder," "Harlequinade" later extended to a cycle (*Settings from Pierrot Lunaire*: "Feerie," "Mein Bruder," "Harlequinade," "Selbstmord") for soprano, fl. (picc.), cl. (bcl.), vln. (vla.), vc., pf., perc. (1987-90, New Music West)

---

[53]Leon Botstein, "Schoenberg and the Audience: Modernism, Music, and Politics in the Twentieth Century," in *Schoenberg and His World*, ed. Walter Frisch (Princeton: Princeton University Press, 1999), 23.

[54]Igor Stravinsky and Robert Craft, *Dialogues and a Diary* (Garden City: Doubleday, 1963), 54.

Ursula Mamlok	"Die Laterne" for soprano, fl., cl., vln., vc., pf. (1988, C. F. Peters)
Stephen Mosko	"Schweres Loos" for alto *Sprechstimme*, picc., bcl., vln. (1990, Leisure Planet Music)
Marc Neikrug	"Köpfe, Köpfe!" for soprano, fl., cl., vln., vc., pf. (1989, unpublished)
Mel Powell	"Die Violine" for soprano, vln., pf. (1988, G. Schirmer)
Roger Reynolds	*Not Only Night* ("Abend," "Nacht" from Schoenberg's *Pierrot Lunaire*, "Morgen") for soprano, fl., picc., cl., vln., vc., pf., tape (1988, C. F. Peters)
Leonard Rosenman	"Die Estrade" later extended to a cycle: *Looking Back at Faded Chandeliers* ("Die Estrade," "Moquerie," "Absinth") for soprano, fl., cl., vln., vc., pf. (1990, Peermusic Classical)
Leonard Stein	"Moquerie" for soprano, fl., cl., vln., vc., pf. (unpublished)

Initiated by Leonard Stein to celebrate the seventy-fifth anniversary of *Pierrot Lunaire* and the tenth anniversary of the Arnold Schoenberg Institute in Los Angeles.

Expressivity, Color, and Articulation in Schoenberg's Seventeen Piano Fragments

Yoko Hirota

The evolution of Schoenberg's concern for timbre, sonority, articulation, and expressivity is nowhere more evident than in his published piano works: *Drei Klavierstücke*, Op. 11, *Sechs kleine Klavierstücke*, Op. 19, *Fünf Klavierstücke*, Op. 23, *Suite für Klavier*, Op. 25, and *Klavierstücke*, Op. 33a and 33b. While some scholarly discussion has been devoted to these aspects of Schoenberg's piano works,[1] the seventeen piano fragments left by the composer are less well known, and have rarely received attention from musicologists and performers. The set of fragments, taken collectively, span the years of the published works; the first was written around the year 1900, and the last after 1933.[2] In this essay, I will undertake a brief overview of Schoenberg's seventeen piano fragments, giving particular attention to the parameters other than pitch and harmonic organization that are so central to the development of his compositional language.[3]

We will pass briefly over the first four fragments (Examples 1-4), wherein the influence of Brahms is clearly evident. Schoenberg freely acknowledges his indebtedness to Brahms at this stage in his development:

[1]For example, see David Burge, *Twentieth-Century Piano Music* (New York: Schirmer Books, 1990); Charles Rosen, *Arnold Schoenberg* (New York: The Viking Press, 1975); and Walter Frisch, *The Early Works of Arnold Schoenberg* (Berkeley and Los Angeles: University of California Press, 1997).

[2]Arnold Schoenberg, *Sämtliche Werke, Abteilung II: Klavier- und Orgelmusik* (Reihe B, Band 4: Werke für Klavier zu zwei Händen. Kritischer Bericht, Skizzen, Fragmente), ed. Reinhold Brinkmann (Wien: Schott/Universal, 1975), xiv, 101-45.

[3]Yoko Hirota, *The Piano Music of Arnold Schoenberg with 17 Fragments*, Phoenix Records Ltd., PHX65122 (CD), 2005.

Yoko Hirota is considered a leading interpreter of contemporary piano repertory in Canada. Her first CD, *The Piano Music of Arnold Schoenberg with 17 Fragments*, was released to critical acclaim and was recently listed as an "essential track" by *The Globe and Mail*. Her performances are often broadcast on Radio-Canada and have been praised by critics as "precise and keenly projective" and demonstrating "the highest level of proficiency." Dr. Hirota recently performed as featured soloist with the Sudbury Symphony Orchestra in the world premiere of *Oiseau de givre*, a new work for piano and orchestra by Robert Lemay. She is currently a Professor of Piano and Chair of the Department of Music at Laurentian University in Sudbury, Ontario. She is also co-founder and co-artistic director of the non-profit contemporary music organization, 5-Penny New Music Concerts

Example 1. Fragment eines Scherzo für Klavier, mm. 1-5. All examples are from *Sämtliche Werke, Abteilung II: Klavier- und Orgelmusik* (Reihe B, Band 4).

(Used by permission of Belmont Music Publishers. Copyright © 1975)

Example 2. Fragment eines Klavierstücks, mm. 1-4.

Example 3. Fragment eines Klavierstücks (1900-01), mm. 1-5.

Example 4. Fragment eines Klavierstücks (1905-06), mm. 1-5.

I had been a "Brahmsian" when I met Zemlinsky. His love embraced both Brahms and Wagner and soon thereafter I became an equally confirmed addict. No wonder that the music I composed at that time mirrored the influence of both these masters.[4]

The composer assigned a characteristically Brahmsian title, *Scherzo*, to the first fragment (Example 1). This eighty-measure fragment opens somewhat dramatically with dynamic octave doublings in the left hand establishing the key of F-sharp minor, and a strong melody in the right hand punctuated by colorful four-note chords. The expressive and dynamic language here is largely that of the nineteenth century, with occasional crescendo and decrescendo markings corresponding to melodic and phrase contours. After seventeen measures of this opening section, Schoenberg moves through a lyrical interlude, still in F-sharp minor, to modulate somewhat conventionally to the relative major, A major. A rather poetic B-section follows, featuring a more melodic and polyphonic texture. The entire fragment oscillates between these two textures, each of which explore the employment of wide registers, a characteristic associated with so much of Brahms's piano music.

In the opening passage of the second fragment (Example 2), in C-sharp minor, Schoenberg further explores a vaguely Brahmsian lyricism. The fragment opens with a six-measure introduction on the subdominant, before finally establishing a clear melody on the tonic at measure 7. This seventy-seven-measure fragment features wide-ranging dynamics and more or less conventional triadic harmonic vocabulary throughout. The first climax arrives in measure 41 with a fortissimo F-sharp minor triad in the right hand, and a secondary climax appears at measure 63 with a forte chordal texture seemingly derived from the opening section of the first fragment. The fragment closes with a glorious chorale texture in E major, the relative major.[5]

Qualities similar to those that characterize the first and second fragments continue to dominate in the third fragment (Example 3). An exquisitely contemplative melody in the plaintive upper register of the cello is projected above a rich chordal texture. Copious dynamic, phrase, articulation, and tempo indications are employed throughout, and the fragment centers on a poignantly expressive "molto rit." at measures 21-22. Hastily written notes scrawled in February 1901 across the bottom corner of the manuscript of the fragment indicate Schoenberg's frustration with his inability to develop and complete this incipient piece to his satisfaction: "A continuation will follow? If I only knew

---

[4]Schoenberg, *Style and Idea* (Berkeley and Los Angeles: University of California Press, 1984), 80. See also Ethan Haimo, *Schoenberg's Serial Odyssey: The Evolution of His Twelve-tone Method, 1914-1928* (Oxford: Clarendon Press, 1990); and Walter Frisch, *The Early Works of Arnold Schoenberg* (Berkeley and Los Angeles: University of California Press, 1997).

[5]See measures 68-76 of the second fragment.

how it will go! I have already made two aborted efforts. I can only dare to hope to find a suitable continuation, if I am able."[6]

The fourth fragment (Example 4), thought to be written around 1905-06, shows a marked advancement in the direction of extended chromaticism, yet maintains a Brahmsian repose and gestural language.

Fragments five to eight (Examples 5-8) are thought to have been started around 1909, the year of the *Drei Klavierstücke*, Op. 11. In the fifth fragment (Example 5), Schoenberg's middle-period contrapuntal technique—a style that emerges with still more maturity in Op. 11—is nascent. Here his harmonic language becomes increasingly acerbic and atonal, and his exploration of the range of the keyboard is broad, dynamic, and coloristic. In the sixth fragment (Example 6), the first chord provides a germinal harmonic idea for the piece, while active unison passages are played in the lower register, and the distinct juxtaposition of the two registers becomes a thematic element throughout.

This registral play becomes the main subject of the seventh fragment (Example 7). Here pitches are deposed in different registers in every measure, an early foreshadowing of Webern's pointillistic technique. Schoenberg's developing preoccupation with specific articulation indications is evident throughout the fragment. In the third movement of Op. 11, written a very short time after this fragment, precise specifications of articulation are seen on almost every note, placing ever increasing demands upon the performer.

The eighth piano fragment (Example 8), written during a period of turmoil in Schoenberg's life (ca. 1909), seems somewhat less successful than the previous three fragments in its exploration of piano color and articulation. While registral play is still a foreground concern, articulation indications are notably absent (with the exception of a single accent in measure 8). Schoenberg opts to proceed no further with this fragment, abandoning it in measure 20. Reinhold Brinkmann has suggested that this fragment may, in fact, be an initial sketch for an orchestral work.[7]

When he wrote his ninth fragment (Example 9), Schoenberg had already completed Opp. 11 and 19. In this fragment, the composer's demand for articulation becomes ever more intensified. Details such as the following require the utmost delicacy of execution: in measure 1, there is a staccato sign on the ornamental note at the end of the measure; in measure 2, the accent and staccato sign appear together on the pianissimo chord; and there are both crescendo and decrescendo signs on the following sixteenth-note chord. While such meticulous specifications may seem better suited to string writing, for example, they

---

[6]"Fortsetzung folgt . . . Wenn ich nur wüsste, wie die Fortsetzung sein wird! Zweimal habe ich mich darin schon getäuscht. Jetzt wage ich nichts mehr zu hoffen, noch zu befürchten. – Folgt Fortsetzung?"

[7]Schoenberg, *Sämtliche Werke, Abteilung II* (Reihe B, Band 4), 120.

Example 5. Zwei Fragmente eines Klavierstücks (1909), mm. 1-3.

Example 6. Fragment eine Klavierstücks(1909), mm. 1-3.

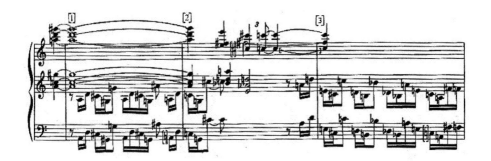

Example 7. Fragment eines Klavierstücks (1909), mm. 1-4.

Example 8. Fragment eines Klavierstücks (1909), mm. 1-7.

Example 9. Fragment eines Klavierstücks (1918), mm. 1-2.

Example 10. Fragment eines Klavierstücks (1920), mm. 1-10.

demonstrate Schoenberg's quest for new coloristic effects on the piano during this period.

An intensified exploration of dynamic range also becomes evident in both the ninth and tenth fragments (Examples 9 and 10). Schoenberg frequently applies piano-pianissimo indications in both of these fragments. Dynamic shading is a preoccupation in the ten measures of the tenth fragment, where tenuto signs (such as those in measures 1-3) are applied to individual notes to give them subtly delicate stress. Again Schoenberg applies crescendo/decrescendo indications on two notes in measure 5, and on the three very short phrases in measure 8.

Example 11. Fragment eines Klavierstücks (1920), mm. 1-10.

The exploration of sonority is particularly sophisticated in the tenth fragment, and it becomes Schoenberg's principal preoccupation in the eleventh fragment (Example 11), which requires extreme expressivity in performance. In this twelve-measure fragment, Schoenberg often applies accent, tenuto, and staccato signs, and crescendo/decrescendo are written over single notes and small three-note phrases.

Here we are reminded of Schoenberg's tendency to conceive of dissonant intervals and sonorities as things of value in themselves, rare diamonds that must be contemplated for their own sake, and from every perspective.[8] This orientation ultimately led to serial thinking, where melody and harmony are conceived "as in Swedenborg's heaven (described in Balzac's *Seraphita*) [where] there is no absolute down, no right or left, forward or backward."[9] Ernst Krenek tells us how "serial thinking" tends to focus the composer's attention on the merits of "the single sound": "The atomizing effect of serial thinking concentrates one's attention on the single sound, the texture and color quality of which gains new importance."[10] Karol Szymanowski likewise corroborates this view with respect to Schoenberg's harmonic theory and project: "The concept of an absolute vertical sound as a *value in itself* . . . became the transition to [Schoenberg's] essential atomism."[11]

[8]James K. Wright, *Schoenberg, Wittgenstein, and the Vienna Circle* (Bern: Verlag Peter Lang, 2007), 95-96.

[9]Schoenberg, *Style and Idea,* 223.

[10]Ernst Krenek, "Schoenberg the Centenarian," *Journal of the Arnold Schoenberg Institute* 1/2 (February, 1977): 89.

[11]Leon Botstein, "Schoenberg and the Audience: Modernism, Music, and Politics in the Twentieth Century," in *Schoenberg and His World*, ed. Walter Frisch (Princeton: Princeton University Press, 1999), 47-49 (emphasis added). Botstein's article includes a full English translation of Karol Szymanowski's essay "On the Question of Contemporary Music" ["*W sprawie muzyki współczesnej,*" 1925].

1. *r* means: accented like a strong beat.

ᵥ " unaccented like a weak beat.

2. ‑ At . it must be light and elastic; but at *r* the staccato must be expressed in a hard, heavy manner.

— means that the note should be lengthened. Often when the signs *r* to *L* appear, it means that the notes should be accented and made longer (tenuto and portato). When the staccato point is placed above (·) it means that the note must be well held on, but separated from the next one by means of a slight pause.

A at least means to be held on. Also it often means to bring out (in this manner upbeats have been specially marked).

3. Arrowheads have been placed on the arpeggio signs (wavy lines) to indicate whether the arpeggios are to be played upwards ⊦ or downwards ⊦ .

4. The Metronome marks are not to be taken literally, they merely give an indication of the tempo.

5. Trills must always be played without gracenotes and appogiaturas should be regarded as upbeats.

6. In general the best fingering is that which allows an exact interpretation of the note groups without the aid of the pedal. On the other hand the soft pedal will often be found useful.

Figure 1. Suite für Klavierstücke Op. 25, Preface.

(Copyright © 1995 Ausgewählte Klaviermusik. Used by permission of Belmont Publishers)

The composer's concern with color and articulation led him to pen his well-known preface to the scores of Op. 23 and Op. 25 (Figure 1), written shortly after these fragments. Here Schoenberg explains the thirteen nuanced accents that he employs in the piece, and the upward and downward directions on the arpeggio signs.[12] Color and articulation continued to be a central preoccupation for Schoenberg in the twelve-tone works of the twenties, and in his late-period works written in America. He describes his abiding interest in expressivity and sonority in a 1941 lecture given at the University of California at Los Angeles:

> I am much less irritated than amused by the critical remark of one Dr. X, who says that I do not care for "sound." "Sound," once a dignified quality of higher music, has deteriorated in significance since skillful workmen—orchestrators—have taken it in hand with the definite and undisguised intention of using it as a screen behind which the absence of ideas will not be noticeable. . . . Today, sound is seldom associated with idea. . . . It is true that sound in my music changes with every turn of the idea–emotional, structural, or other. It is furthermore true that such changes occur in a more rapid succession than usual, and I admit that it is more difficult to perceive them simultaneously.[13]

The twelfth fragment (Example 12), which stands between Schoenberg's Op. 25 Suite and the Op. 33 *Klavierstücke*, contains a character dissimilar to the previous pieces and fragments. Here, the harmonic idiom becomes relatively tonal (even reminiscent, in places, of the language of Prokofiev), and accents and dynamics are employed much more sparingly. In contrast to fragments 10 and 11, Schoenberg seems to have shifted his focus from expressive articulation, and the "single sound," to more general problems of form, motive, melody, and harmonic language.

Fragments 13 to 16 were written around the time Schoenberg composed Op. 33. In fragment 13 (Example 13), he returns again to his preoccupation with coloristic effects. Steady sixteenth notes weave throughout this thirty-five-measure excerpt, with Schoenberg employing sixteenth-note groupings of various lengths to form phrases and gestures. Diverse nuances of articulation, tenuto, staccato, and staccato with accent are evident throughout, and require the most detailed attention by the pianist. The fragment is performed rather dryly, with little pedal. Here Schoenberg's expressive indications become increasingly fastidious, and, as in fragment 11, we again see crescendo and decrescendo indications on a single note (as in measures 22 and 23).

---

[12]Arnold Schoenberg, *Fünf Klavierstücke,* Op. 23 (Copenhagen: Edition Wilhelm Hansen, 1923), 2; ibid., *Suite für Klavier,* Op. 25, in *Selected Works for Piano* (Vienna, Schott/Universal Edition, 1995), 33.

[13]Schoenberg, *Style and Idea,* 240.

Example 12. Fragment eines Klavierstucks (1925), mm. 1-3.

Example 13. Fragment eines Klavierstücks (1931), mm. 1-8.

In the fourteenth fragment (Example 14), Schoenberg begins to explore sonorities involving thicker chordal structures (Example 14a) and writing in octaves (Example 14b), ideas which were perhaps ultimately manifest in the octaves and massive chordal writing found in his last completed piano works, the *Klavierstücke* Op. 33a and b.

The fifteenth fragment (Example 15) shows Schoenberg returning to explore the lyrical phrasing and expressive melody that we more customarily associate with his early works. After the first two measures, Schoenberg continued to compose his melodic line, while adding subtle phrase, staccato, and tenuto markings. A close examination of this fragment—and Schoenberg's piano music, generally—reveals something that sensitive interpreters of his music have always known (Herbert Henk, Paul Jacobs, Peter Hill come to mind),[14] namely that expressivity is always Schoenberg's priority. His concern for expression is equally evident in fragments sixteen and seventeen (Examples 16 and 17), the last two fragments. Only three measures of the lyrical sixteenth fragment do not contain detailed dynamic, articulation, and pedal indications. As in fragment 15, Schoenberg writes careful phrasing indications in both left- and right-hand voices, each of which have melodious contours. The lyricism and more or less traditional expressivity of the seventeenth fragment is equally striking, with Schoenberg writing "cantabile" above measure 8. While this final fragment does not contain many dynamic and articulation indications, his signs are as precise as in the previous fragments. Fragment 17, written sometime after 1933, is the only fragment that is composed with Schoenberg's evolving twelve-tone technique.[15] This fragment reveals that lyrical thinking continues to be central for him as he ventures outward on his twelve-tone odyssey. Rather than depriving his works of their expressivity, Schoenberg felt that the development of his method promised an enhancement of expressivity, and a more rigorous and thoroughgoing exploration of harmonic sonority and color.

While this overview of Schoenberg's seventeen piano fragments has been limited in nature, my goal has been to raise awareness of the importance of the fragments, and of their potential contribution to our understanding of the evolution of Schoenberg's compositional thought, method, and expressive intent.

---

[14]Herbert Henck, *Arnold Schönberg: Klavierstücke, Op. 11, 19, 23, 33a/b, Suite Op. 25, und Fragmente von 17 Klavierstücken*, Wergo WER 6268-2 (1995); *Schoenberg: Piano Music*, Electra/ Asylum/Nonesuch 9.71309-2 (1975); Peter Hill, *Schoenberg, Berg and Webern: Piano Music*, Naxos 8.553870 (1999).

[15]See *Schoenberg: Sämtliche Werke, Abteilung II* (Reihe B, Band 4), xiv, 145.

Example 14a. Fragment eines Klavierstücks (1931), mm. 21-26.

Example 14b. Fragment eines Klavierstücks (1931), mm. 1-4.

Example 15. Fragment eines Klavierstücks (1931), mm. 1-6.

Example 16. Fragment eines Klavierstücks, mm. 1-3.

Example 17. Fragment eines Klavierstücks, mm. 1-10.

Critical Reception, Performance, and Impact of Schoenberg's Music and Thought in Canada Prior to 1960

Elaine Keillor

In August 1960 the International Conference of Composers took place in Stratford, Ontario. Fifty-five composers, representing twenty countries (including twenty-eight composers from Canada), were in attendance at the event. At the time, international music critics expressed astonishment at the range of compositional approaches that were employed by Canadian composers, and wondered why they lacked previous awareness of Canadian chamber and orchestral music, some of it composed with serial techniques inherited from Arnold Schoenberg and the Second Viennese School.[1] I will endeavor to describe some of the performers, composers, and music critics who played a role in raising awareness of Schoenberg's theories and music in Canada prior to 1960. A summary of these findings can be reviewed in Table I.

Early Twentieth-Century Toronto

In the early twentieth century, many Canadian musicians and critics took an active interest in musical developments abroad, and had become aware of the stir being created by the performances of Schoenberg's works through

---

[1]Listings of the concerts, summaries of the round tables, and selected press coverage can be found in John Beckwith and Udo Kasemets, eds., *The Modern Composer and His World: A Report from the International Conference of Composers, August 1960* (Toronto: University of Toronto Press, 1961).

Elaine Keillor is a Distinguished Research Professor Emerita at Carleton University, Ottawa. She has contributed articles to various encyclopedias and dictionaries including *The New Grove, Die Musik in Geschichte und Gegenwart,* and *The Garland Encyclopedia of World Music.* She wrote the essay on music for the widely used third edition of *Profiles of Canada* (2003), and edited four volumes in the twenty-five-volume *Canadian Musical Heritage* series. Dr. Keillor authored *John Weinzweig and His Music: The Radical Romantic of Canada* (Scarecrow Press, 1994), and *Music in Canada: Capturing Landscape and Diversity* (McGill-Queen's University Press, 2006). She is also widely known as a concert pianist, frequently performing premieres of contemporary music. She can be heard on sixteen CDs as pianist and chamber musician, and in DVDs produced for the Piano Research Laboratory of the University of Ottawa.

European periodicals.[2] E.R. Parkhurst, the music and drama critic for Toronto's *The Globe,* whose early references to Schoenberg consisted of information culled from foreign publications, was one of them.[3] In his column dated 24 May 1913, Parkhurst writes about a Vienna performance of Schoenberg's Chamber Symphony, Op. 9, employing a correspondent from London's *Daily Telegraph* as his informant. He reports that, unlike the warm reception the work received at the Promenade Concerts in London in 1912, the Vienna performance created a scandal:

> [T]umult in the auditorium broke loose. Blows were exchanged and people among the audience were slapped by the arrangers of the concert. Later on, Schoenberg attempted to conduct the work of a pupil, Anton von Webern, but it was impossible to go on owing to the noise made by a section of the audience. . . . It is to be hoped that such protests will not become common; and, after all, the Viennese public has it in its power to show its dislike of Herr Schoenberg's methods by staying away.[4]

A year later (13 June 1914) the widely read New York *Musical Courier* was similarly unkind to Schoenberg: "Schoenberg's art is anarchy."[5]

For nearly two hundred years, Canadians have tried to launch music periodicals,[6] but most of them have been ephemeral. The *Canadian Journal of Music,* launched in 1914, was one such venture; it managed to stay afloat for five years. In its second issue, an article written by editor Charles Britten on the Canadian composer Gena Branscombe (a student of Humperdinck) ends: "The composer tells me that she admires Reger, but wonders whether 'we shall go along with Schonfeld.' "[7] (In his next editorial Britten offered an abject apology for misprinting Schoenberg's name.)[8] In December 1914 Luigi von Kunits

---

[2]Augustus S. Vogt, founder of the Toronto Mendelssohn Choir, visited various European cities attending as many musical events as possible from early October 1912 to mid-April 1913. In his series, "Music in European Capitals" written for *Saturday Night,* he states that there were 633 concerts given in Vienna during 1912 and 1600 in Berlin. Although he speaks of contemporary compositions that he heard such as those of Armas Järnefelt in Scandinavia, and recent works by Mahler in Warsaw, Sibelius in Berlin, Richard Strauss in Stuttgart, Elgar in London, he never once referred to Schoenberg.

[3]*The Globe* was founded in 1844 and merged with *The Mail and Empire* in 1936 to become *The Globe and Mail.*

[4]E.R. Parkhurst, "Music and the Drama," *The Globe* (Toronto), 24 May 1913, p. 15.

[5]Ibid., 13 June 1914, p. 13. The author claims to be paraphrasing Glazunov.

[6]The earliest of these was one announced in the Quebec City newspaper, the *Quebec Mercury* (24 March 1818). Stephen Codman declared that he "plans to begin a monthly publication of musical selections of the most approved masters, occasionally interspersed with original compositions founded on the most advanced melodies of this country."

[7]Clarence Britten, "Gena Branscombe," *Canadian Journal of Music* 1/2 (June 1914): 25.

[8]Clarence Britten, "Editorial," *Canadian Journal of Music* 1/3 (July-August 1914): 56.

assumed the editorship of the journal.[9] In a September 1914 article by von Kunits on the contemporary composer Camillo Horn (1860-1941), the following passage (in which he describes Schoenberg as an "impressionist") appears:

> Our contemporary composers may roughly be divided into three "schools." There are first the *classicists* (Brahms and his followers) who strictly adhere to the traditional forms and harmonic structures which they consider as essential to a musical composition as a skeleton is to a vertebrate animal. On the other extreme, there are the *impressionists* (Debussy, Ravel, Schönberg, etc.) who abandon all that is traditional in form and structure for the sake of the most immediate realistic presentation of mood and color; and, in a sense, the *descriptionists* (Strauss, Dukas) have been their fore-runners. Between the two extremes stands the Neo-German School characterized by its continuation of the traditions of the Wagner and Bruckner style.[10]

The next issue contained a lengthy sympathetic review, by Paul Varasdin, of Schoenberg's newly published Six Little Piano Pieces, Op. 19:[11]

> Whoever abandons himself, unbiased and unprejudiced, to these charming thought-flashes and meaningful mood-pictures, painted with the most delicate brush and with a most subtle coloring, will find himself amply rewarded; he will acquire, if not the in-"sight," at least, the in-"feeling," into the new style—if we are permitted to employ such literal translation of a familiar term of German aesthetics, meaning the "interjection of subjective sentiment into the objective presentation of any art." Unfettered by tonality, and unhampered by formal modulation of any sort, or by an *a priori* law of architectonic symmetry, the rhythm pursues its spontaneous, fanciful

[9]Originally from Vienna, von Kunits (1870-1931) came to the United States in 1893 to play violin with an Austrian orchestra at the Chicago World Fair. After teaching violin in Chicago he became in 1896 concertmaster and assistant conductor of the Pittsburgh Orchestra, but when that Orchestra collapsed he returned to Europe in 1910. Two years later he accepted a teaching position in Toronto at the newly established Canadian Academy of Music and became first violinist of the Academy String Quartet. In 1922 he became the conductor of the newly organized Toronto Symphony Orchestra.

[10]Luigi von Kunits, "Camillo Horn," *Canadian Journal of Music* 1/4 (September 1914): 74-75. Alan Gillmor (personal communication) has pointed out that "perhaps this description of Schoenberg as an 'impressionist' is not as odd as it may at first seem, considering that von Kunits was writing in 1914. Contemporary listeners might well have heard the decorative instrumental color of many passages of the Five Orchestral Pieces, Op. 16, for example, as a kind of 'Germanic impressionism.'"

[11]As Kathleen McMorrow has pointed out, this may be a pseudonym of Luigi von Kunits, particularly when Schoenberg is once again described as an impressionist composer. See Kathleen McMorrow, *Répertoire Internationale de la Presse Musicale: The Canadian Journal of Music 1914-1919* (Baltimore, Maryland: NISC, 2005), iii. If it is a pseudonym, von Kunits would not have taken the "Varasdin" from the famous song, "Komm mit nach Varasdin" as Imre Kálmán's operetta *Countess Maritza* did not premiere until 1924 in Vienna. In the United States many immigrants came from the Croatian county of Varasdin. Possibly von Kunits had become aware of that while living in the United States.

inspiration, even where its peculiar aspects are most willfully elaborate and seem, perhaps, over-minute. There is an immediateness of establishing at once the mood, of communicating at once an individual emotion, of which only the impressionistic school is capable. . . . We shall not venture to say that this style is the new style, or that the beauties of classical music are in any danger of fading at its meaning . . . ; but it is undoubtedly a new style, with which we must become familiarized under peril of stagnation, and which if rightly approached, at once reveals itself as a curiously faithful interpreter of all those highly complex and innumerable nameless feelings, moods, and sensations which make up the consciousness of the Modern Man.[12]

During this period von Kunits's editorials sometimes deal with the evolutionary aspects of Western musical development. In a 1915 editorial on "Modern Musical Aesthetics" he writes:

Before we are initiated into Schoenberg's style, we do not "understand" his music, let alone consider it "beautiful"; and some of the music of past ages, we understand "no more." . . . Many works we now consider beautiful, would have horrified the past generation; and we by no means claim to create permanent types for all future. Where, then, is Kant's "universal validity and necessity"?[13]

The first documented public performance of a work by Schoenberg in Canada took place on 31 May 1915. As first violinist in the Academy String Quartette, von Kunits was the driving force behind this performance of Schoenberg's String Quartet No. 1, which received widespread coverage in Canadian periodicals and newspapers. According to an anonymous review that appeared in the *Canadian Journal of Music*, a large audience attended the concert, and gave a rousing ovation to the performers after the final chord.[14] E.R. Parkhurst describes the reception of the work in his review:

The Academy String Quartette introduced Schoenberg to Toronto last night at their concert in the recital hall of the Canadian Academy of Music. Schoenberg is the most discussed musician of the present day. His compositions have met with tremendous opposition and abuse from many influential quarters, but notwithstanding this outcry, they are gradually forcing recognition of their real merit. One cannot presume to give criticism of such colossal work at first hearing. The first impressions were in the main rather chaotic, although there are certain parts, particularly in the latter half of the work, which are strikingly noble and

---

[12]Paul Varasdin, "Piano Futurism—Schönberg," *Canadian Journal of Music* 1/5 (October-November 1914): 114.

[13]Luigi von Kunits, "Modern Musical Aesthetics," *Canadian Journal of Music* 1/9 (March-April 1915): 160, 163.

[14]Anon., "Academy Quartet," *Canadian Journal of Music* 2/3 (July 1915): 44. The performers were von Kunits and Arthur Ely on violins, and brothers Alfred Bruce and George Bruce on viola and cello respectively.

beautiful. The introductory lecture by Mr. von Kunits and the issuing of slips to the audience with the motives printed were new and distinctly welcome innovations worthy of repetition on many other occasions. Mr. von Kunits and his associates must have spent a great amount of thought and time preparing this work, which from a technical point is one of the most difficult ever written. They have had an arduous season and are to be congratulated on their accomplishment.[15]

Echoes of this rare and historic "accomplishment" appeared from time to time in reviews of the Quartette as they returned to more mainstream repertoire in subsequent seasons.[16]

Alberto Guerrero, the extraordinary Chilean pianist and teacher who settled in Toronto in 1918, was another important proponent of Schoenberg's music in early twentieth-century Canada. Although largely an auto-didact, Guerrero was known to have read many of the French music periodicals of the day. Domingo Santa Cruz, one of Guerrero's early students, praised his teacher for the insights he offered his students through his analyses of Schoenberg's First and Second String Quartets (ca. 1916).[17] Guerrero is known to have performed the piano works of Schoenberg frequently in Toronto during the 1920s and 1930s, but efforts to locate those concert programs have not been successful.[18] We know that Guerrero performed the piano part in Stravinsky's *Petrushka* with the Toronto Symphony Orchestra in March 1934, but for his solo recitals—which included works by Tailleferre, Hindemith, Villa-Lobos, Berg, and Schoenberg, among many others—he preferred to play for small groups in his own studio or at the Malloney Gallery (a commercial art gallery).[19]

[15]E.R. Parkhurst, "Music and The Drama," *The Globe* (Toronto), 1 June 1915, 6. This review and others are also to be found in Appendix IV of the dissertation by Robin Elliott, "The String Quartet in Canada." (Ph.D. diss., University of Toronto, 1990).

[16]An anonymous review entitled "Toronto Concert Notes: The Schoenberg Recital," in the *Canadian Journal of Music* 2 (January 1916): 157 includes: "Was there a soul who had ever a fugitive hankering for a snatch of Schoenberg? We guess—not. The Beethoven number was a benediction in itself."

[17]John Beckwith, *In Search of Alberto Guerrero* (Waterloo: Wilfrid Laurier University Press, 2006): 22. Daniel Guerrero, Alberto's oldest brother, did make trips to Europe so it is likely that he was able to bring back to Chile the latest scores available for Alberto who wished to keep current for his own compositions.

[18]Ibid., 75.

[19]Carl Morey, "The Beginnings of Modernism in Toronto," in *Célébration: Aspects of Canadian Music*, ed. Godfrey Ridout and Talivaldis Kenins (Toronto: Canadian Music Centre, 1984), 83.

Early Twentieth Century Montreal: Alfred Laliberté and Léo-Pol Morin

While it is possible that Canadians may have been present at some of the premiere performances of Schoenberg's works in the early twentieth century, firm evidence has not been forthcoming. The young Alfred Laliberté (1882-1952), for example, may well have been one of them, as he attended Berlin's Stern'sches Konservatorium in 1903, where Schoenberg was teaching at the time.[20] At the Conservatory, Laliberté studied piano with Paul Lutzenko, harmony with Ernst Baker, and composition with Wilhelm Klatte.[21] Unlike most of his Quebec contemporaries who sought further musical training in Europe, Laliberté had opted to study in Germany rather than France.

Laliberté's work earned him the Conservatory's top scholarship, allowing him to remain in Berlin for further studies. In 1911 he opened teaching studios in Montreal and New York. Laliberté's studio attracted a literary and musical circle that included the young Rodolphe Mathieu (1890-1962) and Léo-Pol Morin (1892-1941). As Laliberté had become a close personal friend to Alexander Scriabin during his time in Europe and Russia, he developed something of a reputation as a North American proponent of contemporary Russian music. In Laliberté's studio, Mathieu and Morin were able to hear, play, and study contemporary scores including those by Scriabin, who had dedicated his *Poème de l'extase* (1908) to Laliberté. These were undoubtedly formative influences upon Mathieu as he composed his *Trois Préludes* between the years 1912 and 1915. In 1920, Mathieu departed for composition studies in Paris, where his friend Léo-Pol Morin, had been performing his *Trois Préludes* (which are dedicated to Morin) in recital. In 1921, Alexandre Tansman reviewed these pieces in *La Revue musicale*, noting the markedly "Schoenbergian and Stravinskian" touches underlying Mathieu's compositional technique.[22]

Winning the *Prix d'Europe* in 1912, Morin studied for two years in Paris with Isidor Philipp, Raoul Pugno, and Ricardo Viñes, the pianist who premiered many works by Satie, Debussy, and Ravel. Morin was in attendance at the archetypical *succès de scandale* of early twentieth-century music: the 1913 premiere of Stravinsky's *Rite of Spring*.[23] With the outbreak of the First World War, Morin

---

[20]Marie-Thérèse Lefebvre, *Rodolphe Mathieu: L'émergence du statut professionel de compositeur au Québec 1890-1962* (Sillery: Cahiers des Amériques Septentrion, 2005), 35.

[21]Ibid.

[22]Ibid., 99.

[23]A striking difference is seen between Toronto and Montreal with respect to the awareness of Stravinsky in the early 1920s. Stravinsky's name appears only once in the *Canadian Journal of Music* during this period, in an essay by Paul Rosenfeld on "Rimsky-Korsakov" (5/2 [June 1918]: 26-30). The first time Stravinsky was heard in Toronto was a performance of *Petrushka* (cont.) by the Cincinnati Orchestra in March 1926. See Carl Morey, "The Beginnings of Modernism in Toronto," 81.

Figure 1. Cartoon of Léo-Pol Morin, *Le Canada musical*, 23 May 1921.

returned to Montreal to perform, teach, and write. In 1918 he was one of the founders of the radical arts periodical, *Le Nigog*.[24] From 1919 to 1925 he based himself in France and toured as a performer, sometimes in the company of Ravel.

Beyond the efforts of Laliberté and Morin, Montrealers had an opportunity to become familiar with contemporary music through the visits of the Russian musicians Modeste Altshuler (1873-1963) and Leo Ornstein (1892-2002). In 1903, Altshuler founded the Russian Orchestra of New York, with which he made several visits to Canada. The orchestra performed frequently in Montreal between the years 1916 and 1920, giving Canadian premieres of works by

---

[24]*Le Nigog* only survived for a year with twelve issues, but it contained interesting essays dealing with currents in contemporary literature, architecture, painting, and music. Mathieu contributed "Perceptions" (n.p.) and Morin prepared several essays including those on contemporary English music (Mackenzie, Sullivan, Cowen, Vaughan Williams, Holst, Cyril Scott, Percy Grainger, etc. pp. 55-58, 91-98), French composers (Dukas, Ravel, Roussel, p. 105, and Debussy, pp. 137-38), modern Spanish music (Falla, Albéniz, Granados), and an extensive history of modern Russian music (pp. 225-37) including almost two pages on Stravinsky's *Le Sacre du printemps*. There is no reference to Schoenberg in the musical coverage, however. For further details, consult Hélène Paul's "La musique dans *Le Nigog*," in *Le Nigog: Archives des lettres canadiennes,* Tome VII, ed. Paul Wyczynski et al. (Montreal: Fides, 1987), 317-42.

Glazunov, Kalinnikov, Mussorsky, Rachmaninov, Rimsky-Korsakov, Scriabin, Sibelius, and Stravinsky (*Scherzo fantastique*) among others.[25] During an appearance in Montreal in March 1917, Ornstein gave a lecture on modern composition in which he compared the brouhaha created by the works of Schoenberg and other early twentieth-century modernists to the reception Wagner received when he first propounded his theories. According to the reviewer of the *Montreal Daily Star*, Ornstein's discussion proceeded as follows:

> Then, passing over Vincent d'Indy, Mr. Ornstein arrived quickly at a group which he paired off in twos: Debussy and Ravel, Schönberg and Stravinsky, Scriabine and himself. Debussy, he claimed, saw life very clearly; but was afraid of it, "fearfully," and wrote from the outside, but always poetically. Ravel, on the other hand, plunged into all the experiences of life to write about them. Schönberg was rather the man to calculate; Stravinsky was not. Scriabine stood alone, suffering the intensest grief.[26]

Ornstein ended his presentation by stressing that composers have a duty to write music that reflects their present time and concerns. The following day, 13 March 1917, Ornstein gave a piano recital that included works by Franck, Chopin, Albéniz, Debussy, Ravel, Korngold, Cyril Scott, himself, as well as Schoenberg's Six Short Pieces, Op. 19.[27] This was in all probability the first live performance of Schoenberg's music in Montreal.

It was probably through Ornstein that Léo-Pol Morin became aware of Schoenberg's works. Morin soon added Schoenberg's Op. 11 and Op. 19 to his piano solo repertoire. In a recital given at the Salle Pleyel, Paris, on 10 May 1921, he not only performed Op. 19, but gave the Paris premiere of Berg's Op. 1 Piano Sonata.[28] While in Europe, Morin undoubtedly had the opportunity to hear performances of other works by Schoenberg (possibly the 16 January 1922 Paris premiere of *Pierrot Lunaire*, for example, conducted by Darius Milhaud).[29]

At home in Montreal, the periodical *Le Canada musical*, edited by Charles-Onésime Lamontagne, took note of Morin's activities and began to include items with references to Schoenberg. On 5 August 1922, "Que fera Arnold Schoenberg?" refers to a group of New York musicians wondering whether Schoenberg would come to North America. Apparently when Walter Damrosch last visited Vienna, the first thing he wanted to do was to meet the composer of *Gurrelieder*.[30] The next flurry of entries concerning Schoenberg was in connection

---

[25]Lefebvre, *Rodolphe Mathieu* (2005), 46.

[26]"Music Writers Should Express the Current Age," *The Montreal Daily Star*, 13 March 1917, 2.

[27]"Piano Playing of Ornstein Has Always New Side," *The Montreal Daily Star*, 14 March 1917, 2. The anonymous reviewer does not make any comment about the Schoenberg performance.

[28]*Le Canada musical* 21 (May 1921): 4.

[29]Lefebvre, *Rodolphe Mathieu* (2005), 84.

[30]*Le Canada musical*, 5 August 1922, 12. This periodical had its first seven volumes published bimonthly from 1917 until 1924. It was revived for one year in 1930.

with the first performance of *Pierrot Lunaire* in New York that took place under the direction of Louis Gruenberg and the International Composers' Guild on 4 February 1923.[31] In an unsigned article about musical activities in Vienna, three composers are singled out, Richard Strauss, Korngold, and Schoenberg:

> Arnold Schoenberg is the oldest [sic] and most radical of the three. He shows no sign of abandoning the direction that he has chosen. Since publishing his problematic theories, Schoenberg has had his popularity diminish considerably among old admirers and most musicians. Nevertheless, with the assistance of the Society for the Protection of Modern Works [sic] that he has founded, he has attracted several new disciples.[32]

After Morin returned to reside in Montreal, he continued performing and also began writing regularly for publications such as *La Patrie* and later *La Presse*.[33] As Kristina Anderson has pointed out, Morin viewed himself as a *musiographe* (musicologist, historian, and teacher).[34] On 17 March 1927, Mrs. H.M. Little presented a lecture on Schoenberg, Bartók, Berg, and Korngold in her series *Causeries musicales*, with musical illustrations by Morin. It is likely that Morin provided Little with much of the material for the lecture. Two days later Morin published an essay titled "Bartók contre Schoenberg" in *La Patrie*. The article begins by referring to the recent lecture/performance, and then proceeds to a discussion of Schoenberg, which bears citing here at length:

> How does one come to know Schoenberg, this musician who has had such a strong influence on modern music in Austria, and about whom we have heard so many "artistic" scandals? It is excusable that we do not know in depth about this last great Romantic even though he has been celebrated in Europe for almost twenty years and is now age 54.

[31]*Le Canada musical*, 16 December 1922, 16; 3 February 1923, 7.

[32]"De Vienne," *Le Canada musical*, 21 April 1923, 5. Translation by the author: "Arnold Schoenberg est le plus âgé et le plus radical des trois; il ne manifeste aucun désir d'abandonner une voie qui pouvait lui devenir funestes. Depuis qu'il a brûlé ses vaisseaux pour se livrer à ses théories problématiques, sa popularité a diminué considérablement chez les anciens admirateurs et chez la plupart des musiciens. Toutefois, à l'aide de La société pour la protection des oeuvres modernes, qu'il a fondée, il s'est attiré quelques adhérents nouveaux."

There are several inaccuracies here. Strauss (b. 1864) was considerably older than Schoenberg (b. 1875), and Schoenberg's society was named the *Verein für musikalische Privataufführungen* (Society for Private Musical Performances), and not *La Société pour la protection des oeuvres modernes* (Society for the Protection of Modern Works). In citing the recent publication of Schoenberg's "problematic theories," the author is referring to Schoenberg's *Harmonielehre* (Leipzig/Vienna, 1911).

[33]For more details on Morin's activities, see his entry in the *Encyclopedia of Music in Canada*: http://www.thecanadianencyclopedia.com/index.cfm?PgNm=TCE&Params= U1ARTU0002453 (25 October 2008).

[34]Kristina Beth Anderson, "Léo-Pol Morin and *Papiers de musique*: A Critical Introduction and English Translation" (Master's thesis, McMaster University, 1994), 36.

His music cannot charm either the public or our musicians. It takes too many liberties . . . that shock the ears and the spirits attuned to the more common grammatical rules of music. Besides, he himself has advised us that "art is not the consequence of talent but of necessity." He has also stated: "The artisan has talent. He has developed his gifts and that is sufficient to attain his goal. All that he wishes, he can attain. Whether his work be good or bad, superficial or profound, new or out-of-date, it does not matter when he reaches his goal. . . . Nature guides the artist of genius; the talented artist allows himself to be guided by art."

. . . The theories of Schoenberg are as numerous and troubling as his works. However, it must be said to give credit to his theories, that he formulated them after having written his compositions. This man who for some is lost in a foggy metaphysics, and who for others is a romantic lost in the twentieth century, writes music full of logic. And this music is lyrical. It seems that all of his melodies are made to receive texts, even in the instrumental music. His works often involve "chanted words" as in the String Quartet [No. 2] with voice. *Pierrot Lunaire* is one of the most illustrous examples of a chanted poem, at times very curious but extraordinary, accomplished, audacious, and troubling on the part of its creator.

The Six Short Pieces, Op. 19, played at this concert, mark the moment when Schoenberg found his definitive style. Brief melodic phrases consisting of broken contours, some harmonies examined under a microscope suffice to express all of the drama. The longest piece has only two pages. The last one, the shortest, has ten measures. It is almost a blank page, so much so that chords have little stature. But it is great through its economical substance. It was written under the influence of Mahler's funeral. Schoenberg admired him greatly and it was Mahler, the composer, to whom he dedicated his important treatise on harmony. It is the discretion and the extent of his sorrow that he has expressed. The romantic himself is defeated.

There is less brevity in the three pieces, Op. 11, where lyricism ennobles and even overflows. Rather these three pieces mark the emancipation of Schoenberg. It is the point of departure for the flowering that quickly follows.

Is this music viable? It is not assuredly to the extent that one finds with that of Bartók, for example. These little points of music, these scientific tablets which certainly hold an enormous quantity of substance pale before the tumultuous, rhythmic, and powerful wave of a Bartók. . . . The latter is not a scholar in the manner of Schoenberg.

. . . Schoenberg and Berg are cerebral romantics. Bartók is anti-romantic by nature.[35]

[35]*La Patrie* (19 March 1927, 34); also available online at http://bibnum2.banq.qc.ca/bna/ patrie/. Translation by the author: "Connaissait-on Schoenberg, ce musicien que a eu sur la musique actuelle en Autriche une si grand influence, ce musicien qui dût dans son pays si combattu, qui dût lutter si font pour se faire entendre et que fut la cause de tant de scandales 'artistiques?' Nous sommes excusables de ne pas connaître ce grand dernier des romantiques, bien qu'il soit célèbre en Europe depuis près de vingt ans et qu'il soit âgé de cinquante-quatre ans.

Sa musique ne peut charmer ni notre public ni nos musiciens. Elle prend . . . de trop grands libertés que choquent les oreilles et les esprits habitués aux plus infimes jeux-communs de ces illustres grammariens. D'ailleurs, lui-même prend soin de nous avertir que 'l'art n'est pas le conséquence du talent mais de la nécessité.' Et il dit encore: 'L'artisan a du talent. Il a (cont.)

In 1930 Morin selected a number of the essays that he had published in *La Patrie* (1926-29) and in *La Presse* (1929-31) to be published in *Papiers de musique*.[36] In one of them, he comments on Schoenberg's approach in the context of a discussion of the compositions of Mathieu:

As for the musician's harmonic system, it is atonal, as we say in trade jargon. It depends strictly upon his melodic system, which has a disturbing chromatic flexibility that comes and goes without bothering to resolve itself in accordance with the accustomed dictates, nor even for that matter to follow the straight and narrow paths, incompatible with chromaticism in this case. A natural system in that it does not irritate the nature of its author whatsoever. But a system full of dangers in that it foregoes the magnificent glow and vivid manifestations of the tonal system. While the atonal system is full of richness and possibilities, descended from Wagner and Franck, from which Schoenberg made his credo, used for a time by Scriabin and

---

développé ses dons innés et il lui suffit de vouloir pour atteindre son but. Tout ce qu'il veut, il le peut. Que son oeuvre soit bonne ou mauvaise, superficielle ou profonde, neuve ou démodée, peu importe: il atteint son but. . . . La nature guide l'artiste de génie; l'artiste de talent se laisse guider par l'art.'

Les théories de Schoenberg sont aussi nombreuses et troublantes que ses oeuvres. Mais il faut lui rendre cette justice que ces théories, il ne les a formulées qu'après avoir fait les oeuvres.

Cet homme qui pour certains est perdu dans une métaphysique brumeuse, qui peur d'autres est un romantique égaré au 20e siècle, écrit pourtant une musique pleine de logique. Et cette musique est lyrique. Il semble que tous les thèmes soient faits pour recevoir des paroles, même dans la musique instrumentale. Son oeuvre recourt d'ailleurs très souvent à la parole chantée (Quatuor à cordes avec voix). *Pierrot Lunaire* est un des plus illustres exemples de poème chanté: l'oeuvre à la fois la plus curieuse, la plus extraordinaire, la plus achevée, la plus audacieuse et la plus troublante de l'auteur.

Les *Six pièces morceaux*, Op. 19, joués à ce concert, marquent le moment au Schoenberg a trouvé son style définitif. Quelques phrases mélodiques aux contours accidentés, quelques harmonies étudiées au microscope suffisent à exprimer tout un drame. Le plus long a deux pages. Le plus court, le dernier, est de dix mesures. C'est presque une page blanche, tant les accords y tiennent peu de place. Mais il est grand, celui-là, par la substance économisée. Il fut écrit sous l'influence des obsèques de Mahler que Schoenberg admirait profondément et à qui il a dédié son très important traité d'harmonie. Il y a de la discrétion et de la mesure dans la douleur qui s'exprime ici. Le romantique s'est vaincu soi-même.

Il y a moins de raccourci dans les trois pièces, Op. 11, où le lyrisme s'exalte et deborde même. Ce sont cependant ces trois pièces qui marquent l'affranchissement de Schoenberg. C'est le point de départ d'une manière qui devait s'épanouir très vite par la suite.

Cette musique est-elle vivante? Elle ne l'est assurément pas dans la mesure où l'est, par exemple, celle de Bartók. Ces petits instantanés de musique, ces comprimés scientifiques où tient, certes, une quantité énorme de substance, pâliment devant le flot tumultueux, rythmique et puissant d'un Bartók. . . . Ce n'est pas un savant à la manière de Schoenberg. . . . Schoenberg et Berg sont des cérébraux romantiques. Bartók est anti-romantique par nature."

In this article Morin lists the pieces by Bartók played two days before as *Allegro Barbaro, Chansons paysannes hongroises,* the Op. 14 Suite, and the Bagatelles.

[36]Preface to Léo-Pol Morin's *Papiers de musique* (Montreal: Librairie d'action canadienne-française, 1930).

217

still used by many musicians, it is no less a contradictory and indistinct system of grisaille [greyness], where sonorous energy and triumphant assertion are excluded. This system lacks structure. But Rodolphe Mathieu occasionally escapes from it and without committing a tonal sin, he knows how to suddenly settle on perfect concords at certain encumbered bends. But all systems are good if they are mastered.[37]

From this passage it would appear that Morin had little or no awareness that Schoenberg had developed the twelve-tone method during the 1920s.[38] Indeed for at least another decade there was little available published information about the method in the English language, or any other language for that matter.[39] Furthermore, Morin seems to have had little awareness of the stylistic bifurcation that was emerging in European modernism during the 1920s and 30s,[40] with Schoenberg's serialism standing in stark contrast to the neoclassicism of *Les Six* and Stravinsky, a schism that had widened with the publication of Schoenberg's *Three Satires*, Op. 28, in 1925.

As for Mathieu, it is difficult to ascertain how familiar he was with Schoenberg's music and approach, apart from hearing Morin's performances. In his *Parlons ... Musique* (1932), Schoenberg's name appears on page 191 in a list of composers whose compositions were familiar to Debussy.[41] Mathieu refers to Schoenberg in an undated hand-written document (probably dating from

---

[37]Anderson, "Léo-Pol Morin and *Papiers de musique* (1994), 188. Anderson elaborates in a footnote on page 192: "In his search for a fresh scalic organization, Mathieu's exploration of the pre-serialist vein led him to a process subsequently termed 'complementarity.' This solution established the resolution of melodic lines or harmonic progressions through the exhaustion of the twelve-tone series, a clearly serial melodic outline. It has been suggested, although not proven, that Mathieu might have been influenced in this by Scriabin's theory of the attraction of unstable harmonies by stable ones." The original French appears in *Papiers de musique* on pages 95-96. Other references to Schoenberg in this book are to be found on pages 19, 32, 35, and 37.

[38]It must be emphasized that in the case of Schoenberg his mature twelve-tone system had not been reached until the Variations for Orchestra, Op. 31 (1928); see Ethan Haimo, "The Mature Twelve-tone Method," in *The Arnold Schoenberg Companion*, ed. Walter B. Bailey (Westport, Conn. and London: Greenwood Press, 1998), 129.

[39]Elaine Keillor, *John Weinzweig and His Music: The Radical Romantic of Canada* (Metuchen, N.J. and London: Scarecrow Press, 1994), 18.

[40]The Fonds Robert de Rocquebrume [Library and Archives Canada] contains scrapbooks largely filled with cut-out articles written by Morin and programs in which he participated. Although Morin gave a few recitals in both Europe and Canada during the 1930s, there was no evidence in this Fonds of further performances of works by Schoenberg. After Morin's death Robert de Rocquebrume was largely responsible for printing a collection of Morin's later writings in *Musique* (1944) [Léo-Pol Morin, *Musique* (Montreal: Beauchemin, 1944)]. This includes two essays on Austrian music entitled "I. De Bruckner à Schoenberg," (217-20) and "II. Schoenberg et ses disciples" (221-25). Both were written in Switzerland, 30 July 1934. In the latter, Morin refers to twelve different works by Schoenberg as well as *Wozzeck* and Op. 15 of Berg, and Webern's Chamber Symphony. The passages on *Pierrot Lunaire* are almost word for word similar to "Bartók contre Schoenberg." He does not mention the term serialism or offer any explanation of Schoenberg's theories.

[41]Rodolphe Mathieu, *Parlons...Musique* (Montreal: Editions Albert Levesque, 1932), 191.

the early 1950s) that is archived in the Fonds Famille Mathieu. The document, entitled "La composition musicale: Musique moderne," not only discusses Schoenberg, but it also gives some indication of why Mathieu's own compositions became more conservative following his return to Canada in 1925, and his period of study with Vincent d'Indy:

> It is nearly a half-century that the principal method of musical composition has been called serial. Several composers, above all, Schoenberg, use this procedure that they have designated "dodecaphonic." That is to say it is a system built on the twelve chromatic pitches.... Composers before Schoenberg such as Bach, Beethoven, Wagner, etc. have all used dodecaphonic without knowing it. The difference between them and Schoenberg is that the latter makes no change in the order of the twelve melodic pitches used ... [and gives no] special attention to the sound employed for writing melodies. Schoenberg presents any sound of the chromatic ladder and calculates a melody with these sounds. Instead of elucidating a perfection in the relations of the sounds and trying to preserve a beautiful theme, he offers to the ears and to reason nothing properly musical. This series of sounds does not carry the quality of supporting analysis.[42]

Although his intent is clearly to denigrate Schoenberg and his method, Mathieu appears to be emphasizing the same verdict that Schoenberg stressed so often in his discussions and teaching about his method: it is not the tone-row itself, but rather the aural qualities of the music, that is important.[43]

Schoenberg's Years in Los Angeles

When Schoenberg first moved to California from the east coast of the United States in 1934 (largely for health reasons), an advertisement in the local newspaper came to the attention of a number of students, and his first class

[42]Library and Archives Canada, Fonds Famille Mathieu, MUS 165/A7, 14/ box 2. Translation by the author: "Il y a depuis près d'un demi-siècle un principe de composition musical appelé sériel. Des auteurs, surtout Schönberg utilisent ce procédé qu'ils ont désigné 'dodecaphonique.' C'est à dire système basé sur les 12 sons chromatique. . . . Les auteurs avant Schönberg, Bach, Beethoven, Wagner, etc. feraient du dodecaphonique sans le savoir. La difference entre eux et Schönberg, c'est que ce dernier ne fait aucun change des 12 sons mélodiques qu'il utilise [. . . ou donne] une attention spéciale au choix des sons employés pour écrire des mélodies.

. . . Schönberg present n'importe quel son de l'échelle chromatique et compte une mélodie avec ses sons. Plutôt d'élucider un perfection dans les rapports de les sons et essayer de conserve un beau thème, il offre aux oreilles et à la raison rien proprement musicale. Cette série de sons n'a mène pas la qualité de supporter l'analyse." In another file (MUS 165/ A7, 20/ box 2) one can find Mathieu's remark that no Scriabin was taught in Paris. Before his studies with d'Indy he knew Scriabin's Second and Third Piano Sonatas, and the Preludes, and had worked out chords built on fourths. In Paris though, d'Indy opened up for him the magic that could be found in tertian harmony, and considered quartal harmony to be "fluff."

[43]See Bryan R. Simms, "Schoenberg: The Analyst and the Analyzed," in *The Arnold Schoenberg Companion*, ed. Walter B. Bailey (Westport, Conn. and London: Greenwood Press, 1998), 223-50.

was soon formed. Among Schoenberg's earliest students in California was Gerald Strang (1908-83) from Claresholm, Alberta, who soon became the composer's assistant.[44] Schoenberg's presence at the University of Southern California (USC) was rather quiet at first, but his reputation as a teacher soon grew. Leonard Stein relates the story of how, when the committee seeking a professor of composition at the University of California at Los Angeles (UCLA) visited the eastern United States, Maurice Zorn asked Vern Knudsen, a member of the committee, why they were carrying out their search in the east, when "the greatest of all living composers is in Los Angeles, teaching at the University of Southern California."[45]

To the surprise of some of his students, Schoenberg did not stress his own compositions, or regularly discuss his serial technique, in his teaching.[46] (Stein relates how the students had to beg him to discuss his Third String Quartet [1927] during the spring session of 1935.)[47] Rather, Schoenberg always sought to develop the individuality of each student by examining the masterpieces of the past to show the creation of clear phrases, logical constructions and continuations, along with fluency and "unity in variety."[48]

Back in Canada, occasional performances and references to Schoenberg occurred in the media during the years immediately prior to the Second World War. In Toronto, the Hart House String Quartet (1923-1946)—Canada's first professional, fully subsidized group—had been formed. Under the leadership of its first violinist, Geza de Kresz, the Quartet performed Schoenberg's Op. 7 on 13 April 1935 along with a work by Amice Calverley, an English composer working and studying in Toronto at the time. In their program, the Hart House String Quartet referred to the earlier Toronto performance and included the same notes prepared by von Kunits.[49] Raymond Mullens of *Saturday Night Magazine* praised both the performance and the work:

---

[44]Strang had obtained a degree in philosophy at Stanford University and had become active in Henry Cowell's New Music Society in San Francisco. He received a scholarship to study with Schoenberg at USC, and then followed him to UCLA where he was his teaching assistant from 1936 to 1938. After the incarceration of Cowell in 1936, Strang also took over the editorship of *New Music Edition* to 1940. He began teaching at Long Beach City College in 1938 and eventually finished a Ph.D. at USC in 1948. As a consultant for building design and acoustics, he became well known. In 1963 he began working on computer music at the Bell Laboratories, under the guidance of James Tenney. He soon became a lecturer in electronic music at UCLA. He was co-editor with Leonard Stein of Schoenberg's *Fundamentals of Composition* (London, Faber and Faber, 1967). For more information on his compositions, consult Jean-Claude Risset, "Gerald Strang: 1908-1983," *Computer Music Journal* 8/4 (1984): 5.

[45]Marko Kawabata, "Schoenberg at UCLA: Reminiscences from Leonard Stein," *Echo* 2/2 (Fall 2000): 5.

[46]See, for example, Lovina May Knight, "Classes with Schoenberg," *Journal of the Arnold Schoenberg Institute* 13/2 (November 1990): 156.

[47]Marko Kawabata, "Schoenberg at UCLA," 3.

[48]Leonard Stein, "Schoenberg as Teacher," in Bailey, ed., *Arnold Schoenberg Companion* (1998), 252-53.

[49]See Appendix IV of Elliott, "The String Quartet in Canada" (1990).

The Schoenberg quartet, as is the case with all of this composer's earlier work is a mystery when viewed in the light of what he considers his most mature expression. If ever a man was born into this world equipped to write music of Titanic proportions it is this same Schoenberg. His earlier works seem to impress and move everyone who hears them. In writing them he obviously followed the only true method of composition; he shut his eyes, opened wide his ears and waited to see what God would send him. And God, or a remarkable memory, sent him something very good indeed. This something he used with great technical skill and the result was a work that only genius could have produced. Then upon an evil day Schoenberg thought he had begun to think; he was seized with a THEORY. This was, probably, his undoing, for music has its own special kind of logic the one great rule of which is that what is written down shall sound effective. You can't write music to a formula no matter how much you know about music and how much erudition has entered into the preparation of your formula. And so, except for a few zealots, the later Schoenberg is a dreary fellow.

But he was anything but that when he wrote his Quartet, opus 7. Here is a man torn with emotion and steeped in romance. If he is fond of recollections of Wagner he transforms them into a musical fabric that is not in the least Wagnerian. The quartet must be very long, but its inspiration is so unflagging, its melodic beauties so many and its writing so eerily skilful that it seems to pass by like a flash.

It has been written a good many years now and most of us have had a chance to hear it before. I don't think many would say that they heard a finer performance than the Hart House Quartet gave it. Together with their playing of the Debussy quartet the playing of this Schoenberg music will stay in my memory as one of the finest things the quartet has done. And how many fine things it has done![50]

Only occasional references to Schoenberg had appeared during the war years in the Canadian press. Some of these involved descriptions of sensational performances such as the Philadelphia premiere of the Violin Concerto.[51] An article describing Schoenberg's decline of an offer from Irving Thalberg to write the score for the movie *The Good Earth* concludes with Schoenberg's rebuttal: "With so much going on, what do you want with music?"[52]

A few Canadian composers had fleeting direct encounters with Schoenberg in Los Angeles in the 1940s. Jean Coulthard describes her three meetings with Schoenberg in 1942 as follows:

[I said] I had never used his twelve-tone system and that I'd heard that he taught traditionally too and I'd be very interested to have some criticisms of my work. He

[50]Raymond Mullens, "Musical Events," *Saturday Night*, 20 April 1935, 18.

[51]"Shocked by Schoenberg Score Walk Out of Hall" *The Globe and Mail*, 7 December 1940, 19. Of course, this article did not explain how Stokowski had battled with the management of the Philadelphia Orchestra to give this premiere. See Gunther Schuller, "Schoenberg's Influence," in Bailey, ed., *Arnold Schoenberg Companion* (1998), 266.

[52]Roly Young, "Rambling with Roly," *Globe and Mail*, 28 June 1945, 9. This item does not explain that Schoenberg had demanded a higher salary than first offered and certain artistic control which was denied. See Walter B. Bailey, "Biography," in Bailey, ed., *Arnold Schoenberg Companion* (1998), 35.

said, "Oh you don't need to write in the twelve-tone system. You should write how you feel." I'll always remember that. He went over a string work and some early piano preludes which I had written. . . . I was terribly pleased at the end; he offered to send them to Schirmer for me. . . . He was a delightful man, . . . very cultured and we discussed at one session, what he was aiming to do with the twelve-tone system. By that time he had written the lovely 1920s piano pieces and all those things that I knew, of course.[53]

Subsequently Coulthard occasionally called upon the twelve-tone method as an organizational technique, and taught it to her students at the University of British Columbia.

Canadian composer Eldon Rathburn (born 1916 in Queenstown, New Brunswick) had a memorable encounter with Schoenberg in 1945. In 1944, as a young man in Saint John, Rathburn learned that he had won a composition competition judged by three Los Angeles composers: Arnold Schoenberg, Alexandre Tansman, and Arthur Lang. As a result, Rathburn was invited to spend two weeks in Los Angeles, where a performance of his submission (*Symphonette*) was given by Alfred Wallenstein and the Los Angeles Philharmonic. During his stay in Los Angeles, Rathburn was invited back to the Schoenberg's Rockingham home, where he met the family,[54] chatted with Schoenberg, showed him more music, and performed some Schumann (with compliments from Schoenberg, apparently) on the family piano. Figure 2 shows a selection of photographs taken by Rathburn during the visit. During a long and distinguished career as a film composer for the National Film Board of Canada, Rathburn occasionally tried to incorporate twelve-tone technique into his film scores (to the consternation, apparently, of some of his collaborators).[55] Later in his career, he wrote a humorous and programmatic character piece for piano solo, titled *Schoenberg versus Gershwin* (1991), depicting Schoenberg embroiled in an aggressive tennis match with Gershwin, complete with leitmotifs for each composer taken from their works.

Schoenberg's works seem to have received very little performance or attention in any of Canada's major cities during the 1940s. In the first half of the twentieth century, it was very rare in Canada for tributes and editorials about prominent composers to be published upon their death. However, on 17 July 1951, a tribute to Schoenberg appeared in Toronto's *Globe and Mail*. It began:

---

[53]Jean Coulthard, "Jean Coulthard," in *Canadian Music in the 1930s and 1940s*, ed. Beverley Diamond Cavanagh (Kingston Ont.: School of Music, Queen's University, 1986), 44.

[54]Rathburn encountered the three Schoenberg children again in 2007 in Ottawa, sixty-two years after this first meeting in 1945. Just over a year later, on 30 August 2008, Rathburn died in Ottawa.

[55]James Wright kindly provided this information, citing personal communication with Rathburn in June 2007.

Figure 2. Above Left: Eldon Rathburn in front of the Beverley Hills hotel, 1945. Above Right: Rathburn's photograph of Schoenberg with his children Nuria, Lawrence, and Ronald. Below Left: Rathburn (far left) dining with M.G.M. mogul Louis B. Meyer (to his left), actor Walter Pigeon (far right), and an unidentified guest. Below Right: Schoenberg dining with other adjudicators at the same reception. All photographs were taken during Eldon Rathburn's visit to Los Angeles in 1945.

The death of Arnold Schoenberg . . . will not end the controversy started half a century ago by his campaign "to free harmony from all rules." The composer and music theorist lived long enough to see disciples of his twelve-tone scale installed in high places, as authors, teachers and performers. But his estimate that it would take fifty years before his aims would be understood was too optimistic. There still is a small world audience for performances of his type of music—and from the popular point of view the revolution which he introduced is still in blueprint form.[56]

[56]"Arnold Schoenberg," *Globe and Mail*, 17 July 1951, 6. It should be noted that the editorialist's claim that Schoenberg's intent was "to free harmony from all rules" would have inflamed Schoenberg, as the truth was the contrary.

Perhaps this editorial was also a signal for the dramatic changes in the 1950s. Three strong new voices would promote Schoenberg's works and thought in Canada for the next several decades: John Weinzweig, Glenn Gould, and Serge Garant.

John Weinzweig

Although he had received musical training only through childhood summer camps, piano lessons, and the extracurricular orchestra at Toronto's Harbord Collegiate Institute, John Weinzweig (1913-2006) resolutely determined to become a composer at the age of nineteen.[57] However in the 1930s there was no center for advanced training in composition in Canada. Of Jewish heritage, the Weinzweigs knew that sojourning to Europe was out of the question, due to the rise of Nazism. Having obtained an undergraduate degree at the University of Toronto and saved enough money, Weinzweig registered at the Eastman School of Music, University of Rochester, in 1937. At Eastman, Weinzweig studied composition with Bernard Rogers (who had been a student of Ernest Bloch, Nadia Boulanger, and Frank Bridge), and spent many hours studying contemporary scores and listening to available recordings in the Sibley Music Library. There, one afternoon when he first heard Berg's *Lyric Suite* (1926), Weinzweig had a life-altering experience. While he knew that Berg was a student of Schoenberg, he otherwise knew nothing about the Second Viennese School, its aesthetics, and its methods. When his queries to professors at Eastman provided no answers, he sought information in journals such as *Modern Music* and *The Musical Quarterly*.[58] With these meager guidelines, and his study of Schoenberg's string quartets and piano pieces, Weinzweig wrote his first composition based on a twelve-tone series on 30 June 1938: a short piano piece titled *Spasmodia*.

When Weinzweig returned to Toronto after graduating from Eastman, he slowly built up a class of theory and composition students. Like Schoenberg, he always stressed sonic results rather than adherence to rigid rules in his teaching. He occasionally tried to revisit the idea of working with a row in his own compositions during this period, but it was not until the appearance of Krenek's *Studies in Counterpoint* (1940) that he developed a clear idea of the theoretical framework for twelve-tone technique.[59] In 1941 he began to fulfill commissions from the Canadian Broadcasting Corporation (CBC), and to write original music for radio dramas. As these dramas generally involved non-fictional accounts of

---

[57]This was entirely a new concept in Canada at the time as musical composition was viewed as a sideline activity to one's main occupation as a musician. See Keillor, *John Weinzweig and His Music* (1994), 2.

[58]Ibid., 271.

[59]Ernst Krenek, *Studies in Counterpoint Based on the Twelve-Tone Technique* (New York: G. Schirmer, 1940).

individuals fleeing persecution in Europe, Weinzweig felt that intense emotional impact was required of the supporting music. He discovered that twelve-tone technique could both provide this emotional intensity, and stand in contrast with the diatonic materials of the musical quotations that he employed to sonically identify the cultural backgrounds of his subjects.[60] Accordingly, Canadians began to hear dodecaphonic music more frequently, though they may not have been aware of it.

Like von Kunits and Morin, Weinzweig understood contemporary compositional language as something that evolved from earlier styles and reacted to present conditions. In an article that appeared in the *Canadian Review of Music and Art* (June 1942), entitled "The New Music," he wrote:

> The canonic devices of Josquin Des Prez and the tonal implications of Scriabin's mystery chord built on superimposed fourths; the polyphony of Bach and the vertical thinking of Debussy; the diatonic scale of Haydn and the twelve-tone technique of Schoenberg; the semitonal inflection of Wagner's "Tristan" and the rhythmic counterpoint and polytonality of Stravinsky's "Rite of Spring":—these all are masterful and valid. Each exemplifies one possible way in which the mind can comprehend coherent patterns of tone and rhythm. Each, too, is a product of a changing social environment.[61]

This was the essential outlook that Weinzweig adopted in his teaching of several generations of music students. He encouraged each student to find his or her own voice. While his own approach was an outgrowth of that of the Second Viennese School, he did not insist that serial technique was the only way to the future. When some of Weinzweig's students nonetheless adapted the technique to their own purposes, Weinzweig was no longer isolated as a serial composer in Canada. In addition, a number of European musicians who had emigrated to Canada during the 1930s, and during and following the war years—including Franz Kraemer (a private student of Berg), Otto Joachim, Istvan Anhalt, Emmy Heim,[62] Karl Steiner (who had studied with Wellesz and Webern),[63] and Udo Kasemets (who had worked with Krenek),[64] for example—were proponents of serialism.

---

[60]See Keillor, *John Weinzweig and His Music* (1994), 124-27. The Appendix 261-68 lists some 100 radio and film scores by Weinzweig.

[61]John Weinzweig, "The New Music," *Canadian Review of Music and Art* 1/5 (June 1942): 16.

[62]Heim, who had performed at Schoenberg's *Verein*, spent several months teaching and performing in Canada in the 1930s before permanently moving to Toronto in 1936.

[63]Albrecht Gaub, "Karl Steiner, Canadian Apostle of the Second Viennese School," *Newsletter of the Institute for Canadian Music* 1/2 (May 2003); 3-7 (online edition: http://www.utoronto.ca/icm/0102a.html)

[64]The dates of their arrival in Canada were respectively Kraemer (1940), Joachim and Anhalt (1949), and Kasemets (1951). Kraemer became a very influential producer at CBC of music productions, while both Joachim and Anhalt had significant influence through their teaching in Montreal. Kasemets also became fascinated with the ideas of John Cage and has been one of those Canadians who has drawn together disparate approaches to composition.

Glenn Gould

No account of the Canadian Schoenberg legacy before 1960 would be complete without reference to Canada's iconic pianist, Glenn Gould. Gould's teacher, Alberto Guerrero, introduced him to the piano music of Schoenberg by 1948 or earlier. Gould was fascinated with "row technique" (apparently somewhat to the consternation of Guerrero), and employed it in the first two of his Five Short Piano Pieces, probably written in 1950.[65] Gould first performed these compositions in January 1951. Some of Guerrero's other students became advocates of the music of Schoenberg and his school. Anahid Alexanian, for example, organized the first Canadian performance of *Pierrot Lunaire* in Toronto on 27 May 1962, fully fifty years after its composition.[66]

Gould's subsequent numerous performances of works by Schoenberg began with a Memorial Concert given at the Royal Conservatory Concert Hall in Toronto on 4 October 1952. Together with Robert Fulford, Gould organized this event under the banner of the New Music Associates, an organization they had created in order to promote contemporary music. On this occasion he performed the Suite for Piano, a work that Gould considered one of the great masterpieces of the piano repertoire.[67] Ten days later Canadians had the opportunity of hearing Gould perform this work on a CBC radio broadcast. The following year Gould performed Schoenberg's Piano Concerto with the CBC Symphony on 9 March 1953. New Music Associates organized a concert on 9 January 1954, celebrating the Second Viennese School. The first Canadian performance of the *Ode to Napoleon* took place at this event.

Elsewhere in this volume Gould's important tour to Russia in 1957 is examined, particularly with regard to Gould's promotion of the works of the Second Viennese School. Only recently has it been realized how much Gould wrote about Schoenberg, as many of these writings remained in manuscript during his lifetime. Serge Garant would have more success than Gould in disseminating his writings on Schoenberg's theoretical and aesthetic ideas.

---

[65]Carl Morey has prepared an edition of Glenn Gould's *Klavierstücke: Piano Pieces* (Schott 1995). In his preface Morey points out that Gould uses the Schoenberg method of "Principal" and "Secondary" statements to a certain degree in the first two of the Five Short Piano Pieces (1950). The Two Pieces for Piano (1951-52) have a single twelve-note series as their basis and reflect a systematic application of the Schoenberg technique. As for Gould's fascination with the manipulation of twelve pitches, I personally heard this observation of Guerrero's consternation from his wife, Myrtle Rose Guerrero, in 1982, and John Beckwith refers to this as well in his book, *In Search of Alberto Guerrero* (Waterloo: Wilfrid Laurier University Press, 2006), 107.

[66]John Kraglund, "Music in 1962: Pierrot Worth Wait of 50 Years," *Globe and Mail*, 28 May 1962, 39.

[67]"I can think of no composition for solo piano of the first quarter of this century that can stand as its equal. . . . [In its] rare joie de vivre, and blessed enthusiasm for the making of music, [it] is among the most spontaneous and wickedly inventive of Schoenberg's works" ("The Piano Music of Arnold Schoenberg," in *The Glenn Gould Reader*, ed. Tim Page [New York: Alfred A. Knopf, 1985], 127).

Serge Garant

After Morin's untimely death in 1941, no other Quebec composer seemed ready or able to carry the torch for contemporary music in the province. Laliberté had even denigrated Morin for his lack of training as a composer, his support of folk music as a possible resource for serious music, and his continued championing of contemporary composers.[68] As Quebec artists began to denounce the conservative society around them in the late 1940s (in a foreshadowing of the "quiet revolution" of the 1960s), new voices for contemporary currents in the arts arose. Among them were Serge Garant (1929-86) and Pierre Mercure (1927-66). Mercure had studied composition with Luigi Dallapiccola in 1951 and thoroughly assimilated the principles of the twelve-tone method in his early works.

Beginning as a clarinetist and saxophonist and largely playing jazz, Garant discovered contemporary music on his own. In his hometown of Sherbrooke, he gave a performance of Schoenberg's Op. 11 in 1950 and the following year he arranged for the performance of the Op. 43 Theme and Variations by a Sherbrooke band.[69] Later that year Garant departed for Paris where he became a student of Messiaen, devouring and analyzing the score of Berg's *Wozzeck*, among other Second Viennese masterworks.[70] Settling back in Montreal in 1953, Garant began to employ serial techniques in his compositions. Through Pierre Boulez, he had become much more aware of Webern, and began to program his works in 1954.[71] Garant soon became something of a lightning rod in Quebec, vigorously debating reactionary opponents to the compositional avant garde. One such conservative was Jean Vallerand, who wrote a column titled "La vie musicale" for *Le Devoir*. In an article headlined "La Public et la musique moderne" (*Le Devoir*, 13 February 1954), Vallerand attacked dodecaphonism in general,

---

[68]After Morin's death in a car accident, several encomia appeared in Quebec newspapers. Laliberté on 30 August 1941 criticized the one by Jean Désy by saying that Morin was mistaken for saying music began with Debussy [Library and Archives Canada, Fonds Laliberté, MUS 266/67, B1, 32]. Also in the Library and Archives Canada [Fonds Laliberté, MUS 266/68 B1, 34, 2] is a 112-page typescript of Laliberté conducting an interview with "Moi," but the details reveal that he had in mind Morin as Moi. On page 3 there is a favorite composer list for Moi that begins with Stravinsky, has Berg as No. 8, and Schoenberg as No. 9. After Scriabin's death, Laliberté had become a great admirer of the late romantic Russian composer/pianist, Nikolai Medtner (1880-1951), who referred to Laliberté as his son.

[69]If the author's experience was typical of a number of young musicians in Canada in the early 1950s, Garant was not the only young musician obtaining Schoenberg's music and learning it on his own without the guidance of a teacher like Guerrero in Toronto. Even Guerrero did not have all of his students learn Schoenberg, but he did play the piano works for his students (John Beckwith, e-mail message to author, 9 January 2008).

[70]Lefebvre, *Serge Garant et la revolution musicale au Québec* (Montreal: Louise Courteau, 1986), 40.

[71]Ibid., 48.

and Schoenberg in particular.[72] Garant's rebuttal disputed several aspects of Vallerand's argument, including his dating of the twelve-tone method from 1913-14, and his argument that serialism was merely an abstract theoretical idea that had no concern for the sonorous quality and character of the music itself.[73] Subsequently Vallerand wrote four columns entitled "La Musique de douze sons" in which he tried to explain the basic technique with reference to the analyses of René Leibowitz (particularly that of Schoenberg's Variations for Orchestra).[74] Regardless of where one stood in the debate, it is clear that these very public polemics served to raise the general awareness of Schoenberg in mid-century Quebec.

Schoenberg on CBC Radio

As Gould in Toronto and Garant in Montreal organized more live performances of Schoenberg's music, radio broadcasts including Schoenberg were also heard with increasing frequency in Canada.[75] Schoenberg's early *Transfigured Night*, his most frequently performed score in Canada as elsewhere, appears to have received its Canadian premiere on 19 August 1949 in a CBC radio broadcast from Toronto (probably of the original sextet version).[76]

---

[72]Jean Vallerand, "La Vie musicale: Le public et la musique moderne," *Le Devoir*, 13 February 1954, 5.

[73]All of the writings (1954-84) of Garant including transcriptions of his radio commentaries on contemporary music can be found in Lefebvre, *Serge Garant* (1986), 73-205.

[74]Jean Vallerand, "La Vie musicale: II. La musique de douze sons," *Le Devoir*, 29 May 1954, 5. The publication by René Leibowitz is *Schönberg et son école: l'étape contemporaine du langage musical* (Paris 1947). The main argument that Vallerand uses to say that Schoenberg's approach lacks validity is that contemporary listeners expect recognizable vertical combinations in a contrapuntal texture. In the third essay, he states that Schoenberg is admired for his recipes, but not his compositions, and in the fourth he quotes Furtwaengler who apparently told him that young composers had to use this system of composition as they knew no other ("La Vie musicale: La musique de 12 sons," *Le Devoir* (1954): 22 May, 7, 5; 29 May, 5; 5 June, 7; 12 June, 7.

[75]Periodically, Canadians could hear on the CBC, broadcasts from abroad that included Schoenberg's works. A premiere broadcast from NBC in 1944 was that of the Piano Concerto which John Beckwith recalls as his first introduction to Schoenberg (e-mail message to the author, 9 January 2008), the New York Philharmonic's premiere of the *Ode to Napoleon* from CBS in 1944, the St. Louis Symphony Orchestra playing *Transfigured Night* on 9 November 1948, and on 14 February 1951 the Oklahoma Symphony Orchestra playing the Theme and Variations, Op. 43. A portion of the *Gurrelieder*, "Song of the Wood Dove," with the New York Philharmonic, was broadcast on 8 July 1951. The Violin Concerto with the Hessian Radio Orchestra on 29 August 1951 and the New York Philharmonic on 30 November 1952, the Handel-Schoenberg Concerto for String Quartet and Orchestra on 22 October 1951, and again on the French network 27 January 1952, appear listed in the *CBC Times*. Then Canadian performers get into the act: Trudy Carlyle singing "Song of the Wood Dove," 21 May 1952; Glenn Gould performing the Piano Suite, 14 October 1952, and the Piano Concerto with the CBC Symphony, 9 March 1953. Adar Charlton kindly did the research to obtain this information.

[76]Although Walter Kaufmann, the conductor of the Winnipeg Symphony at the time, appears to be connected with this performance according to the *CBC Times*, programs of the (cont.)

According to the *CBC Times*, the first Canadian orchestral performance took place under the baton of Heinz Unger in Toronto on 23 January 1952 for CBC Wednesday Night. In June of the same year, it was performed by the CBC Vancouver String Orchestra. A live performance given by Ethel Stark's Symphonetta at the Montreal Summer Festival on 30 August 1954 was very likely the Montreal premiere of the work (see the programme of this concert, shown in Figure 3).[77]

Only with a series of radio programs initiated and hosted by John Beckwith did Canadians finally have the opportunity to hear a wide range of works by Schoenberg. The nationally broadcast CBC series "Music in Our Time" began with a program on Bartók on 15 August 1953. The September 24 listing in the *CBC Times* also includes "Schoenberg" but does not specify the works or performances heard. Beckwith recalls that he played the String Trio (1946) on an early program.[78] Over the next four years, Beckwith incorporated thirteen different works by Schoenberg into his programming. In 1956 he began hosting a new CBC program called "World of Music." Its first broadcast on 9 October 1956 paired *Pierrot Lunaire* with fourteenth-century music. In all, Beckwith played recordings of twenty-three works by Schoenberg including a four-week series on the string quartets in 1957.[79]

Winnipeg Symphony do not indicate that he ever conducted the orchestral version of this work. Perhaps he conducted the sextet or commented on the work for the broadcast.

[77]Ethel Stark (b. 1916) had an extensive career as a solo violinist. In Montreal she formed and conducted the Montreal Women's Symphony Orchestra which was the first Canadian orchestra to play in New York (22 October 1947).

[78]E-mail message to the author (9 January 2008). The time slot of this series varied considerably in its opening weeks moving between Saturday and Thursday evenings at either 10, 10:30 p.m., or 7:30 p.m. until it settled on 6 October at Tuesday evenings, 10:30 p.m. I am indebted to Adar Charlton for this information.

[79]Beckwith's inclusion of Schoenberg on CBC Radio Programs: "Music in Our Time" 1952-56, and "World of Music" 1956-59: Chamber Symphony No. 1: 05/11/1958; 06/07/1959; Chamber Symphony No. 2: 05/11/1957; Five Pieces for Orchestra: 22/02/1955; *Kol Nidre*: 12/10/1954; 24/07/1956; *Ode to Napoleon*: 14/06/1955; Piano Concerto: 18/05/1954; Piano Suite, Op. 25: 13/09/1955; 28/01/1958; *Pierrot Lunaire*: 09/10/1956; Serenade, Op. 24: 20/08/1957; Six Piano Pieces, Op. 19: 08/01/1956; String Quartet No. 1: 29/01/1957; String Quartet No. 2: 05/02/1957; String Quartet No. 3: 3rd movement 19/07/1955; 12/02/1957; String Quartet No. 4: 1st movement only, 24/11/1953; 19/02/1957; String Trio: (cont.) 24/09/1953; 21/09/1954; Suite, Op. 29 or portions thereof: 02/04/1956; 22/05/1956; *A Survivor from Warsaw*: 01/02/1955; Three Songs, Op. 48: 03/09/1957; Variations for Orchestra, Op. 21: 17/06/1958; Variations for Organ, 24/11/1953; Violin Concerto or portions thereof: 22/02/1955; 25/08/1956; 01/11/1959; Violin Fantasy: 13/09/1955; Wind Quintet, Op. 26: 02/06/1958.

Conclusion

Beckwith's efforts to enlighten Canadians about Schoenberg's legacy prepared the ground for further work, mainly done at Canadian universities, in the 1960s. Readers could also find thoughtful commentaries and reviews of recordings in a newly minted journal, *The Canadian Music Journal*, that had emerged in 1957. The very first issue of this journal featured Glenn Gould's essay, "The Dodecacophonist's [sic] Dilemna."[80] Even so, Canadian listeners and performers continued to have difficulty comprehending what this music meant and how its composers intended them to listen to it.[81] As Garant had so often stated in his writings, music students were rarely given the opportunity to hear and learn these works, and thus could not readily understand the most recent trends in contemporary music that had built upon foundations laid in the early twentieth century by Schoenberg, the Second Viennese School, and others.[82]

Since 1960, artists of the stature of Glenn Gould, and contemporary music organizations such as the *Société de musique contemporaine du Québec* (SMCQ, founded 1966) in Montreal and New Music Concerts (founded 1971) in Toronto (among others), have made great strides in bringing intelligent, rigorous, informed, and sensitive performances of Schoenberg's works before Canadian audiences. Only through such insightful performances will Schoenberg's legacy be fully appreciated in Canada and elsewhere.

[80]*The Canadian Journal of Music* 1/1 (Autumn 1956): 2-29. Other important articles from this journal showing aspects of the debate around Schoenberg and his followers are: Maurice Lowe's "The Labyrinth of Modern Music" (1/2 Winter 1957: 17-20); Harry Adaskin's "Review of Leonard Ratner's *Music—The Listener's Art* (2/1 Autumn 1957: 59-60); Istvan Anhalt's Review of "New Records" (2/3 Spring 1958: 50-54); A.G. Ross's "Festival Fever in Europe" (3/1 Autumn 1958: 38-43); and Austin Clarkson's Review of Rudolph Réti's *Tonality, Atonality, Pantonality* (4/1 Autumn 1959: 81, 83).

[81]As revealed in the early issues of *The Canadian Journal of Music* and the performance of Schoenberg's String Quartet No 1.

[82]Lefebvre, *Serge Garant* (1986), 101, 116-17, 146, 149, 155.

Monday, August 30   Lundi, 30 août

AT L'ERMITAGE HALL

9 p.m.

Chamber Music Concert

THE ETHEL STARK SYMPHONIETTA

Conductor
ETHEL STARK

PROGRAM

Symphony in E flat . . . . *Carl Friedrich Abel*
    Allegro
        Andante
            Presto

Concerto in E major . . . . *Karl Ditter Von Dittersdorf*
      for Contre Bass and Orchestra
    Allegro moderato
        Adagio
            Allegro
           Soloist: **NATALIE CLAIR**

Transfigured Night (Verklärte Nacht) . . . . . *Arnold Shoenberg*

INTERMISSION

Mass in G major No. 2 . . . . *Franz Schubert*
      for Chorus and Orchestra

    Kyrie
      Gloria
        Credo
          Sanctus
            Benedictus
              Agnus Dei

    Soloists: **ANN WATSON**, soprano
          JEAN-PAUL JEANNOTTE, tenor
          ROBERT SAVOIE, baritone.

BERLIOZ CHOIR — Director. **MARCEL LAURENCELLE**

— 53 —

Figure 3. Program of Ethel Stark Symphonietta.
(Library and Archives Canada, Fonds Ethel Stark, MUS 242, 1993-19, box 1)

Table 1. Chronicle of critical reception, performance, and impact of Schoenberg's music and thought in Canada prior to 1960.

1903	Canadian Alfred Laliberté studies at Berlin's Stern'sches Konservatorium, where Schoenberg is teaching
24 May 1913	Parkhurst in Toronto's *Globe* writes about a Vienna performance of the First Chamber Symphony, Op. 9 (1906).
June 1914	Reference to Schoenberg in Britten's article on Gena Branscombe in the first volume of the *Canadian Journal of Music* (June 1914).
October 1914	"Piano Futurism – Schonberg," a review of Op. 19 (1911), in *Canadian Journal of Music* 1/5.
May 1915	*Musical Canada* features an item on the upcoming performance of String Quartet No. 1, Op. 7 (1905).
31 May 1915	Academy String Quartette of Toronto performs String Quartet No. 1, Op. 7 (1905).
13 May 1916	*Le Canada* states that Leo Ornstein, the Russian composer-pianist, shows an interest in the methods and aesthetics of the European modernists (Schoenberg, Stravinsky, et al).
13 March 1917	Leo Ornstein performs Six Short Pieces, Op. 19 (1911), during his Montreal recital.
August 1918	Alberto Guerrero settles in Toronto after reportedly giving performances of Schoenberg's Op. 11(1909) and analytic presentations on String Quartets Nos. 1, Op. 7 (1905) and 2, Op. 10 (1908) in Chile.
10 May 1921	Canadian pianist Léo-Pol Morin performs recital at Salle Pleyel in Paris that includes works by Schoenberg (Op. 19, 1911) and Berg (Sonata, Op. 1, 1908). The latter was a premiere performance for Parisian audiences.
21 May 1921	Cartoon in *Le Canada musical* associates Morin with Schoenberg.
4 August 1922	*Le Canada musical* (p. 12): "Que fera Arnold Schoenberg?"
November 1922	Review of Rodolphe Mathieu's *Trois Préludes* (1912-15) in *La Revue musicale* by Alexandre Tansman refers to "Schoenbergian and Stravinskian touches."
16 December 1922	*Le Canada musicale* (p. 16): "*Pierrot Lunaire* [Op. 21, 1912] de Schoenberg."

3 February 1923	*Le Canada musical* (p. 7): Notice of first New York performance of *Pierrot Lunaire* [Op. 21, 1912] taking place on 4 February under auspices of International Composers' Guild.
21 April 1923	*Le Canada musical* (p. 5): "De Vienne" (discussion of R. Strauss, Korngold, Schoenberg, et al).
17 March 1927	Mme. H.M. Little presents Schoenberg, Berg, Bartók, and Korngold for Pro Musica, Montreal, with illustrations by Léo-Pol Morin.
19 March 1927	*La Patrie* (p. 34): Léo-Pol Morin, "Bartók contre Schoenberg."
1932-35	Franz Kraemer (later an important producer at CBC) studies with Alban Berg.
30 July 1934	Morin writes "I. De Bruckner à Schoenberg," and "II. Schoenberg et ses disciples" in Switzerland. Both were published later in *Musique*.
October 1934	Canadian Gerald Strang (1908-83) is among Schoenberg's first students at the University of Southern California. Strang later assists him in teaching classes at the University of California at Los Angeles, and jointly edited *Fundamentals of Musical Composition* (1967) with the composer.
13 April 1935	The Hart House String Quartet performs the String Quartet No. 1, Op. 7 (1905) by "the leader of the modern German school of composition" [*The Globe*, 13 April 1935, 17].
2 October 1937	*Le Canada*: Morin writes from Venice on 12 September 1937 that he has met the American composer Roy Harris and attended performances of works by da Falla, Bartók, Prokofiev, Schoenberg, Milhaud, and Stravinsky, among others.
16 October 1937	In a review of a performance of Shostakovich's Symphony No. 1, Op. 10 (1925) in Montreal, Morin states that disciples of Schoenberg are now to be found in the USSR.
1937-38	Torontonian John Weinzweig becomes familiar with works of Schoenberg through recordings and scores in the Sibley Music Library of the Eastman School of Music. His first serial work, *Spasmodia*, for piano solo, is written on 30 June 1938.
21 June 1939	Letter to the Editor, Toronto *Globe and Mail*: Mr. Clement Hambourg would not "publicly advocate . . . that Arnold Schoenberg be returned to Nazi Germany."

7 December 1940	American Press item appears in Canadian newspapers "Shocked by Schoenberg Score Walk Out of Hall" on premiere of Violin Concerto, Op. 36 (1936) in Philadelphia.
June 1942	Weinzweig's "The New Music" appears in the *Canadian Review of Music and Art*. He argues that the creation of "new music," including Schoenberg's works, is part of an "evolutionary process."
1942	Jean Coulthard of Vancouver has private lessons with Arnold Schoenberg in California.
1943	Glenn Gould begins his nine years of study with Alberto Guerrero. His repertoire included the piano works of Schoenberg, ca. 1948. Gould wrote his first dodeca-phonic compositions two years later and performed his own Five Short Piano Pieces in January 1951.
25 November 1944	Upcoming CBS broadcast with the world premiere by the New York Philharmonic of *Ode to Napoleon*, Op. 41 (1942) noted in Canadian newspaper radio listings.
1945	Canadian composer Eldon Rathburn visits Schoenberg in Los Angeles
28 June 1945	Story in Toronto's *Globe and Mail* of Schoenberg turning down musical score for *The Good Earth*.
1946	Emmy Heim who had done premieres of Arnold Schoenberg's works in Europe settles in Toronto and teaches voice to Mary Morrison among others.
19 August 1949	CBC Summer Concert 7:00 pm Schoenberg's *Transfigured Night*, Op. 4 (1899/1917) performed in Toronto under conductor Walter Kaufmann
3 October 1950	Serge Garant performs Op. 11 (1909) at Mont Notre-Dame, Sherbrooke, Quebec.
14 February 1951	CBC broadcasts Oklahoma Symphony Orchestra performing Schoenberg's Theme and Variations, Op. 43 (1943).
1 May 1951	*Harmonie de Sherbrooke* performs Schoenberg's Theme and Variations, Op. 43 (1943).
17 July 1951	Toronto's *Globe and Mail* features editorial titled "Arnold Schoenberg": "There still is a small world audience for performances of his type of music—and from the popular point of view the revolution which he introduced is still in blueprint form."
25 January 1952	Heinz Unger conducts orchestral performance of *Transfigured Night*, Op. 4 (1917) broadcast on CBC.
16 June 1952	The CBC Vancouver String Orchestra performs Schoenberg's *Transfigured Night*, Op. 4 (1917).

5 July 1952	In a report on the Salzburg Festival published in the *Globe and Mail*, John Beckwith points out that Five Orchestral Pieces, Op. 16 (1909) received their first performance in Schoenberg's native Austria. "The moral seems to be that since Schoenberg has become a classic everyone is embarrassed by the fact that they never got round to playing his music when he was alive."
15 August 1952	Béla Böszörményi-Nagy gives lecture/recital at Banff, Alberta, about modern music including works by Schoenberg.
1952	John Beckwith begins hosting CBC radio series, "Music In Our Time" that includes a number of works by Schoenberg over the next four years.
4 October 1952	New Music Associates at the Royal Conservatory Concert Hall, Toronto, present two Canadian premieres, *Ode to Napoleon*, Op. 41 (1942) and Suite for Piano, Op. 25 (1923), the latter performed by Glenn Gould.
9 January 1954	New Music Associates, Toronto, founded by Glenn Gould and Robert Fulford, present a Second Viennese School concert that includes *Das Buch der Hängenden Garten*, Op. 15 (1909) and Variations for Organ, Op. 40 (1941).
13 February 1954	Jean Vallerand writes an article in *Le Devoir* on modern music.
20 February 1954	Serge Garant writes an article, "Non Monsieur Vallerand," in *L'Autorité*, criticizing his explanation of Schoenberg's technique.
22, 29 May, 5, 12 June 1954	Series of articles on serial music in *Le Devoir* by Jean Vallerand.
30 August 1954	The Ethel Stark Symphonietta gives performance of *Transfigured Night*, Op. 4 (1917) at the Montreal Summer Festival (30 August 1954).
4 September 1954	In an article in *L'Autorité*, Serge Garant points out how Claude Champagne's String Quartet (1954) bears a strong affinity to the sonorous world of the Second Viennese School, though the composer's knowledge of Schoenberg, Berg, and Webern was limited.
9 October 1954	In an article in *L'Autorité*, Garant bemoans the fact that music students are graduating with limited knowledge of works after Debussy, particularly those of Schoenberg and his school.

February 1955	Serge Garant writes essay on the Second Viennese School for *Le Journal musical canadien*.
July 1955	The Canadian Federation of Music Teachers Association (CFMTA) Convention in Vancouver includes a presentation on "Schoenberg and the 12-tone System" by Stephen Balogh.
January 1956	Serge Garant writes an article, "l'Émission 'Premières,'" in *Le Journal musical canadien*, pointing out how Schoenberg and Berg are important influences for Otto Joachim.
9 October 1956	John Beckwith begins a new CBC radio series, "World of Music," with Schoenberg's *Pierrot Lunaire*, Op. 21 (1912). *Pierrot* would not be performed in Canada until 1962 (see footnote 66, above).
Autumn 1956	The first issue of the *Canadian Music Journal* features Glenn Gould's essay, "The Dodecacophonist's [sic] Dilemna."
May 1957	Gould tours the Soviet Union, and gives important concerts at the Moscow and Leningrad Conservatories featuring the music of the Second Viennese School.
Spring 1957	Austin Clarkson writes a lengthy review in the *Canadian Music Journal* of a Columbia recording of Schoenberg's Opp. 20, 28, No. 3, 29, 33a and b, and 48.
Winter 1957	In *Vie des Arts*, Serge Garant argues that the public must hear more of the music of Webern, Schoenberg, Berg, Messiaen, Boulez, Stockhausen, Nono, and Cage.
1958	In *Cahiers d'essai*, Garant criticizes critics who either like or dislike all of Schoenberg's works on the basis of barely being familiar with one or more.
28 July 1958	*Globe and Mail* features article "Festival Poorly Attended - Dutch Explore Schoenberg Fare."
September-October 1959	Garant writes an article, "Un Esprit de genèse," for *Liberté*, in which he argues that Stravinsky, Berg, and Schoenberg have one foot in the eighteenth and nineteenth centuries, while Webern does not.
Fall 1959	Serge Garant writes a review of Glenn Gould's recording of Schoenberg's Op. 11 (1909) for the *Canadian Music Journal*.

Glenn Gould, Arnold Schoenberg, and Soviet Reception of the Second Viennese School

James K. Wright

Gould and Schoenberg

The year 2007 marked not only the seventy-fifth anniversary of Glenn Gould's birth and the twenty-fifth anniversary of his all-too-early death, but also the fiftieth anniversary of his historic concerts and lecture-recitals in Moscow and Leningrad.[1] In this essay, I will reflect on the extraordinary impact Gould's Russian tour had on the appetite for musical modernism in the Soviet Union, in the middle of the Cold War, at a time when Soviet culture was beginning to emerge from the brutal artistic repressions of the Stalin years.

Gould was a passionate advocate for the music of Arnold Schoenberg. Lawrence Schoenberg has noted that "Canada has always been friendly to Arnold Schoenberg."[2] At mid-century, while most of Schoenberg's Canadian apostles were Austro-German expatriates—Otto Joachim, Lothar Klein, Alfred Rosé, Karl Steiner, and Gould's friend Franz Kraemer, for example–Gould was the most passionate among a new generation of home-grown Canadian Schoenbergians. He truly loved this important but difficult music, and he admired the rigour and rationality underlying its construction. Gould described Schoenberg

---

[1]For the most detailed treatment of Gould's 1957 tour of Russia, see Kevin Bazzana, *Wondrous Strange: The Life and Art of Glenn Gould* (Toronto: McLelland & Stewart, 2003), 162-72.

[2]Opening address to the Symposium "*I Feel the Air of Another Planet: Schoenberg's Chamber Music, Schoenberg's World*," Carleton University, Ottawa, Canada, 26-29 July 2007.

James Wright has pursued a broad-ranging career as a composer, pianist, and musicologist. Upon completion of his Ph.D. in 2002, McGill University awarded him a Governor-General's Gold Medal for his dissertation on Schoenberg and Wittgenstein, the first time in McGill's history that this distinction was conferred upon a musicologist. Dr. Wright's research interests encompass areas as diverse as music philosophy and aesthetics, music perception, twentieth-century music history, post-tonal music theory and analysis, dance and music, Glenn Gould, and the history of music theory. In 2006, his book, *Schoenberg, Wittgenstein, and the Vienna Circle* (Bern: Verlag Peter Lang, 2005, 2007) received a coveted Lewis Lockwood Award from the American Musicological Society. Dr. Wright is also widely known as a composer of choral music whose works have been commissioned, performed, and recorded by choirs throughout North America. He is an Associate Professor, and Supervisor of Performance Studies, in the School for Studies in Art and Culture (Music), Carleton University, Ottawa.

as "a colossus of biblical proportions,"[3] and considered twelve-tone technique the only truly valid innovation in twentieth-century musical language. Seeking a rapprochement between hostile audiences and the music of their time, Gould performed and recorded Schoenberg's music more than any other musician of his stature. Schoenberg fascinated him—as did Gibbons, Sweelinck, and Richard Strauss—because he was "one of the crucial pivot composers in music history."[4]

Like Schoenberg, Gould had an interest in music that was stripped of adornment. He felt that one of Schoenberg's achievements was to have effectively simplified compositional language after the chromatic excesses of the late nineteenth century, much as the composers of the late Renaissance had done with the modal music of their time.[5] Like Schoenberg, Gould felt that music must always point to something mystical, beyond itself; it must always aspire to a higher truth and integrity. His prodigious technique notwithstanding, Gould was therefore strongly opposed to all forms of musical showmanship for its own sake.[6] He felt that his quantum leap from the music of Bach to that of Schoenberg was a logical and natural one, since their music was conceived in primarily linear terms, and Gould had always had a predilection for "contrapuntal thinking."[7] The dialectical curve of Schoenberg's career also fascinated him: from "thesis" in the early tonal works, through "antithesis" in the atonal and twelve-tone works, arriving at a kind of "synthesis" of tonal/atonal reconciliation in the late works of Schoenberg's American period. Gould and Schoenberg were both musical Platonists, pacifists, artistic loners, at once passionate and anti-sensual, who were most comfortable when swimming against the current, and who stood opposed to the competitive model of the Western music industry. Both also knew how the transcendence of music offers a unique form of solace to a troubled world. The war-weary world of post-Stalinist Russia was ready, if cautiously at first, to receive Gould's message.

When Gould decided to champion the works of the Second Viennese School during his Russian tour, the repercussions were profound. A kind of musical "Berlin Wall" had been erected; the revolutionary compositional and aesthetic ideas that had emanated from Vienna decades before had remained largely unknown in the Soviet Union. This music was considered ideologically incompatible with the set of aesthetic precepts that were prescribed by the

---

[3]Glenn Gould, *Écrits* III: *Non, je ne suis pas du tout un excentrique*, ed. Bruno Monsaingeon (Paris: Fayard, 1986), 211.

[4]Glenn Gould, *Arnold Schoenberg: A Perspective* (University of Cincinnati Press, 1964), 10.

[5]Ibid., 3.

[6]Gould dismissed some of the most celebrated pianists of the twentieth century—Rachmaninoff and Horowitz, for example—as "demonic virtuosi." See Martin Meyer, "Glenn Gould on Anton Webern and Sviatoslav Richter," *Glenn Gould Magazine* 1 (Fall 1995): 12.

[7]Eric McLean, "Glenn Gould, Interviewed by Eric McLean," *Glenn Gould Magazine* 9/2 (Fall 2003): 50. Gould goes on to say "There was a time when I admitted the existence of almost no one between Bach and Richard Strauss."

Figure 1. Gould at the family cottage on Lake Simcoe with the Chilean-Canadian
pianist Alberto Guerrero, his teacher, during the summer of 1947.
During his teenage years, Gould spent many hours behind the
wheel of this boat, which he had named "the Arnold S."
(Library and Archives Canada, Glenn Gould Fonds)

totalitarian Soviet regime. Just as it had banned much of Bach's music for its "evangelism," Stalin's Ministry of Culture placed the music of the European avant-garde under strict prohibition, describing it as an unwholesome by-product of bourgeois decadence.[8] Undaunted, Gould bravely featured both Bach and the new Viennese music on his 1957 tour.

Gould's passion for Schoenberg had developed during his ten years of study with the Chilean-Canadian pianist Alberto Guerrero (shown with the young Gould in Figure 1) at the Toronto Conservatory.[9] Guerrero had been a primary proponent of musical modernism in Chile prior to his immigration to Canada in 1919, and it was under Guerrero's tutelage that Gould was first introduced to the music of the moderns. During his period of study with Guerrero (1943-52), Gould tells us that he "came alive to contemporary music,"[10] reporting that he listened daily to Schoenberg's Serenade Op. 24,[11] and developed an abiding love for the Suite for Piano Op. 25, a piece which he later performed and recorded repeatedly.[12] While Gould later tended to be somewhat dismissive of Guerrero's role in his formation, the facts appear to suggest that Guerrero's influence was decisive.[13] We know that Guerrero discussed, performed, and worked through both Schoenberg's Opus 11 and Opus 19 with Gould in 1947 and 1948.

Czech-Canadian composer Oscar Morowetz credits René Leibowitz as another source of Gould's fascination with Schoenberg:

> Glenn was a voracious reader in his adolescence. One day he got hold of René Leibowitz' book. The book made a tremendous impression on Glenn, and after

---

[8]See Boris Groys, *The Total Art of Stalinism: Avant-garde, Aesthetic Dictatorship, and Beyond* (Princeton: Princeton University Press, 1992).

[9]The list of Guerrero's piano students reads like a Who's Who of Canadian Music from the period, including not only Gould but William Aide, John Beckwith, Helmut Blume, Paul Helmer, Edward Laufer, Pierrette Lepage, Bruce Mather, Oskar Morowetz, Arthur Ozolins, R. Murray Schafer, and Ruth Watson Henderson.

[10]Quoted in Peter F. Ostwald, *Glenn Gould: The Ecstasy and Tragedy of Genius* (New York: Norton, 1998), 87 (fn. 14).

[11]See Ghyslaine Guertin, *La Série Schoenberg* (Montreal: Christian Bourgeois, 1998), 18.

[12]Gould considered Schoenberg's Opus 25 one of the great masterworks of the piano repertoire: "I can think of no composition for solo piano of the first quarter of this century that can stand as its equal. . . . [In its] rare *joie de vivre*, and blessed enthusiasm for the making of music, [it] is among the most spontaneous and wickedly inventive of Schoenberg's works" ("The Piano Music of Arnold Schoenberg," in *The Glenn Gould Reader*, ed. Tim Page [New York: Alfred A. Knopf, 1985], 127).

[13]See John Beckwith, *In Search of Alberto Guerrero* (Waterloo: Wilfrid Laurier Press, 2006); John Beckwith, "Shattering a Few Myths," in *Glenn Gould by Himself and His Friends*, ed. John McGreevy (Toronto and Garden City, New York: Doubleday, 1983), 65-74; John Beckwith, "Glenn Gould, the Early Years: Addenda and Corrigenda," *Glenn Gould Magazine*, 2/2 (Fall 1996), 56-64.

that it was only Schoenberg, Berg, and Webern. He talked about them constantly, listened to recordings of their music, and began playing it himself.[14]

Schoenberg's influence is clearly manifest in Gould's early compositional efforts. He hand-copied Schoenberg's early songs, as if to better understand this music from the inside out. Both his early Sonata for Bassoon and Piano, and his earliest compositions for piano solo—including this attempt at a twelve-tone fugue (see Figure 2)—show the integration of Schoenberg's method. He also cites Schoenberg's Second String Quartet, Op. 10, as the primary inspiration for his own String Quartet of 1953.[15] Young composers of the post-war period were eager to forge an alternative path to the future. "Most of us were hard-edged constructivists,"[16] Gould would write in his later years, reflecting on his aesthetic ideals in the early 1950s. "All of us, no matter in what way we compose, compose differently because of Schoenberg," he was fond of saying to all who would listen.[17] Some of Gould's compositional sketches from later years reveal that he continued to experiment with the twelve-tone method until the end of his life (Figure 3). Gould was also a passionate analyst of the twelve-tone repertoire,[18] though he did not share Schoenberg's view that it is unnecessary for the performer or listener to understand row-structure in order to appreciate it.[19]

When Schoenberg died in 1951, Gould eulogized him at a special commemorative concert held at the Toronto Conservatory.[20] The following year he and his friend Robert Fulford formed a group called the New Music Associates, which organized a memorial concert devoted entirely to Schoenberg's music (Figure 4). In 1953, he gave the Canadian premiere of the Schoenberg Concerto, Op. 42, in a performance that was broadcast nationwide by CBC radio.[21] Through 1953 and 1954, Gould performed a number of concerts

[14]Quoted in Ostwald, *Glenn Gould*, 87. Morowetz is referring to Leibowitz's *Schoenberg and His School: The Contemporary Stage in the Language of Music*, trans. Dika Newlin (New York: Philosophical Library, 1949).

[15]Liner notes from Columbia MS 6178 (1960), featuring Gould's Quartet performed by the Symphonia Quartet. See also Tim Page, ed., *The Glenn Gould Reader* (New York: Alfred A. Knopf, 1985), 228.

[16]Glenn Gould, "A Festscrift for 'Ernst Who?'" in Page, ed., *The Glenn Gould Reader*, 189.

[17]Gould, *Arnold Schoenberg: A Perspective*, 16.

[18]See, for example, Glenn Gould, "A Consideration of Anton Webern," *Glenn Gould Magazine* 1 (Fall 1995): 4-8; Glenn Gould, "The Piano Music of Arnold Schoenberg," in Tim Page, ed., *The Glenn Gould Reader*, 122-28; Glenn Gould, "Piano Concertos by Mozart and Schoenberg," in ibid., 128-34; Glenn Gould, "Arnold Schoenberg's Chamber Symphony No. 2," in ibid., 134-42; Glenn Gould, "Piano Music of Berg, Schoenberg, and Krenek," in ibid., 194-200; Glenn Gould, "The Dodecacophonist's Dilemma," in ibid., 207-16.

[19]See Humphrey Burton, *Conversations with Glenn Gould: Schoenberg* (April 19, 1966). Part IV of a four-part BBC television series.

[20]Gould cites this eulogy in his essay "The Dodecacophonist's Dilemma," in Tim Page, ed., *The Glenn Gould Reader*, 207-16.

[21]With the CBC Symphony Orchestra, conducted by Jean-Marie Beaudet, 21 December 1953.

Figure 2. Sketch of a twelve-tone fugue, circa March 1952, by the young Glenn Gould.

(Library and Archives Canada, Glenn Gould Fonds)

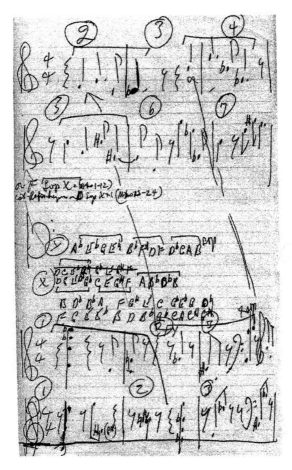

Figure 3. Gould continued to sketch twelve-tone compositions until the end of his life. This sketch, from April 1978, appears to be for a twelve-tone piece for soprano and accompaniment.

(Library and Archives Canada, Glenn Gould Fonds)

dedicated wholly or largely to works of Schoenberg, Webern, and Berg. In 1955 and 1956, the years that brought Gould to international prominence through his landmark recording of the *Goldberg Variations*, he continued to proselytize on Schoenberg and his students in a series of published articles and polemical program notes.[22] Even if we disregard the Russian tour, 1957 was by any standard a banner year for Gould, with major performances in New York, San Francisco, Cleveland, Washington, Pittsburgh, Montreal, Toronto, Miami, Berlin,

[22]See Nancy Canning, "Gould's Published Writings," in Otto Friedrich, *Glenn Gould: A Life and Variations* (New York: Random House, 1989), 422-26.

NEW MUSIC ASSOCIATES
Present
S C H O E N B E R G – B E R G – W E B E R N

A program of music by Arnold Schoenberg and his two most distinguished pupils, Alban Berg and Anton Webern

ANTON WEBERN   Five Movements for String Quartet, Opus 5 (1909)

        Heftig Bewegt
        Sehr Langsam
        Sehr Bewegt
        Sehr Langsam
        In Zarter Bewegung

Morry Kemerman, Victor Feldbrill, violin; Eugene Hudson, viola; Donald Whitton, cello

ARNOLD SCHOENBERG   Das Buch der Handenden Garten, Opus 15 (1908)
        (The Story of the Hanging Gardens - 15 songs to poems by Stefan George)

Roma Butler, mezzo-soprano; Glenn Gould, piano

INTERMISSION

ANTON WEBERN   Variations for Piano, Opus 27 (1936)

Glenn Gould, piano

ANTON WEBERN   Quartet for tenor saxophone, clarinet, violin and piano, Opus 22 (1930)

        Sehr Massig
        Sehr Schwungvoll

Morris Weinzweig, tenor, Ezra Schabas, clarinet, Morry Kemerman, violin; Glenn Gould, piano.

(Because this work is, on first hearing, difficult, it will be played twice)

ALBAN BERG   Sonata in One Movement, Opus 2 (1908)*

Glenn Gould, piano

* This work has been recorded by Mr. Gould for Hallmark Records.

Arnold Schoenberg's Variations for Organ, announced as part of this program, have regrettably been cancelled.

Figure 4. A program devoted entirely to the works of the Second Viennese School, Royal Conservatory of Music, Toronto, 9 January 1954 (Glenn Gould Fonds, Library and Archives Canada). This concert was presented by the New Music Associates, an organization established by Glenn Gould and Robert Fulford to promote the performance of "modern music." The program notes for this concert, titled "A Consideration of Anton Webern," are among Gould's earliest writings on music.

Figure 5. Glenn Gould demonstrating from the piano during his 1963 lecture-recital on Schoenberg at the University of Cincinnati (published as *Arnold Schoenberg: A Perspective*, University of Cincinatti Press, 1964).

(Library and Archives Canada, Glenn Gould Fonds)

and Vienna, many of which featured works of the Second Viennese School. Throughout the 1960s and 1970s Gould created several radio and television programs on Schoenberg, including what is perhaps his most reverential tribute, the monumental ten-episode "Schoenberg Series" of 1974, in honor of the centenary of the composer's birth.[23] In 1963 he gave an important lecture-recital on Schoenberg at the University of Cincinnati (Figure 5), a presentation deemed so significant that the University of Cincinnati Press published the transcripts under the title *Arnold Schoenberg: A Perspective*.[24] From 1964 to 1974 he recorded Schoenberg's complete solo and chamber works involving piano for Sony Classical. "I thought of myself as a valiant defender of twelve-tone music, and of its leading exponents," Gould wrote.[25] Both music critics and the listening public were likely to concur with Yehudi Menuhin: "perhaps no one in the world knows as much about Schoenberg as Glenn does."[26]

Schoenberg Reception in Russia

Before discussing Gould's Russian tour in substance, let us consider the ideological context into which he entered so dramatically in 1957. In light of subsequent history, one can easily overlook the vigorous avant-garde culture that existed in Russia prior to the 1917 Revolution. Cubism, Rayonism, Primitivism, Futurism, Geometric Constructivism, and Abstract Expressionism all had significant Russian representatives, including the celebrated ballet scores of Stravinsky, and the paintings of Goncharova, Malevich, Klutsis, Kandinsky (see Figure 6),[27] and other Russian proto-modernists. This was the cultural

[23]See Nancy Canning, "Gould's Radio and TV Programs," in Otto Friedrich, *Glenn Gould: A Life and Variations* (New York: Random House, 1989), 385-421.

[24]*Arnold Schoenberg: A Perspective* is the only monograph Gould would publish during his lifetime. Geoffrey Payzant has noted that "nothing more clearly illustrates the prevailing reluctance to accept Glenn Gould as author than the almost total neglect of his writings about the music of Arnold Schoenberg" (*Glenn Gould: Music and Mind* [Toronto: Van Rostrant Reinhold, 1978], 142).

[25]Cited in Bazzana, *Wondrous Strange*, 110.

[26]Yehudi Menuhin, *Unfinished Journey* (London: MacDonald and Janes, 1976), 333. Lest the reader conclude that Gould was a card-carrying Schoenbergian in every respect, it should be noted that he did not share the composer's views on all aspects of music aesthetics. In a lecture associated with an all-Second-Viennese-School programme performed in Toronto on 3 October 1953—the first written document we have which offers insights into Gould's view of Schoenberg—he points to "contradictory influences" in Schoenberg's music: namely vestigial remnants of traditional formal and tonal procedures in twelve-tone contexts. These early comments by Gould are astonishingly aligned with some of the views expressed by Pierre Boulez in his notorious manifesto, "Schoenberg is Dead," in *Stocktakings from an Apprenticeship*, ed. Paule Thévenin, trans. Stephen Walsh [Oxford University Press, 1952], 209–14). In this early lecture Gould also suggests that Schoenberg's fundamental compositional nature and persona "was, in many respects, incompatible with the twelve-tone technique" (Bazzana, *Wondrous Strange*, 100). Finally, Gould never accepted Schoenberg's contention that his own approach was inevitable, and that the only true path to the future of music was revealed by his music and ideas.

Figure 6. Vassily Kandinsky's *Impression III/Concert* is a striking example of both the painter's early abstractionism, and his attempt to capture synesthetic perception on canvas. It was painted immediately after attending a concert featuring Schoenberg's music in Munich on 2 January 1911. Kandinsky's long correspondence with Schoenberg began with a letter addressed to the composer a week following this concert.

(Städtische Galerie im Lenbachhaus, Munich)

landscape that welcomed Schoenberg when he visited St. Petersburg in December of 1912, to conduct his symphonic poem *Pelleas und Melisande* (Figure 7). When he arrived, Schoenberg was already known in Russian music circles as an *enfant terrible* of sorts. In 1911, the Second String Quartet, Op. 10 had been heard in St. Petersburg in a performance featuring soprano Sandra Belling, and Sergei Prokofiev had performed his *Drei Klavierstücke*, Op. 11. Wiatscheslaw Karatygin, the contemporary Russian musicologist and critic, tells us that Op. 11 was not warmly received: "[it] caused a part of the audience to laugh until they collapsed."[28] The Second String Quartet, a work Karatygin found to be "laconic, thoroughly original, wildly bold yet rigidly logical," was heard with "less

---

[27]Schoenberg's relationship with Kandinsky is well documented in Esther da Costa Meyer and Fred Wasserman eds., *Schoenberg, Kandinsky, and the Blue Rider* (New York, Scala Publishers, 2003).

[28]From an essay by V.G. Karatygin written for the influential newspaper *Ryech*, reprinted in V.G. Karatygin, *Zhizn' deyatel' nost', statii i materialy* (Leningrad, 1927), 222-24 (cited in Boris [cont.]

Figure 7. Arnold Schoenberg in the back yard of the St. Petersburg Philharmonic Society, December 1912. The fur coat was a gift from the pianist, conductor, and impresario Alexander Siloti, who had invited Schoenberg to the city to conduct his symphonic poem *Pelleas und Melisande.*

(Archives of the Arnold Schoenberg Center, Vienna)

obstruction."[29] Finally, reviewing a performance of Schoenberg's *Pelleas* the following year, Karatygin writes: "Yesterday there were no cat calls—on the contrary, there was vigorous applause."[30] Another critic was more effusive: "I can confirm with the highest conviction that since the time of Wagner's visit in 1863 . . . there has been nothing equal to it here."[31] In a letter to Karatygin, Stravinsky was enthusiastic:

> I have just read your review of the Siloti concert where Schönberg conducted his *Pelléas*. I gathered from your lines that you really love and understand the essence of Schoenberg—that truly remarkable artist of our time. Therefore I believe that it might interest you to become acquainted with his latest work which reveals most intensely the unusual character of his creative genius. I am speaking of *Pierrot Lunaire*, op. 21, which I recently heard in Berlin.[32]

Soon after Schoenberg returned to Berlin, he corresponded with Siloti about the possibility of future performances of his music in St. Petersburg. A performance of *Pierrot Lunaire* was planned, but abandoned, probably due to resistance by soprano Albertine Zehme, who owned the performance rights. Similarly, plans for a 1915 performance of the Chamber Symphony, Op. 9, were thwarted by the outbreak of the First World War. Although their exposure to Schoenberg's music had been tantalizingly brief, some Russians understood the profound importance of his 1912 visit. Inspired by Schoenberg's example, a number of young Russian composers of the period would become champions of the most progressive elements in European music. Chief among them was Nikolai Roslavets, who has been described as "the Russian Schoenberg" for having independently developed his own quasi-serialistic techniques.[33] In 1923, Roslavets published an important article on *Pierrot Lunaire* which showed a

---

Schwarz, "Arnold Schoenberg in Russia," *Perspectives of New Music* 4/1 [Autumn/Winter, 1965], 87). Karatygin's description of Schoenberg (conducting) is evocative: "As lively as quicksilver. . . . A little man with a bald head and a burning, restless look, nervous gestures, and demonic passion, even in the quieter moments."

[29] Ibid.

[30] Cited in Hans Heinz Stuckenschmidt. *Arnold Schoenberg: His Life, World and Work*, trans. Humphrey Searle (New York: Schirmer Books, 1977), 159.

[31] "Venturus," the Russian music critic, is cited by Iris Pfeiffer in "Arnold Schoenberg in St. Petersburg" (Arnold Schoenberg Centre: http://www.schoenberg.at/1_as/bio/petersburg_e.htm).

[32] Stravinsky's letter of 26 December 1912 is cited in Schwarz, "Arnold Schoenberg in Russia," 87. Toward the end of his life, Stravinsky again showered praise on Schoenberg's *Pierrot*, famously referring to it as "the solar plexus as well as the mind of early twentieth-century music" (Igor Stravinsky and Robert Craft, *Dialogues and a Diary* [Faber: London, 1968], 108).

[33] Detlef Gojowy, "Half Time for Nikolai Roslavets (1881-1944): A Non-Love Story with a Post-Romantic Composer," in Malcolm H. Brown ed., *Russian and Soviet Music: Essays for Boris Schwarz* (Ann Arbor: UMI Research Press, 1984), 211-20.

thorough understanding of Schoenberg's approach to melody, harmony, and rhythm. "Schoenberg's principles and methods of creativity," he wrote, "will gradually conquer the thoughts of contemporary artistic youth. . . . The Schoenbergian School is of decisive importance for the immediate future of music."[34]

Socialist Realism

Though the First World War and the Revolution clearly stifled dialogue between the Russian and Western European art worlds, Soviet artists continued to embrace a wide variety of forms of artistic expression for much of the first decade of the post-revolutionary period. During the twenties, Russian pianist Maria Yudina championed the piano music of Hindemith, Honegger, Bartók, and Stravinsky,[35] and Leningrad performances of both Schoenberg's *Gurrelieder* and Berg's *Wozzeck* ("a tumultuous success," Berg reports) were given in 1927.[36] Lenin had initially sought to guarantee freedom of artistic expression, and the early Bolsheviks felt that revolutionary politics and non-traditional art forms might be complementary, a view championed by science-fiction author Alexander Bogdanov who established the cautiously pro-modernist *Proletkult* movement in 1917.[37] Pre-revolutionary "Evenings of Contemporary Music" in both Moscow and St. Petersburg were broadened by the Moscow-based Association of Contemporary Music to promote the most recent and innovative music from the Soviet Union and Western Europe.[38] As late as 1928, pianist Mikhail Druskin would praise Schoenberg's Op. 25 *Suite für Klavier* as "a sample of highest mastery, on a level with the best polyphonic achievements of J.S. Bach."[39] Ivan Sollertinsky, Shostakovich's closest friend, likewise published a sympathetic study on Schoenberg during this period.[40] But Trotsky and others soon argued that artistic modernism was antithetical to Marxist principles which condemned bourgeois elements in art. Following Lenin's death in 1924, Stalin's ascent to power ushered in an era of aggressive artistic repression that would last thirty years.

Under Stalin, a set of aesthetic principles that became known as "Socialist Realism" was soon established as state policy. From 1932 until the dictator's

---

[34]Nikolai Roslavets, "Lunnyi P'ero Arnolda Shenberga," *K Novym beregam* 3 (July/August, 1923): 33 (cited in Schwarz, "Arnold Schoenberg in Russia," 88).

[35]Yudina's recordings are largely unknown in Europe and North America; they are available in a 33-volume CD set from Mariayudina.com.

[36]Helene Berg, *Alban Berg: Letters to his Wife*, ed. and trans. Bernard Grun (London: Faber and Faber, 1971), 360.

[37]See Schwarz, *Music and Musical Life in Soviet Russia*, 20-22.

[38]The "ASM" (*Assotsiatsiia Sovremennoi Suzyki*). See Amy Nelson, *Music for the Revolution: Musicians and Power in Early Soviet Russia* (University Park: Pennsylvania State University Press, 2004), 42, 49.

[39]Mikhail Druskin, *Novaya fortepiannaya muzuka* (Leningrad, 1928), 88-90 (cited in Schwarz, "Arnold Schoenberg in Russia," 88).

[40]See Caroline Brooke, "Soviet Music in the International Arena, 1932-41," *European History Quarterly* 31/2 (2001): 231-64.

Figure 8. In 1946, Stalin put Andrei Zhdanov (1896-1948) in charge of Soviet cultural policy. Until the late 1950s, Zhdanov's repressive ideological aesthetic code, known as Zhdanovism (zhdanovshchina), defined the parameters of permissible cultural production in the Soviet Union.

death in 1953, this policy was ruthlessly enforced in all spheres of artistic endeavour. Artists who strayed from it were severely punished. The fortunate ones were simply labeled non-persons and excluded from artistic circles and activities. The less fortunate among them were sent to the Gulag labor camps.

Even Soviet ideologues never quite agreed on what the slippery term "Socialist Realism" actually meant. The principles of Socialist Realism dictate that wholesome artistic expression must depict and glorify the proletariat's struggle toward socialist progress. The doctrine was originally intended to control the content and style of Soviet literature, but it was quickly adapted to the visual arts, film, and music. In 1933, new statutes adopted by the Union of Soviet Composers included directives such as the following:

> The spiritual world of Soviet man . . . must be embodied in musical images full of beauty and strength. Socialist Realism demands a struggle against modernistic directions that are typical of the decay of contemporary bourgeois art.[41]

In reference to music, the term "formalism" was soon adopted to denote all abstract instrumental music that was putatively self-absorbed, excessively cerebral, concerned principally with its own formal construction, and devoid of all ideological content. In private, composers such as Prokofiev were at first dismissive: "Formalism is music that people do not understand at first hearing!"[42] But in 1948, Andrey Zhdanov, then Soviet Minister of Culture (Figure 8), publicly denounced Prokofiev, Shostakovich, Khatchaturian, and Miaskovsky, alleging that they had fallen victim to the temptations of formalism, "the cult of atonality, dissonance, and disharmony . . . [and] the confused, neuro-pathological combinations that transform music into cacophony, into a chaotic conglomeration of sounds."[43] The declaration seemed to be aimed most particularly at the "pernicious" modernist trends emanating from Vienna.[44] Among the numerous ironies in the Soviet anti-modernist stance: many of the so-called decadent Western modernists (Eisler, Adorno, and Nono, for example) were leftist ideologues, while most of the composers the Soviets held up as exemplary models were avowed Tsarists (Tchaikovsky, for example).[45]

---

[41]From the statutes of the Union of Soviet Composers (1933), cited and translated in Boris Schwarz, *Music and Musical Life in Soviet Russia* (Bloomington: Indiana University Press, 1983) 114.

[42]Israel V. Nestyev, *Prokofiev*, trans. Florence Jonas (Stanford University Press, 1960), 278.

[43]Central Committee resolution, published February 1948, cited and translated in Schwarz, *Music and Musical Life in Soviet Russia*, 220.

[44]Scholars have noted that Norman Rockwell's somewhat ideologically-driven depiction of American lifestyle can be understood as America's propagandistic counterpart to Soviet Social Realism. See Tomas Pospiszyl, "Socialist Evening Realistic Post," *ART Margins: Contemporary Central and Eastern European Visual Culture* (online journal), 12 November 2003.

[45]See, for example, William H. Parsons, "Tchaikovsky, the Tsars, and the Tsarist National Anthem," in Alexander Mihailovic, ed., *Tchaikovsky and his Contemporaries* (Oxford: Greenwood, 1999), 221-32. Tchaikovsky employs the melody "God Save the Tsar," by Alexis Lvov, in no less than six of his works.

Glenn Gould's 1957 Tour of Moscow and Leningrad

Such was the prevailing Soviet view of Western art and artists that greeted Gould when he performed in Moscow and Leningrad in May of 1957. He was the first North American pianist to appear in the Soviet Union.[46] Menuhin had visited in 1947,[47] and Stern in 1955,[48] but it was not until 1958, with the establishment of a formal cultural exchange program, that Western artists started to appear in Russia with any regularity. For Americans, Van Cliburn's triumph at the 1958 Tchaikovsky Competition provided the world with unequivocal evidence of the superiority of their socio-political path,[49] just as John Glenn's Mercury mission had done following the Russian Sputnik satellite launch of 1957. Although Cliburn's Tchaikovsky prize attracted more attention in the Western media, the record shows that Gould's visit had much longer and deeper resonance for Russians and Russian musical culture.[50]

Figure 9 shows the programs of Gould's Moscow and Leningrad concerts. Apart from the Berg Sonata, the repertoire he performed on May 7, 8, 11, 14, 16, and 18—sanctioned in advance by Soviet officialdom—was relatively conservative. On May 12, however, he gave a lecture-recital at the Moscow Conservatory in which he performed only music of the Second Viennese School.[51] A week later, on May 19, he would repeat this lecture-recital at the Leningrad Conservatory. Gould's goal was to introduce the music of Schoenberg and his school to young Soviet musicians and composers.

In general, the students were attentive and receptive, but several elderly professors walked out when Gould performed works by Berg, Webern, and Krenek, interspersed with some remarks about the new compositional techniques employed by the Viennese school. His program—bravely titled "Music of the West"—was viewed by the establishment as "an attempt to pervert the taste of the young."[52] "I am quite sure that many of the students were uncertain whether it was better for them to remain or walk out," Gould wrote the following year

[46]See Peter J. Schmelz, "Listening, Memory, and the Thaw: Unofficial Music and Society in the Soviet Union, 1956-1974" (Ph.D. diss., University of California, Berkeley, 2002). Pages 51 to 60 of Schmelz's dissertation are devoted to accounts of Gould's lecture-recitals at the Moscow and Leningrad Conservatories.

[47]See Menuhin, *Unfinished Journey.*

[48]See Isaac Stern and Chaim Potok, *Isaac Stern: My First 79 Years* (New York: Da Capo Press, 1999).

[49]When Cliburn mused about programming a Bach Toccata for his first concert in Moscow, a Russian official warned him: "No, you must not do that. Don't forget that we have just had Canada's Gould here!" (quoted in Bazzana, *Wondrous Strange*, 171).

[50]See Yosif Feyginberg, "Glenn Gould and the Russians, Then and Now: A Filmaker's Impressions," *Glenn Gould Magazine* 13/1 (Spring 2008): 38-41.

[51]Most of this lecture-recital was recorded and released by Jimmy Classic as "Glenn Gould in Russia, 1957" (under license of Melodiya, OM 03-101/102, 1996).

[52]John P.L. Roberts and Ghyslaine Guertin, eds., *Selected Letters by Glenn Gould* (Toronto: Oxford University Press, 1992), 12-14.

DATE	CITY	PROGRAM
May 7	Moscow	Bach Partita No. 6; Beethoven Op. 109; Berg Sonata
May 8	Moscow	Beethoven Concerto No. 4; Bach D Minor Concerto (Moscow Philharmonic)
May 11	Moscow	Goldberg Variations, Two Brahms Intermezzi, Hindemith Sonata No. 3
May 12	Moscow Conservatory	Berg Sonata, Schoenberg excerpts, Webern Variations, Krenek Sonata No. 3; *Art of Fugue, Goldberg Variations* (excerpts)
May 14	Leningrad	Bach Partita No. 6; Beethoven Op. 109; Berg Sonata
May 16	Leningrad	Berg Sonata; rest unknown
May 18	Leningrad	Beethoven Concerto No. 2; Bach D Minor Concerto (Leningrad Philharmonic)
May 19	Leningrad Conservatory	Bach, Sweelinck, Webern Variations; Krenek Sonata No. 3 (documentation fragmentary)

Figure 9. Gould's concert programs, Moscow and Leningrad, May 1957.

to Yousuf Karsh. "I managed to keep things under control by frowning ferociously now and then…. It was the most exciting musical occasion in which I have taken part!"[53] The recording of the Moscow lecture-recital reveals that after performing Krenek, Gould addresses the crowd half-apologetically: "I only hope that I haven't bored you with too much of this music; it is very dear to me, and I really wanted to play it for you."[54] "No! No!" a woman yelled out from the audience after the translation, followed by enthusiastic applause. Gould then went on to emphasize his view that twelve-tone music had its origin in the revered masterworks of the past:

> I think the highest compliment that I can pay [to this music] is to say that the principles that one finds here are not new, but are at least five hundred years old. They are principles which reached their heights with the Flemish school, with Josquin des Prez and others in the mid- and late-fifteenth century.[55]

To further demonstrate this historical link, Gould then completed his programme with excerpts from *The Art of Fugue* and, as encores, excerpts from the *Goldberg*

[53]Ibid.
[54]Quoted in Schmelz, "Listening, Memory, and the Thaw," 56.
[55]Ibid.

Figure 10. Gould at the keyboard, with an interpreter standing to his left, during a lecture-recital titled "Music of the West," presented to a standing-room-only crowd of students and faculty at the Small Hall of the Leningrad Conservatory, 19 May 1957.

(Glenn Gould Fonds, Library and Archives Canada, photographer unknown)

Variations. The ovations were deafening, and the route between Gould's dressing room and limousine was jammed with cheering students. Edison Vasilievich Denisov, the young composer, described the performance as "a genuine revelation."[56]

Triumphant in Moscow, Gould continued on to Leningrad, where he also gave his final performance before a student audience (Figure 10).[57] In a recent interview, Boris Tischenko (a young graduate student in 1957) enthused: "Glenn Gould was an explosion. . . . After a man hears Gould, he becomes a different person. . . . He played Bach, Sweelinck, Webern, Schoenberg, and

---

[56]Edison Denisov and Jean-Pierre Armengaud, *Entretiens avec Denisov: Un compositeur sous le régime soviétique* (Paris: Edition Plume, 1993), 66 ("Ce fut une veritable revelation!").

[57]Kevin Bazzana (*Wondrous Strange*, 171) reports that the entire lecture-recital was recorded, but the tapes in the archive of the Leningrad Conservatory were thought to have been either lost or stolen. However, in 2002, while preparing his television documentary ("Glenn Gould: The Russian Journey), Yosif Feyginberg located a cassette of Gould's lecture-recital in the possession of the pianist and professor Vladimir Tropp. Unfortunately the tape is of poor quality, and includes only Gould's performances of the Sweelinck, Webern, and Krenek.

Krenek. . . . To see the living Gould—it's as if you had met Moses in the desert!"[58] The Russian students must have felt that an invigorating breeze from another world had blown into their midst. Indeed, echoing Stefan George's portentous words that open the fourth movement of Schoenberg's Second String Quartet ("I feel the air of the another planet"), Gould reported that he felt like "the first musician to land on Mars."[59]

Some students resisted Gould's precocious efforts, viewing his near-obsession with the Viennese School as just one of his many apparent eccentricities. After he played the Webern Variations, voices from his audience exclaimed "It would be better to play Bach! Rachmaninov!" At this point Gould leapt up from his piano bench. "I am playing the *best* music of the twentieth century," he shouted back. "It is not only new, but it is deeply connected with the *very old* classics; the roots of this music are *very old*."[60] After interpreting Gould's reply, the translator added: "Students, behave yourselves!" According to one account, Comrade Barsodanov, a professor of Marxist aesthetics and chairman of the conservatory's Communist Party Committee, then came to the stage and remarked dismissively, "Surely it is something of an exaggeration to make such a strange parallel between the music of these contemporary dissonant decadent composers and the music of Bach!"[61] According to all witnesses, the atmosphere at the recital was "viscerally emotional."[62] A strange commixture of elation, fear, incredulity, uncertainty, and awe must have hung palpably in the air. Gould had "always been attracted to states of transition and musical brinksmanship"[63]— it is this aspect of Schoenberg's life and work that he admired most. In his Russian conservatory lecture-recitals of 1957, he knew that one of the world's great musical cultures was on the threshold of a major paradigmatic change, and he was determined to exercise a form of musical brinksmanship of his own.

The impact of Gould's lecture-recitals at the Moscow and Leningrad Conservatories would become the stuff of legend, due not only to the content of his presentations, but also to the sheer fact that he was saying such things in public. With these initial glimpses of forbidden fruit from the leading composers

[58]Quoted in Schmelz, "Listening, Memory, and the Thaw," 58. Schmelz is citing his 1 December 2000, interview with Boris Tischenko.

[59]Roberts and Guertin, eds., *Selected Letters by Glenn Gould*, 12-14.

[60]Sergey Slomninsky, *Burleski, elegii, difirambi v prezrennoy proze* (St. Petersburg: Kompozitor, 2000), 121.

[61]Vladimir Frumkin (a graduate student who had been assigned to look after Gould during his visit), interviewed on 1 December 2000, by Peter Schmelz ("Listening, Memory, and the Thaw, 58). According to Frumkin, Gould had opened his programme with some Bach, "but then, suddenly, and without any permission from the Conservatory officials, he said 'And now I want to play for you the real heirs of the Baroque geniuses like Bach!'"

[62]Schmelz, "Listening, Memory, and the Thaw," 59.

[63]Transcripts of "The Schoenberg Series, Part 1: Gould's Favourite Schoenberg" (CBC Radio broadcast, 11 September 1974), published in *Glenn Gould Magazine* 10/1 (Spring 2004): 13.

of the Western avant-garde, Soviet music students sensed that a gradual loosening of the strictures of the past would be inevitable, and that the "Kruschev thaw" would become permanent throughout Soviet culture. Indeed, a continuing relaxation of Soviet arts policy did take place through the late 1950s. All of these factors emboldened young Soviet composers as they sought to find their voices in the 1960s, composers such as Denisov, Schnittke, Grabovsky, Gubaidulina, Gershkovich,[64] Arvo Pärt,[65] and Andrei Volkonsky;[66] the latter's *Musica Stricta* and *Mirror Suite* were among the earliest explorations of twelve-tone technique by a Soviet composer. Soviet composers would continue to build on these new techniques from the West. Through the 1960s, Kruschev's regime relented even further, allowing the most promising young Soviet composers to attend the International Summer Courses for New Music in Darmstadt, West Germany.

The discovery by Soviet composers of what they had missed—during four decades of isolation from the latest developments in new music—initiated an upswelling of new compositional ideas, the likes of which Russian culture had not seen since the turn of the century. The floodgates that Gould had opened would continue to pour refreshing water on the compositional culture of the Soviet Union in the decades that followed. His 1957 tour remains enshrined in Russian memory as a pivotal turning point in their cultural history.[67] A new intellectualism was emerging in the post-Stalin era.[68] Many Russians would see Gould as the iconic champion of this new mode of musical thought and understanding, and advocated for his early return.[69] Furthermore, it was clear that Gould's personification of artistic integrity and lofty ideals was hardly consonant with the image of the dissolute, misguided, decadent, and spiritually-bereft Western artist that the Stalinist state had tried to promulgate (see, for

---

[64]Gershkovich had been a pupil of Webern. See Alfred Schnittke, "In Memory of Filip Moiseevich Gershkovich," in *A Schnittke Reader*, ed. Alexander Ivashkin, trans. John Goodliffe (Indiana University Press, 2002), 70-71.

[65]Like so many of his Soviet contemporaries, Pärt went through a prolonged post-Webern phase in the 1960s.

[66]See Peter J. Schmelz, "Shostakovich's 'Twelve-tone' Compositions and the Politics and Practice of Soviet Serialism," in *Shostakovich and his World*, ed. Laurel E. Fay (Princeton University Press, 2004), 303-34; see also Joel Sachs, "Notes on the Soviet Avant-Garde," in Brown, ed., *Russian and Soviet Music: Essays for Boris Schwarz* (Ann Arbor: UMI Research Press, 1984), 287-307.

[67]Yosif Feyginberg, *Glenn Gould: The Russian Journey* (television documentary), Chestnut Park Entertainment Inc. (2002); Yosif Feyginberg, "Glenn Gould and the Russians, Then and Now: A Filmaker's Impressions," *Glenn Gould Magazine* 13/1 (Spring 2008): 38-41.

[68]See Gerard McBurney, "Soviet Music after the Death of Stalin: The Legacy of Shostakovich," in *Russian Cultural Studies: An Introduction*, ed. Catriona Kelly and Devaid Shepherd (Oxford University Press, 1998), 120-37.

[69]Gould mused about returning to the Soviet Union in the 1980s, but this dream remained unfulfilled when he died in 1981.

Figure 11. This 1947 Soviet propaganda poster by Victor Koretsky exemplifies the portrayal of classical music performers from the West by Zhadnov and the Stalinists. Koretsky's poster contrasts a handsome, wholesome, and confident looking young violinist playing in a grand concert hall in the USSR, with a young, disconsolate, impoverished looking violinist in the West wandering downcast through the streets of New York. The captions read: "In Capitalist countries, the path for the talented is bleak ... In Socialist countries, the path for the talented is clear!"

(Courtesy of Art.com. Item #: 12812169A. The 140 x 99 cm

original is in the public domain)

example, Viktor Koretsky's 1947 propaganda poster, Figure 11). Times had changed. Reflecting on Gould's visit, the celebrated Russian cellist Mstislav Rostropovich was effusive: this "God, from Toronto," he wrote, "discovered the new Viennese composers for us [and] changed our musical climate forever."[70] Even to the present day, Glenn Gould is widely regarded in Russia as a prophet, the likes of which may never come again.

---

[70]Feyginberg, *Glenn Gould: The Russian Journey.*